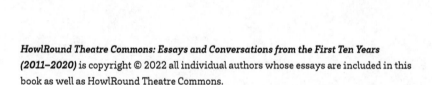
Published by HowlRound Theatre Commons
Office of the Arts
Emerson College
120 Boylston St.
Boston, Massachusetts 02116
United States
https://howlround.com
books@howlround.com

First edition, May 2022

ISBN: 978-1-939006-06-6
Library of Congress Control Number: 2022931582

Book design: Design Action Collective, Oakland, California.
Editor: May Antaki
Anthology Curators: May Antaki, Jamie Gahlon, Deen Rawlins-Harris, Abigail Vega
Publishing Coordinator: Vijay Mathew
Proofreader: Ashley Malafronte

TABLE OF CONTENTS

2013

2014

2015

2016

2017

2018

TABLE OF CONTENTS

ACTING & PERFORMANCE

ANTI-RACIST THEATRE

ASIAN AMERICAN THEATRE

BLACK THEATRE

CLIMATE EMERGENCY

COMMONS-BASED APPROACHES

CRITICISM

DIRECTING

DISABILITY & ACCESSIBILITY

GENDER

INDIGENOUS, FIRST NATIONS, & NATIVE THEATRE

LATINX THEATRE

LEADERSHIP

MIDDLE EASTERN, NORTH AFRICAN, & SOUTHWEST ASIAN (MENASA) THEATRE

PLAYWRITING

PRODUCING

HOW WE GOT HERE

As HowlRound approached its ten-year anniversary in 2021, those of us who steward the platform began thinking about appropriate ways to celebrate a decade of publishing essays, livestreaming events, and bringing theatre practitioners together to amplify pogressive and disruptive ideas. Approaching my own decade of work on HowlRound, as a co-founder and the current director, this seemed to me a monumentally important charge and challenge to take up. How could we offer gratitude within our commons-based frame while reflecting on the immense contributions of so many?

While early in HowlRound's founding we self-published a handful of books and talked about the possibility of releasing HowlRound content in hard copy, the occasion of our tenth anniversary felt particularly ripe to return to this idea. As a commons-based, peer-produced, free, and open platform, HowlRound would not exist without the thousands of theatremakers who have shared their collective wisdom through contributions to our journal, TV, and podcasts over the past decade. And as a primarily digital space, the idea of having a tangible object to hold felt of a permanence that was attractive to us.

We set to work thinking through what a HowlRound anthology could be and how it might act in accordance with our values set. While what has resulted is a people's history of a sort, it in no way claims to be objective or exhaustive. This book is one reflection of the thoughts of many who took up our invitation to contribute to the HowlRound journal. In the early years of HowlRound, this invitation was loosely predicated on personal connection to one of the co-founders or founding editorial board, but over the years we worked to iterate on and expand the invitation into an open-access platform with published curatorial guidelines. HowlRound itself evolved over this time, shifting from a new play development focus in the United States to an intentionally global mandate rooted in advancing progressive and disruptive ideas about theatremaking.

Alongside HowlRound's evolution and growing influence, discourse in the nonprofit theatre sector evolved. Conversations around gender and gender parity met the #MeToo movement. Questions around race and representation surfaced more and more as the field was confronted with its own systemic racism, brought into sharper relief by the racial reckonings catalyzed by the murder of George Floyd. At the time of writing, we find ourselves engaging meaningfully in these conversations, which invite complex, nuanced, and intersectional responses. Throughout the decade, considerations of the climate crisis began to creep in, becoming more urgent and frequent as time went on. Reading back over many of the essays HowlRound published, I was struck by how much our early content focused on the role and possibilities of new technology at the time, as well as the question of theatre's relationship to the digital. Writing now nearing two years into the pandemic, little could we have imagined back then the ways technology would by necessity take center stage thanks to COVID-19. All of these themes are reflected in the anthology, as the chorus of essays speaks to our evolving theatre field and its relationship to broader society and the world at large.

HOW WE PUT THIS TOGETHER

Creating this book necessitated an intentional process of inclusion and exclusion. It must be noted that there are many more essays from the HowlRound journal that merited being in this anthology, but not everything could fit. We had to make some tough choices. Of course, the good news is that every essay HowlRound has ever published is always digitally accessible and will continue to be part of our growing archive of practice and reflection.

Former HowlRound content editor May Antaki, HowlRound associate producer Deen Rawlins-Harris, HowlRound creative producer Abigail Vega, and I served as the co-curators of this anthology. We began by revisiting the essays from each year that had been the most read and most commented upon. To clock how each essay reflected our current curatorial charge, we ran our reading of the essays through the lens of HowlRound's core values:

- Generosity and abundance—all are welcome and necessary
- Community and collaboration over isolation and competition
- Diverse aesthetics and the evolution of forms of theatre practice
- Equity, inclusivity, and accessibility for marginalized theatre communities and practices
- Global citizenship—local communities intersecting with global practice

We thought critically about the diversity of contributors (including age, gender, geography, affiliation within the field, race and ethnicity, sexual orientation) as well as their positionality with regard to the topics they wrote about. We made considerations for repetitiveness of topic and theme and how essays throughout the book were advancing the conversation at hand. We made the terribly difficult choice to not include more than one essay per author to feature a maximum number of voices in this book.

Through three rounds of reading and discussion, we winnowed down a starting list of one hundred and eighty-three essays to seventy-seven essays. We then took a stronger subjective hand to interrogate what felt absent in the existing lineup, knowing that some of our most impactful and important content is not always synonymous with the most read, or clicked, or commented on. We each conducted a series of what we called "investigations" into content areas, bringing in our existing knowledge of the archive and reading with fresh eyes. Coming out of these research forays, we advocated for specific pieces to fill gaps we had identified.

We had hours and hours of joyous and painful conversation about what to keep and what to let go, which led us to a list of fifty essays total, between four and six for each year in the decade. Finally, we asked each author for permission to republish their essay and made final adjustments in accordance with their wishes. What you hold in your hands is our imperfect, subjective, best attempt at representing ten years of incredibly divergent and multiplicitous contributions to the HowlRound journal.

WHO THIS IS FOR

First and foremost, this anthology is a love letter to those who contributed to HowlRound over the past decade. Thank you for co-creating our knowledge commons. HowlRound and the theatre field are all the better for your offering. More broadly, we hope that theatremakers around the globe will benefit from seeing themselves and this decade of theatre practice reflected in this anthology, whether or not they have contributed to HowlRound.

We also hope those teaching the next generation of theatremakers will take up this book as an educational resource for their students. We know that about one half of the HowlRound community self-identifies as educators, and our fervent desire is that this anthology will be a welcome teaching tool. For this reason we have also released a number of free lesson plans that accompany this text for adaptation in a myriad of educational contexts. Finally, this book is for anyone working toward a theatre field where resources and power are shared equitably in all directions, contributing to a more just and sustainable world. It is a much-needed reminder that alternatives to the status quo are possible and that we are making them together by practicing otherwise everyday.

—Jamie Gahlon
HowlRound Director and Co-Founder, March 2022

ACKNOWLEDGEMENTS

HowlRound has been stewarded by an incredible group of theatremakers over the past decade, without whom this platform as we know it would not exist. Similarly, the creation of this book and its contents would not be possible without a host of people.

We offer gratitude to HowlRound co-founders P. Carl and David Dower, who are no longer on staff, as well as current founders on staff, HowlRound director, Jamie Gahlon, and cultural strategist, Vijay Mathew. In particular, we want to lift up the work of previous HowlRound journal content editors, Lynette D'Amico and May Antaki. We also want to thank all current and former HowlRound staff for their contributions: Travis Amiel, Emma Baar-Bittman, Ciara Diane, Hannah Fenlon, Jacqueline Flores, Jax Gil, Armando Huipe, Ramona King, Shannon Knapp, Ashley Malafronte, Srila Nayak, Adewunmi Oke, Deen Rawlins-Harris, Thea Rodgers, J. D. Stokely, Abigail Vega, and Dillon Yruegas. Additionally, we thank the many Emerson students who have worked to support our efforts over the years.

We honor the contributions of our founding editorial board: Jeremy Cohen, Deborah Cullinan, Daniel Alexander Jones, and Ed Sobel. We also thank the many theatremakers who have functioned as our collective brain trust through our advisory council: Claudia Alick, Zenkő Bogdán, Ilana Brownstein, Lizzy Cooper Davis, Deborah Cullinan, David Dower, Olga Garay-

English, Matthew Glassman, Derek Goldman, Rachel Grossman, Michelle Hensley, Melanie Joseph, Fran Kumin, Todd London, Kirk Lynn, Jonathan McCrory, Porsche McGovern, Bonnie Metzgar, Ralph Peña, Diane Ragsdale, Michael Rohd, Vera Starbard, Clyde Valentín, José Luis Valenzuela, Regina Victor, Alexandria Wailes, and Adrienne Wong.

Finally, the publication of this book has been made possible thanks to the support of the Barr Foundation, the Doris Duke Charitable Foundation, and the Mellon Foundation.

THE THEATRE OF THE FUTURE

09 FEBRUARY 2011

MEIYIN WANG

In the future, this will all be under water. Old definitions will be drowned out; new and buoyant ones will float.

The term "theatre"—or the idea of it—will encompass the full spectrum of performance and its possibilities. It will include dances without people, actors without words, visual arts installations, object theatre, high technology and gaming, choose your own adventures, one-on-one interactions, flash mobs, high-sensory interactions, rock concerts, radio shows, Broadway spectaculars, stories told in living rooms and fire-lit caves, full and all-consuming environments that will engulf you, one-minute gestures that will change you.

The work will be idiosyncratic, expansive, and could not be replicated in any other experience or medium. It will not replicate reality but instead turn it on its head to tell us deeper truths.

There will be no titles of playwrights, directors, actors, designers, managers, producers. There will be theatremakers. That will be all that is allowed on a name card. "Theatremaker." People you meet will include a writer/designer. A director/electrician. A sculptor/actor. A film editor/musician. A cook/dramaturg. A plumber/poet.

I think about the work of Richard Maxwell, Young Jean Lee, and Guillermo Calderón in Chile, who are, at first glance, writers/directors. To me they are instead theatremakers—creating total experiences of theatre that cannot be recreated anywhere else, in any other setting.

The notion of authorship, sole authorship, will change rapidly. Theatre will be made in duos, like Big Dance Theater's Annie-B Parson and Paul Lazar; in trios, like Alec Duffy, Rick Burkhart, and Dave Malloy in *Three Pianos*; in ensembles and collectives, like the Rude Mechs, Universes, and SITI Company—where you will not be able to see the edges of creation, generation, and execution. Theatre will be performed and generated by machines, like how New York director Annie Dorsen takes the famous television debate between the philosopher Michel Foucault and linguist and activist Noam Chomsky from the seventies as inspiration and material for a dialogue between two specially developed chatbots: every evening, these computer programs, designed to mimic human conversations, perform a new—as it were, improvised—live text.

Theatre will be performed by audiences—as in Rotozaza's *Etiquette*—where two participants sit across from each other at a cafe table, listening to instructions over headphones, moving around objects and participating in the enactment of a narrative. Or as in Gob Squad's *Kitchen*, where the collective attempts to recreate Andy Warhol's underground movies, where, by the end, the four performers are replaced by four audience members on stage, participating in this quirky meditation of the unknowability of the past and optimism for the future.

Theatre will be made by and for audiences. They can create and choose their own narratives—like in *Sleep No More*, coming to New York in March, where three hundred audience members roam a ninety-three-room installation of the Scottish Play, where they can chase after characters, follow plotlines, roam in Lady M's closet inches from Lady M herself, and open drawers and read.

But, more significantly, we are at a sea change in terms of what might be perceived as us the theatre versus them the audience. I quote Ben Cameron, from the Doris Duke Charitable Trust, who spoke so beautifully at Under the Radar this January, who compared the religious reformation in the fifteenth century and our current arts reformation—

> which is dramatically shaped by new technologies and a massive redistribution of knowledge. With the means for cultural and artistic production and distribution having been democratized. There is a term, pro-am, amateurs who are doing work professionally—a group expanding our aesthetic vocabulary, even as they assault our traditional

*notions of cultural authority and undermine the
assumed ability of traditional arts organizations to
set the cultural agenda.*

With increasing interactivity and participation from
audiences who are no longer satisfied to be on just
the receiving end, content changes. Form changes.
Authorship changes.

***

And as water has to always take the shape of its container,
theatre will become increasingly about place.

Theatres will have to turn into cultural centers, gathering
places for the community. They will continue to open
their doors to the outside world and deepen the dialogue
between arts, culture, and society, bringing the arts back
to the table of civic discourse, leading the conversation in
society, instead of us—artists—having a conversation with
ourselves. More theatres will have bars. Real bars, not just
beer and wine, but actual bars.

Theatre buildings will change; they have to. People will create
theatres that can respond creatively and organically to the
art that goes on inside them. More and more—bars, museums,
parks, living rooms, roof decks, libraries, basements, galleries,
cars—will becomes sites for performances. Theatre will
be taken to the audience, a way to interrupt their daily
perspectives, a way to see a space anew.

Theatre will be local. We will no longer casually import
theatremakers from big cities into other cities to make work
that artists in their own city can. It is no longer responsible
environmentally or artistically for that matter.

New ways of thinking of artistic exchange will emerge. One example is *Ciudades Paralelas*, a form of traveling festival. Lola Arias and Stefan Kaegi invited artists to devise interventions in public spaces—functional places like hotel rooms, factories, shopping centers. As observation stations for situations, the projects make stages out of public spaces used every day. Projects are staged in Berlin, Buenos Aires, Warsaw, and Zurich—in each city with local performers—and are created by local artists.

Theatre will need to become about less waste. Climate change will be part of the discussion in the creation and presentation of the play because it will increasingly insist upon it. There will be no more disposable sets. It will no longer be cheaper to throw something out than to store it. Theatres will account for carbon emissions and pay for carbon offsets. We will have to create with less, and be more creative.

Speaking of recycling, shows can no longer go up for six weeks and disappear forever. I think more festivals will emerge—which will be homes for emerging new work—that cannot sustain six-week runs but are vital nonetheless in the theatre landscape. There is a small movement of experimental theatre festivals including Portland's Time-Based Arts, Philly Live Arts, and Fusebox in Austin that manage for two to three weeks to place cutting-edge art and ideas at the center of the city—changing the dynamic of the cultural dialogue within the city.

And in the same breath I will say that theatre will be global. I think that the artist and the individual are the true and effective unit of cultural exchange and political change.

I am always amused when I am asked to speak to my views on the American theatre, since I possess neither citizenship nor a green card. (I am a legal alien from Singapore.) Definitions of nation, language, and ethnicity will be continually turned over and investigated in the coming years, both in our society and in our theatre. I believe that borders, both artistic and national, will become increasingly porous as artists will move in and out of countries and cities—reflecting a global interconnected world. I cautiously hope that the immigration and tax systems will be able to keep up and change fast enough.

I think we will have increasing relationships with China, Latin America, and the Middle East, and we will need to respond to those relationships. I think about Mike Daisey, who has been sponsored by the state department and through his own indomitable efforts been to the far reaches of the world, from Tonga to the heart of industrial China, bearing witness to changing social and political phenomena and bringing back the stories to us. One person's richly observed examinations have made the political stories personal.

I think about the recent developments with our friends from the Belarus Free Theatre, who have brought us stories of oppression and hope from their country—having escaped under the cover of night to perform their piece *Being Harold Pinter,* a performance that juxtaposed Harold Pinter's Nobel Prize acceptance speech, scenes from his late plays, and testimonies from Belarusian political prisoners to shed light on the effects and fallout of the authoritarian regime of Lukashenko. Theatre is their activism, and it is their form of protest.

It is truly humbling to contemplate this, that these are artists literally willing to die for their art.

But it is only through performance, and being in the same room as these astonishing artists, that you can feel how theatre can move the body politic, one room at a time.

As we reel from talking about changes, and institutions, and models, and funding, and diversity in the coming days, I hope that we will remember to start always with the art. This art form that is immediate, expansive, mythical, powerful—with the power to change and be changed.

People will always crave bodies sweating in the room. Stories will always need to be told. Audiences will be in performances, where they will crave being asked to be still and be present. To gather and to listen deeply.

MEIYIN WANG

Meiyin Wang (she/her) is a producer and curator of live performance, working with global artists who are investigating the urgent questions of our time. She is the producing director of the Ronald O. Perelman Performing Arts Center in New York. She was the co-director of Under the Radar Festival at the Public Theater, the festival director of La Jolla Playhouse's Without Walls, and the curator of the Park Avenue Armory's Artist-in-Residence series. As an independent producer, her work has been seen across four continents. Meiyin was born and raised in Singapore and currently lives in Brooklyn.

NOTES ON GENEROSITY IN THE THEATRE

10 APRIL 2011
P. CARL

"My vocation changed everything: the sword-strokes fly off, the writing remains; I discovered in the belles-lettres that the Giver can be transformed into his own Gift, that is, into a pure object. Chance had made me a man, generosity would make me a book."

—Jean-Paul Sartre

These are the words that open the third chapter, "The Labor of Gratitude," of Lewis Hyde's book *The Gift*[1]—a must-read for any artist. Last week I spent a lot of time thinking about generosity. I don't think there's enough of it in this field and I was reminded of its transformative power as I grappled with the unexpected and untimely loss of a mentor and friend. In that moment of stunned sadness I considered the many gifts this lovely man had given me and wondered about how I might best honor his example.

[1]   Lewis Hyde, *The Gift: How the Creative Spirit Transforms the World* (New York: Random House, 2006).

Hyde talks about a long and cross-cultural tradition of threshold gifts, gifts that we give at moments of transformation in our lives—baptismal celebrations, wedding gifts, funeral flowers. In these moments of transformation when we move from one threshold to the next, when we transform ourselves to join in union with another—for example, when we marry—we let go of a part of ourselves, and the gifts we receive acknowledge what we give up in order to move forward—"they guide us to a new life, assuring our passage away from what is dying." It's hard to tear ourselves away from what we've known, to leave behind where we've been, so difficult to embrace transformation and new life. It's why we don't leap willy-nilly into marriage and struggle to accept the inevitability of death.

In the theatre, I experience this fear in the scarcity mindset that is prevalent in much of the conversations that shape our field. Perhaps it's easy for me to point this out as I sit in the midst of abundance most days, lucky to have infrastructure and means to accomplish the work I am passionate about. But I, too, am prone to the scarcity approach to the work, the ominous sense that there is only so much opportunity out there and that the circumference of the pie is finite and the pieces we divide among ourselves limited. As artists we compete for gigs, attention, recognition, patronage, and opportunities. As organizations we compete for funding, contributions, and audience. As a field we compete to be relevant. We are competing for credit, position, and power, even if we're uncomfortable admitting it, even if we have no taste for blood sports, we are all playing the game. And this competition for our piece of the action can make us all feel victimized by a poverty of the imagination that there just isn't enough to go around. The scarcity mentality relies on victims to flourish.

Certain stories that we tell ourselves over and over rely on the idea that there isn't enough. These are some scarcity narratives in the theatre: The story that plays are developed to death rather than produced. The story that artists are at odds with institutions. The story that nonprofit theatre is beginning to merge with commercial theatre. The story that pits playwrights against directors and directors against dramaturgs and everyone against artistic directors. These are all narratives driven by a feeling of lack—lack of respect, lack of understanding, lack of appreciation. How do we cross a new threshold? How can we start to reimagine new stories?

In Hyde's book he contends, "market exchange will always seem inappropriate on the threshold." When I read this, I know why nonprofit (versus commercial) theatre is where I've decided to maintain my focus. If art is, as I believe it to be, a gift that transforms our lives and transports us from death to life, then the transactional nature of making art will always be an ill fit. It's why we bristle at high-priced theatre tickets and huge disparities between the lowest and highest paid staff in arts institutions. We're products of a market-driven culture but gifts in moments of transformation supersede the forces of the market. Making art falls somewhere in between commerce and transformation. "A man who would buy and sell at the moment of change... will be torn apart. He will become one of the done-for dead who truly die. Threshold gifts protect us from such death." As theatremakers how can we better create the conditions for generosity—where threshold stories can be told and transformations can occur? How can we avoid becoming the "done-for dead?"

Here are some thoughts:

- Regardless of where you are in your career as a theatremaker, seek to mentor. Recognize that you have a responsibility to foster the passions and dreams and aspirations of others and there is almost always someone who has less experience in this business than you. As Hyde says, it's only when we release our own gifts do they become ours—it's in the giving that potential is actualized. Generosity transforms us into artists. To be an artist is a becoming not a being.

- "Once the gift has stirred within us it is up to us to develop it." I have articulated Hyde's sentiment over the years telling artists to become their own arts administrators. No agent, artistic director, or advocate of any kind will make your career for you. Give yourself the gift of access to the means of production. Learn how to raise money and manage budgets. Strategize ways to connect with institutions and other artists you admire. I believe the more control you have over your own career, the more generous you'll feel.

- If you run an arts organization, drop what you're doing immediately and create an ethics statement. Every organization has a mission statement, but the nonprofit arts organization requires an ethical approach. Answer the hard questions, such as what is a responsible spread between the lowest and highest paid person in the organization, inclusive of artists and administrators? Make a clear accounting of the intersection and collision between commercial and nonprofit interests. What values does your organization hold sacred, and are you willing to make them transparent? Are you willing to engage in honest and open communication as you shape and prepare to live by this statement? Honesty and openness are forms of generosity.

- Take the long view.

  For the slow labor of realizing a potential gift the artist must retreat to the Bohemias, halfway between the slums and the library, where life is not counted by the clock and where the talented will be sure they will be ignored until that time, if it ever comes, when their gifts are viable enough to be set free and survive in the world.

  If you take the risk of exercising your gift, you must acknowledge the truth that it may never be recognized and that lack of recognition doesn't take away from your identity as an artist, and it's not a reflection on the quality of the art you make. The long view will give you endurance and protect you from the poison cloud of bitterness that hovers in close proximity to the life of the artist. Bitterness is the enemy of generosity.

- Don't read reviews. I mean this. Really. Don't read your reviews. Compliments are a pleasant distraction but I bet you can find more meaningful kudos from trusted colleagues. Negative reviews will never be constructive because they are just too damn personal. You've made something. It's a reflection of your deepest passions and pains, and then you must give it away to this unknown entity called an audience. Who are they? And what gives them the right to criticize your work? Of course they have every right to their opinions, but these random criticisms will only hinder your evolution as an artist. It's simply impossible not to perseverate over every hint of unkindness coming from some unknown, usually disembodied voice. Random criticisms from strangers eat away at you. The fewer things that eat away at your creative energy, the more productive you will be, the more likely you will have energy for others, the less likely you will be to compare your reviews with those of your colleagues.

- Get over the myth of entitlement. No one owes you anything in this business or in life. The surest way to feeling victimized is to feel owed, and to feel owed is to be at a deficit. Deficits leave you with nothing to give. "The Gift is not merely the witness or guardian to new life, but the creator."

In my very darkest days at the Playwrights' Center, of which there were more than a few in the early going, I felt consistently at a deficit, victimized by other people who felt victimized—it was such an ugly cycle. But I was lucky because I had mentors who were wiser and smarter and more generous than I. One of those was Tom Proehl, my friend who passed away last week. He was on my board of directors and he was sage beyond his years. I feel certain that one year I called him three hundred times and every phone call was received with attention and warmth. Tom always had time. He understood deeply how arts organizations function. He was compelled to share his gift. He always encouraged me to take the high road, to see the good in people and the hope in hopeless situations. He propped me up and he stood by me. He's one of a handful of people who have compelled me to be a better person than perhaps my nature left to its own devices would accommodate. This article, my wish for greater generosity in a field of tremendous abundance, is my labor undertaken in gratitude for the gift received.

P. CARL

P. Carl (he/him) is a senior distinguished artist-in-residence, Department of Performing Arts, at Emerson College in Boston and the author of the memoir Becoming a Man: The Story of a Transition, *published by Simon & Schuster in 2020.*

HOW GOING LOCAL CAN REVITALIZE AMERICAN THEATRE

24 AUGUST 2011
MARSHALL BOTVINICK

Twenty-five hundred years ago in ancient Athens, theatre shaped the body politic. It was a sacred space where commoners and leaders sat side by side and watched their most pressing national questions dramatized and choreographed. In America, however, neither our leaders nor our citizens flock to the theatre, and our playwrights, unlike Sophocles (or Václav Havel for that matter), do not serve as national leaders. So what has changed in twenty-five hundred years? Why has theatre been relegated to the periphery of the national dialogue in America and, more importantly, what can we, American theatre artists, do to rediscover our sense of purpose?

For me, a rediscovery of that purpose begins with a frank admission of what theatre cannot accomplish in twenty-first-century America: it cannot act as a catalyst for a national transformation. I feel confident saying that there is no American playwright who will incite the masses against the King Louis of our day as Beaumarchais' *The Marriage of Figaro* did, foreshadowing the French Revolution. The current social and political conditions make it impossible for a play to take a major role in contemporary political discourse. The manifold reasons for this include the absence of a national theatre; prohibitive ticket prices that have produced a predominantly monolithic, bourgeois audience; and the fragmented nature of twenty-first-century America. Certainly, the immensity of our country makes it exceedingly difficult for a work of art, particularly one that thrives on direct contact between performer and audience, to reach a critical mass of people. Unlike major motion pictures and YouTube videos, live performances cannot replicate themselves and be viewed in multiple locations simultaneously, and, if they are, then their impact is instantly diminished. The magic of theatre derives from its immediacy. Because of this, it can never truly go viral, which means it is doomed to play second fiddle in matters of social change.

So what is theatre to do now that online media and forums such as YouTube and Facebook have become the primary venues for social discourse and public performance? One possible answer is to identify what virtual media cannot provide, such as a sense of community and a connection to a tangible, geographic location, and to offer these things in greater quantity at the theatre. In other words, the theatre must go local. It can take a lesson from the locavore movement, a form of social and ecological activism that champions community and resists the fragmentation brought about by the Information Age, and transform itself into a gathering place for a group of people, not a viewing space for a disparate collection of individuals.

There are three steps that the theatre can take to hasten this transformation: 1) Get out of the theatre more. 2) Produce multidisciplinary works that involve collaboration with local artists. 3) Seek out plays that are more geographically specific.

In the modern era, the theatre has become increasingly private. My use of the word "private" here has two meanings. First, the theatre no longer belongs to the public. The market squares that played host to commedia dell'arte performances have been replaced by formidable buildings where spectators are no more than guests passing through. Today's audience member is a visitor in a place that he should be able to call home. Second, the theatre experience has become completely private and individualized. People, myself included, often go to the theatre expecting to be left alone. They go seeking a personal experience, not a communal one. One possible antidote to this problem is to utilize more nontraditional performance venues.

A theatre company should be connected to the city in which it finds itself, and if it never ventures beyond the confines of its own space, then that relationship is very limited. A major component of Shakespeare in the Park's success is the public venue. That space belongs not to a company, but to the people. Consequently, individuals who do not usually attend the theatre make the trek to watch a play they would otherwise not see. Other successful site-specific performances include the work of Punchdrunk and the Classical Theatre of Harlem's 2007 production of *Waiting for Godot* on a street corner in the Ninth Ward of New Orleans. For me, the latter production is a seminal example of the kind of service and communal healing that theatre can offer. A theatre can also do things to transform itself into a public space. There is no reason that every theatre in the country cannot collect food for local food banks, host blood drives, or serve as a location for Alcoholic Anonymous (AA) meetings. Not only would such actions benefit the community, but they would also deepen the theatre's connection to its audience.

Increasing collaboration with local bands, painters, and dancers is another way for a theatre to expand beyond its walls. Why can't Chekhov be done with live, local music, and is there a good reason not to use paintings and other pieces of visual art in a production design scheme? The Greeks envisioned theatre as a multidisciplinary organism. The segmentation of artistic disciplines is a relatively recent phenomenon. One way to combat this unfortunate turn in history is to tear down the artificial barriers that separate the arts. As long as theatre remains a place for one type of artist, it can only do so much. But if it finds ways to include all the arts, its influence will certainly grow.

When I worked as a script reader in a literary office, I was struck by the paltry number of texts that focused on a specific location, culture, or region. So many realistic plays, including the good ones, take place in offices and apartments that could be anywhere. Even plays that are set in a particular city seldom explore issues of cultural identity and geography. As a result, theatre is almost utterly devoid of regional character. If theatres are unwilling or unable to explore what is happening in their own backyard, then how can they assist in the process of community formation?

One recent innovation, the concept of a rolling world premiere, is a tacit admission that new work need not have any connection to the city/cities in which it is created. In fact, it is encouraging work that is not specific to any one community. (I should note that despite this problem I recognize the economic value of this model as well as its potential benefits for playwrights seeking a larger audience and, certainly, we should do what we can to encourage the spread of our best plays across the country. However, we should be aware that this sometimes hinders a theatre's ability to serve its particular community.) So what would a community-based theatre look like? I point my readers to the 1930s and the Federal Theatre Project. Hallie Flanagan, the national director of the Federal Theatre Project, had the genius to recognize that theatre must target specific populations and be responsive to local issues. As a result, in no other time has our country produced such regionally diverse works and, not coincidentally, in no other time has our theatre been more lively or topical.

Today, American theatre artists are faced with a choice. In our work we must prioritize either breadth of impact or depth of impact. Given the current state of affairs, I argue that we must pursue depth of impact. Our art may no longer be the spark that ignites a revolution, but it can still be the necessary spark in the dark to heal a broken community if we just take the time to connect.

MARSHALL BOTVINICK

 Marshall Botvinick (he/him) is a playwright, dramaturg, and theatre educator. Organizations he has worked with include Seven Devils New Play Foundry, Jewish Plays Project, Palm Beach Dramaworks, South Carolina Repertory Company, American Repertory Theater, Burning Coal Theatre Company, and PlayMakers Repertory Company.

A CULTURE OF TRUST

22 SEPTEMBER 2011
TAYLOR MAC

I t all started with John Wilkes Booth. That's what Uta Hagen suggests in her book *A Challenge for the Actor*. The mistrust for actors all started when an actor used a bullet to break the ultimate fourth wall. Actually, I would guess it started before Booth. Maybe in the Middle Ages with the creation of liturgical/vernacular drama, but certainly somewhere between the honored heyday of Homer and rapscallion commedia street performers whose tipping hats reminded their audience of beggars.

Still it's safe to assume Lincoln's actor assassin didn't elevate the actor's status. A fair generalization might be— in the eyes of those with stable occupations—that actors historically are vagabonds, agitators, vain, not the brightest of breeds, and (the old standard) deceitful. We get paid to lie. And if we do it extraordinarily well, so well that if the lie seems truer than truth, then we're hailed as great at what we do. Great at what we do but not great humans to be trusted with political opinions and societal points of view, and certainly not great enough to be hired without an extensive series of tests (auditions) designed to prove the actor is the right fit for the part.

If a playwright or producer is looking for a director, they do their research. They see the director's work, seek out references, and/or sit down and have tea with a number of directors to find one their vision can commingle with. They do not ask the director to direct two minutes of the play to prove she knows what she's doing. Nor should they. They respect and, better yet, trust the director. The same cannot be said for the actor.

I believe actors (and all theatre practitioners) should be treated with the same respect and trust we tender the director.

Some would argue respect should be earned. Fair enough. One of the great things about the kind of career I've created for myself (with the help of many) is I get to work in a variety of different theatrical environments and with a wonderful assortment of performing artists. I've been in ensemble plays by other playwrights, acted in my own plays with actors I've cast, done the midnight show and the midday matinee. I've worked in the circus, strip club, LORT, street, museum, opera house, basement bar/sex club, and ethical society. And from this experience I've come to believe that, in terms of rehearsal process, actors help perpetuate the cliché that they are the laziest of the performing artists (I think they're the hardest workers when it comes to sustaining a single performance over a long run, though so few of them ever get that opportunity).

In my play *The Lily's Revenge* the third act is dance theatre. Its premiere in New York, at the HERE Arts Center, was my first time working with a group of dancers (as opposed to actors who move or musical theatre performers). They flabbergasted me. They were so... professional. I'd show up twenty minutes early to have quiet time before rehearsal and they'd already be warmed up, focused, and privately working on their roles (I want to write a full-length dance theatre play because I love working with that level of professionalism). I had to ask myself why all these actors I've worked with, whether paid appropriately or not, and regardless of the status of the venue, show up late, rarely remember their blocking from the day before, and wait until tech week to get off book. Why aren't they as disciplined as the dancers? I have a couple theories.

The first has to do with the misuse (and overuse) of naturalism. This misuse asks the actor to *be* the character, not *play* the character. As an actor, whenever I've gotten to play roles far from my own personality or body type (usually roles I've written for myself to play), I couldn't possibly be lackadaisical and pull it off. I'm guessing it was similar with actors from ancient Greece who had to play multiple roles, including roles different from their own being, in each production. Primarily in casting nowadays, we look for an actor to be the right fit for the part, which is just laziness on the parts of the director, playwright, producer, and casting director. Where do trust, process, and craft come in? Isn't it a joy to see the work an actor has put into *playing* the role (even if that work is so good it's barely perceivable)? I love watching an actor *play* a role. Do they have to actually *be* the role? Some would argue, in this market and culture where failure is not celebrated, yes. There is no room for trust, experimentation, or play. But, in my experience, it is almost always more exciting, engaging, and revelatory to see an actor who is wholly miscast triumph in his role.

To be clear, I'm not attacking naturalism. This does not preclude the method actor from doing method work in naturalism, or from sacrificing ego and disappearing into the role, but rather it gives them more opportunities to stretch themselves while allowing those who prefer traditional theatrical styles and techniques (such as commedia, mask work, etc.) the same opportunity. If actors have to stretch themselves, they work harder and, as a result, their craft (and our collective theatremaking craft) gets better. It's worth the risk. Witnessing someone stand in front of a group of people and brave failure is one of the reasons people come to the theatre. It works in tandem with the storytelling and is a major ingredient in what makes the actor/performing arts honorable. In the last century, it seems to me, we've created a lazy system and asked our actors to adapt to it. And, for the most part, they have.

As a playwright I understand the stakes. Usually your play has one shot at having any kind of chance to have a life beyond its first production, so the impulse is to cast as close to the bone as possible. It's hard enough to make a play work in the first place without having to incorporate the process of others. But theatre is, arguably, the most collaborative art form there is and, as a wise man once said, if you're not willing to allow your vision to change, you probably shouldn't be working in the theatre. Treat the actor as a partner in this process. Allow them to serve your play with their craft, not their ability at being appropriately cast. Cast good actors and let them do their job. My experience has been the play has an equal if not a better chance at prospering as a result.

Here's another way the system is lazy and helps perpetuate this laziness: the audition.

I often facetiously joke that producers/directors created the tiers of auditions because actors give you syphilis, so they created the casting director, bought a couch, formed a line of actors, and said, "Let us know which ones give you a rash." Snarky humor aside, I've come to believe auditions are not only harmful to the theatre because they foster mistrust, hierarchy, and barriers between artists, as well as diminish process (if you're casting actors who can play the character from day one, why not eliminate the rehearsal period like film and television?), but they are also less effective than other forms of casting. I've championed actors who were great in the audition room and cast them in my plays only to find they didn't have the craft to rehearse a play and perform it night after night. Auditions are preparing our actors for auditioning (a much easier job than rehearsing and performing an entire play) when they should be practicing the craft of acting. And we've all seen flops where the actors were auditioned. Auditioning does not guarantee you a great production.

But if directors/producers/playwrights stop auditioning, how will they know whom to cast? We won't *know*. We'll trust. The way the actor trusts us to be a good fit as a director/producer/playwright. We'll trust and start to equalize the field by treating actors like the co-creators they are. Of course we can hedge the bet. And we can do it in a more responsible, egalitarian way.

To help me in non-auditioned casting, these are the things I've been doing or at least working at doing better: I scout, ask around, try to see more theatre than anyone else I know in a variety of venues, styles, genres, and forms (it's made me a better director/producer/playwright in the process). When working with casting directors (who, when working without auditions, become more useful and part of the process instead of less), I ask them to let me know when actors we are interested in are in something new (so I can see the range of their abilities). I've started planning my productions further in advance so the entire team has time to scout for roles that require specific skills. I sit in on the rehearsals of productions I'm not associated with (this is also making me a better artist). I audit acting classes (especially useful for finding younger, emerging, and trained actors). Above all, I trust. I trust that if I've stymied my own laziness, done the groundwork, and chosen an actor who knows her craft and has a good attitude, she'll serve the play to great effect.

So far I've cast four of my ensemble productions without a single audition (including two productions of my large ensemble play—thirty-six cast members—*The Lily's Revenge*). Aside from the art itself, it's the aspect of the productions I'm most proud of. Some incredible things have happened and some mistakes have been made (strangely enough, more incredible things and fewer mistakes than when I cast plays solely from auditions). The biggest lesson has been that when I've treated actors as capable from the get-go (before casting them), they work harder. I'm not sure why but I don't think it's only gratitude for not having to audition. It could be that actors who've gone through many callbacks to win the roles feel they've explored their parts enough and so don't work as openly or as much in the rehearsal period. What I've learned is that starting from scratch with actors who weren't asked to audition created a more fruitful process and resulted in my most successful productions artistically and financially. I can only hypothesize, but it seems like the actors dug in more because we treated them from the start like the professionals they'd already spent their lives proving themselves to be. They went about creating instead of treating the rehearsal process as if the hard part (winning the role) was already complete. The success of my non-auditioned productions and the joy-filled experience of them (the Magic Theatre's production of *The Lily's Revenge* being the most recent and exuberantly gleeful) have convinced me to make auditions the exception rather than the rule.

What I'm suggesting is we respect the artist more or at least as much as the art. In the new play realm, theatres like Arena Stage are doing just that. They are interested in building relationships more than reading blind submissions.

I would go one step further and suggest that theatres not read plays until after they've committed to producing them. Instead, get to know artists and their body of work. Specifically for playwrights, theatres should give them a date on the calendar for when their new play will be produced and... trust. If you've liked plays they've written in the past, chances are they'll write something you'll be interested in again. If not, the production will be over in a couple months but the relationship with the artist may last decades. This isn't a new way of working. Joe Papp often offered productions to playwrights on the day before the critics came to their current production. He didn't need to read what they'd come up with. He trusted. Sometimes it didn't work and sometimes it did, but the same goes for theatres that commit to productions solely from having a developed script in their hands. There is no guarantee for success, so let's treat our artists like they know what they're doing and let them do it.

I don't expect auditions (in all their various forms) to become the exception as opposed to the norm any time soon. We're too entrenched in the industry of them to change quickly. I do hope more producers/directors/playwrights will simply call actors up and ask them out to tea instead of sending an email to a casting director or an agent with a side attached. I think you'll find it a liberating, humane, and community-building practice. I've discovered that with better trust, better art has been made. It may not ultimately be your preference, but why not try it? Try casting a production without an audition. Try casting great actors who would need to stretch themselves to play the role. Try it once. If you're weary, try it on a production for a play with a small cast (less risk), and if you, like me, find it a healthier and more productive process, try it on a production for a play with a large cast. It is my challenge to you. I challenge you to challenge your actors with your trust. Give them an opportunity to work harder. Forgive the actor for their vagabond ways. Forgive their life of lies and bullets.

TAYLOR MAC

Taylor Mac (who uses "judy"—lowercase sic—as a gender pronoun) is the author of The Hang *(composed by Matt Ray),* Gary: A Sequel to Titus Andronicus, A 24-Decade History of Popular Music, Hir, *and* The Lily's Revenge, *among others. Taylor is the first American to receive the International Ibsen Award; is a MacArthur Fellow, Pulitzer Prize finalist, and Tony nominee for Best Play; and is the recipient of the Kennedy Prize (with Matt Ray), the Doris Duke Performing Artist Award, a Guggenheim, the Herb Alpert Award, a Drama League Award, the Helen Merrill Playwriting Award, the Booth, two Helpmann awards, a NY Drama Critics Circle Award, two Obies, two Bessies, and an Ethyl Eichelberger.*

CONFESSIONS OF A SERIAL INTERN

22 DECEMBER 2011

ANNAH FEINBERG

B y all measures of intern metrics, my experiences as an intern at seven theatre organizations in New York and Chicago have all been pretty wonderful. I've cultivated crucial relationships with artistic leaders in the new play world I have always aspired to play in. I have had significant insight into the structures and functions of a hefty handful of respected institutions. I've gained access to the work of writers that I would never have known about otherwise.

I've improved my writing and communication skills, become savvy to industry politics, and gained an insider vocabulary that enhances my credibility as a serious theatre practitioner. But the "dark side" of the internship has taught me not to speak up or make independent decisions and demanded my gratitude for the privilege of having my intelligence and labor exploited. I've learned to accept whatever breadcrumbs I'm given. I've learned to apologize incessantly or, even better, shut my trap. I've become accustomed to working outside of the US Fair Labor Standards Act, and gotten used to sucking up sexism.

Internships have been responsible for eroding my sense of my own value. Our nonprofit theatre industry, perhaps more than most of our country's flailing industries, is entirely dependent on the work of under- or unpaid interns. College students, college graduates, graduate students, graduate school graduates, and adults in the midst of career change populate a significant portion of the offices of America's nonprofit theatres. They tackle tasks from photocopying to script reading to special event planning to line producing. Many inhabit the desk and responsibilities of pre-2008 staffers, working part-, full-, or more-than-full-time for a leg up, a way in, an artistic outlet, an inside view, a challenge, a chance. But what kind of chance do theatre internships truly provide? What myths run rampant throughout our theatrical community about the value and purpose of internships? And how much truth is there in these perceived chances? Do the skills acquired as an intern actually translate to impactful artistic leadership?

One troubling myth is that of the post-internship hire. A major tactic for convincing a potential intern that his or her future internship is worthwhile is to provide examples of former interns who have since been hired by the theatre organization of their internship. This is done on internship pages on theatres' websites, in interviews, at the first-day internship welcome session, at intern seminars, and in one-on-one conversations with appointed mentors. I've been sold on this myth more than a few times—that there is some sort of causal link between being an awesome intern and getting a job. In my own experience, and the experience of many of my peers, this is an impossibly rare occurrence. I've been told more than once that I was the best intern such-and-such ever had, or was the best intern since so-and-so years ago, and had glowing written evaluations about my work in my months of intern-hood. I am not, nor have I ever been, a full-time paid staff member at any of those seven theatres. And I know I'm not alone in this. Though my amount of internship experience is certainly on the high end of our industry's spectrum, I have many friends and acquaintances that have held between three and seven theatre internships. Many of them have excelled in these internships, formed great relationships, and then been tossed out at sea. While there are a handful of examples of this dreamy hire happening (largely due to extremely random circumstances), there are many, many more examples of great interns not getting hired. Their only options are to continue to intern at other theatres until some extremely random circumstance works in their favor, start a flailing theatre company of their own, or leave the field altogether.

The most troubling aspect of this paradigm centers on access. When we have conversations about diversity of voices and perspectives in new plays, we should start by looking at the demographic most likely to receive internships. In my experience, most of the other interns I've worked with have looked suspiciously similar to me. If we are attempting to carve out a place for a multiplicity of voices to create the future of theatre, we must carve out a place for a multiplicity of voices in the institutions that are giving a platform for these voices. I am lucky to have grown up in a comfortable middle-class community, gone to an in-state public college where I received scholarships, lived at home in the summers I interned while also working some terrible jobs at burger restaurants and day camps. I was lucky to go to school part-time my last semester of college and work full-time at a coffee shop so I could save money and move to New York and sustain myself (eating lots of canned beans) for another year of interning. My relatively comfortable circumstances made choosing the poverty of internships possible.

To me, there are two possible solutions to the intern's dilemma: get rid of internships altogether or create more sustainable ways (both for theatres and interns) to nurture them. Theatres cannot view interns as a way to pad the budget with free or cheap labor, moving bodies in and out over a period of months as if interchangeable and disposable. The most valuable experiences I've had as an intern have worked against this sense that I'm easily traded in for a cheaper model—whether it was a supervisor introducing me as her colleague, or being brought into a meeting, or a rehearsal, or a reading and asked what I thought. The closer I was to the act of art-making, the less disposable I felt. But I have traded in my financial well-being for these ephemeral moments of feeling esteemed. But what is the alternative for theatres confronting financial scarcity? Hiring an unpaid intern is definitely the most obvious solution to increase the efficiency of an organization. But since when did our art form thrive on the obvious choice? There are surely other ways to squeeze an intern's minimum wage out of a budget. One of the plays at one of the theatres that I interned for had two dogs in it. These dogs cost $800 per week to employ (including their handlers, personal dressing rooms, and trainers). The dogs came on stage for less than a minute in the second act to walk in a circle around the stage and demonstrate the wealth and eccentricity of the characters. At this time, there were fourteen interns employed by the theatre, about half of whom were working full-time. The full-time interns made $50 a week; the part-timers made nothing. In what world is this fair, productive, or just? If a budget is the reflection of the priorities of an institution, it is time for a shift in priorities.

How we treat personnel must be as considered as the work we put on our stages. There is no artistic justification for exploiting desperate and aspiring theatremakers. An intern needs to work with some sense of security and respect just as much as any artist. We must begin to put our egos aside and see the intern as artist if we are going to have a future for our beloved art form. As a young person entering this field, and hoping to develop my voice as a leader within it, there is very little that I can depend on. What can I expect and assume about my future? Of course, I did not enter this field to live a life of affluence, but if I am to keep working at attaining what I've always hoped to attain, I need to be able to see a little further in front of me. I need to have a realistic post-intern road to take, even if that means paving my own. If I were to begin my short career over again, it is hard to say whether I would do anything differently. I don't have any regrets over my choices thus far, but I do wish I had known more about what I was getting myself into and that internships would be my only option for many years post college. I wasn't prepared to jump from place to place to string together my sustenance and didn't expect that my work from job to job would not always translate. I wish I had had some hard data about internships in the theatre industry so I could make an informed decision for myself rather than relying on persuasive mythology.

We need to take a long, hard look at where interns fit in the ecology of our industry. If you work at a theatre that employs interns, think selflessly and shamelessly about how you view and value them. If you are an intern, think honestly and provocatively about your importance to the institution you are working in. At the heart of intern mythology exists a sense of desperation about, and fear of, the future. For most interns, it is a fear for their individual future. In shaky economic times, there also exists a fear on the part of institutions for the future of the art form. Let's get to the heart of intern mythology. This could come through a research study of the state of internships in our field. It could come through structural or budgetary changes from all sides of the industry. Theatre does not begin in the rehearsal room and end on the stage. It begins much earlier than that, in the seeds of dreams we plant in the minds of the next generation of theatremakers.

ANNAH FEINBERG

Annah Feinberg (she/her) was impossibly young when she wrote this essay and is proud to be embarrassed that it exists. In the years since it was published, she completed her MFA in dramaturgy at Columbia University, where she had the debt-riddled realization that she didn't want to be a dramaturg. She moved to Los Angeles, co-founded feminist theatre collective the Kilroys, and promptly ditched the theatre to work toward becoming a screenwriter and cartoonist. Her comics and humor writing have been featured in the New Yorker's Daily Shouts, McSweeney's, Awry, *the* Hairpin, *and the collection* Notes from the Bathroom Line. *At the time of writing this bio, she is in development on multiple TV and film projects in the adult animation space.*

THE BENEFITS OF SLAVERY

30 JANUARY 2012
TIMOTHY DOUGLAS

In the 1970s Dr. Howard Washington Thurman, a theologian and mystic—and mentor to Dr. Martin Luther King Jr.—gave a lecture on the "benefits of slavery." In it he focused on the mindset of the African people and how the creative center of their "being" developed because of their closeness with nature and "the presence," which they experienced everywhere and in everything. He also talked about the fact that, as a result of slavery, their creative, intuitive, compassionate, and forgiving mindset was spread throughout the world. He went on to suggest that the "hand of evolution" had something to do with the spread of this mindset so that it would be everywhere on the planet as the guiding influence for the next leap in human evolution.

My recent resignation as artistic director of Chicago's Remy Bumppo Theatre Company has decidedly struck a chord in this theatre community with regard to the entrenched reticence to talk openly and candidly about matters of (and perceptions of) race relations between Blacks and whites. This discordant dance of avoidance is not unique to Chicago, as evidenced by my body of experience as a practitioner of theatre across America. A prolific freelance career wherein much of the time I'm engaged as the director for a theatre company's ethnic production in a given season. And while I absolutely treasure the relationships I've cultivated with artistic directors across the country—all of whom I know engage me first and foremost because of my talents as an artist—my resume tells a very precise statistical story, which ensures that my primary professional conversation consistently surrounds issues of race.

While it is true that my principal reason for moving on from Remy Bumppo was based on artistic differences, perspectives on race and culture did indeed factor into my decision. As part of my agreement in merging with the company, I inherited six longtime artistic associates—all actors, and all of whom are white (as is the entire board and staff). During the rehearsal-, performance-, and season-planning processes it became abundantly clear that we had fundamentally differing ideas about effective leadership and how to create stories for the stage.

When pressed for details by the media and the genuinely curious here in Chicago on how race may have impacted my departure, I answer in this way: If you liken my creative self to a gumbo, the specificity of my race and primary cultural influence is the equivalent of a dominant spice. Its presence is formidable, and yet its inherent function is to complement and enhance the other ingredients. And though you can clearly taste and identify the specificity of the spice, once it has been added to the gumbo and allowed to simmer, it can never be extracted because it has fully blended itself into, through, and around the other ingredients, altering their nature forever. There were aspects of the "spice" I inherently bring to my work and leadership style that the prevailing palate at Remy Bumppo was unable or unwilling to digest.

The majority of mainstream American theatre has built its reputation by producing highly literate Eurocentric plays and, as a direct result, the majority of mainstream American centers for actor training build their pedagogical paradigms upon Eurocentric principles. I had the good fortune of receiving my classical actor training at Yale School of Drama and was blessed to do so during the tenure of Lloyd Richards, and I counted as my primary acting teacher and mentor the visionary Earle Gister (who just recently made his transition). In those days, one did not audition but was simply cast in roles that the faculty felt would be best for the acting student to wrestle with at that point in their development. Of the thirty-three productions I performed in during my three years at Yale, only once was I cast in a leading role actually designated for a Black man.

I'll confess that I used to hold racial resentment about this until I had a revelation a few years back. It struck me that the most influential aspect of my training was in getting to deeply explore—by default—what it is to be "other" while at the same time having to convey a genuine authenticity in each role. My white counterparts always got to "be white" without ever having to bring the concept of whiteness to conscious mind. They were allowed to simply build a character as part of, and on top of, who they innately were. In my acting I wasn't playing "white" per se, but in each case I was most definitely (subliminally, but not subtly) asked to suspend my innate "Blackness" in order to accomplish the task at hand, and it was expected that I appear as authentic in my characterizations as my fellow actors who were melanin-challenged.

My latent revelation lay in the fact that I actually received a phenomenally comprehensive exploration of cultural craft at a depth far beyond those of my classmates, who rarely, if ever, were asked to explore outside of race and/or culture. Further (if I'm to believe the assessment of my acting instructors), it actually makes me a more accomplished theatre practitioner than my classmates because I succeeded in being able to authentically bring forth a living, breathing cultural equivalence through craft. It's why today I feel as confident in my approach to William Shakespeare, Jane Austen, and Beth Henley as I do when approaching Alice Childress, August Wilson, and Robert O'Hara... I know both creative worlds intimately and equally.

It is also why, when dragged into discussions about race and diversity in the theatre, and the seemingly inexhaustible question surrounding "Who has the right to tell whose story?" that I hold firm to a seemingly paradoxical double standard of expressing full confidence and qualification in my directing the European classics while holding suspect the motivation and abilities of my white counterparts when at the helm of an Afrocentric work. My objection isn't across race lines, per se, and I am most definitely not saying that white directors should not direct Black works—not at all. What I am standing up for is the integrity of storytelling itself, and insisting that the director possess the fundamental capacity to fully realize the foundational bottom layers of a culturally specific work, and I don't know how one does this effectively if one has not "lived" inside of it. I can tell you all about the properties of honey—its sweetness, stickiness, sensuousness of flavor, and truly indescribable sensation on the tongue until blue in the face—but you will never "know" honey until you taste it!

In the recent case of the Broadway revival of *Joe Turner's Come and Gone*, I went on record defending every director's right to helm any project they feel passionately drawn to, including Bart Sher—whom I consider to be a truly visionary, gifted, and accomplished director. As a colleague and admirer of his work, I fully defend every artistic choice he made on that production. That being said, I felt there were fundamental layers missing as a result of a basic misunderstanding of, or disregard for, the cultural specificities inherent in that play. I had the benefit of having this discussion with some of the folks at Lincoln Center and remain clear that from the best of intentions one aspect of Mr. Sher's appointment as the director was an act of a kind of diversity, which I can fully get behind. In my opinion, though, American audiences cannot yet claim they've seen so many productions of August Wilson's plays directed by Black directors that the time has now come for an interpretation or deconstruction of the work from a white perspective as the way of unearthing the deeper and nuanced meanings in the plays.

I do ultimately think it unreasonable to believe that the theatre can or should be expected to satisfactorily and/or effectively address all the social ills of the world. For sure, part of our designated mission as its practitioners is to shed the light, ask the provocative questions, teach the hard lessons... and, oh yes, entertain. Still, the pressure is far too great to expect we can collectively bring forth meaningful paradigm shifts given the extremity of current world events. This is why I try to remember to regularly seek perspective by scrutinizing my work in the theatre within the context of the world we currently live.

With regard to perceived differences, whites seem always to be looking to Blacks for the answer to the "race problem." The reason that Black people so often appear to be frustrated about engaging in that dialogue is simply that we do not have the answer and are achingly weary of the question. The task remains for all of us as Americans to emerge from our psychic amnesia surrounding the unresolved legacy of slavery, and on a mass level finally admit that the ongoing conundrum between Blacks and whites is a direct result of the overwhelming and desperate need for the healing of that festering wound—our shared former atrocity. Until the moment comes when there is a genuine attempt on the part of dominant culture to offer a symbolic apology on par, say, with the profound and prolific response to the Jewish Holocaust, we will continue to perpetuate the manufactured and ultimately imaginary rift between the races—on our stages and off.

The answer that whites are looking for is within themselves. If dominant culture could summon the integrity, grace, desire, and wisdom to "go inside" and get underneath that ancestral vibe that believed it was okay to enslave another people, all confusion about the nature of why and how Blacks and whites have been relating to one another would be erased in that instant of revelation. I often wonder why this event has not yet happened. In turning the focus away from Blacks to engage in their own soul's search, do whites fear that we would rise up and engage in a massacre of retaliation? I happen to know the opposite would be true, because we as a people would be too busy enjoying the relief from all the scrutiny we're perpetually under to provide answers we don't have and have never had. Indeed we'd be too busy chillin' with profound gratitude for the much-needed break!

Perhaps this is the next phase of evolution that Dr. Thurman alludes to.

TIMOTHY DOUGLAS

Timothy Douglas (he/him) has staged over one hundred productions globally including for Off-Broadway, ACT, Actors Theatre of Louisville (former associate artistic director), Arena Stage, Berkeley Rep, Boston Lyric Opera, Cincinnati Playhouse (associate artist, board member), the Guthrie, Center Theatre Group, Roundhouse, Steppenwolf, the Great Theatre of China, Downstage (New Zealand), and many others. He is a recipient of the Lloyd Richards Director Award and serves as a distinguished artist-in-residence at Emerson College. timothydouglas.org.

A NEW REVOLUTION?

09 FEBRUARY 2012
JAAN WHITEHEAD

"If the very fabric of our thought had not changed, we would not have been able to change reality."

—*Zelda Fichandler*

Our field was born of a dream, and that dream created a revolution. Fifty years ago, a group of artists dared to believe they could create theatre outside the confines of Broadway and New York that could respond to the needs of art, rather than the needs of commerce. They wanted to produce the classics and new work Broadway was no longer willing to produce and, in doing so, reclaim their art form. It took time and imagination; they were working in a void and had to start from scratch creating the structures and funding to support their art. But they did it, and the rich tapestry of the regional theatre movement was the result.

Today, it is time for a new dream and a new revolution. Propelled by the forces of technology and globalization, we live in a radically changed—and changing—world. Boundaries are dissolving between art forms, between art and audiences, between countries and cultures, and between actual space and cyberspace. The internet is breaking down historic modes of production and changing peoples' expectations of how they interact with each other and with the arts. A new generation of artists has entered the field, many of whom are rejecting our traditional theatre structures as too hierarchical and restrictive and want to create new ways of working. And, although hard to believe, for the first time since our founding we actually have the possibility of major new funding, as the great individual wealth amassed in this country during the past few decades starts to flow into philanthropy. This is an environment filled with remarkable possibilities for the American theatre.

Today, we have the opportunity to change the lives of our artists and audiences, to revitalize our art form and to create revolutionary new institutional and funding structures. But to do this we need to learn to dream again, to free ourselves from established attitudes and historical constraints and open our minds and imaginations to new and exciting possibilities.

But we've become handicapped in our ability to dream. As our field matured, two problems emerged that theatres weren't able to overcome. One is an imbalance between artists and theatre institutions. As theatres grew, they increasingly controlled the resources—the funding and access to audiences—that artists needed to do their work. At the same time, artists became hired workers, jobbed in on a play-by-play basis. Having little to say in the theatre's financial or artistic decisions, artists lost authority over their art. As a result, artists started working for institutions, rather than the other way around, a reversal of the founders' dream and a striking change in the mindset of what role artists would play in the theatre world.

The other problem theatres couldn't solve was that their sources of funding weren't able to keep up with the growth of the field. Particularly in hard times, a squeeze on revenues left theatres open to commercial pressures to cut costs and provide more audience-pleasing work. This squeeze led to two other imbalances creeping into the field that were also alien to our founding. Traditional audiences became accustomed to being consumers rather than collaborators, and we became accustomed to accepting that the art form was tied to the exigencies of funding and institutional constraints rather than to the vitality of its times.

These three assumptions—that audiences are consumers, that artists work for institutions, and that the art form is tied to its financial and institutional limitations—limit our ability to dream. How can we dream if the fundamental elements of our art are so constrained? And how can we dream if we don't believe in our hearts that change is possible in the first place?

As Zelda Fichandler, one of our founders and always our most articulate spokesperson, said on looking back on the history of the field, the founders could not have created a revolution or changed reality if they had not changed "the very fabric of our thought." That is our challenge today: to change the very fabric of our thought, to release our art from the restraints of the past and imagine new realities—a new humanism for audiences, a new freedom for artists, and a new vitality for the art.

IMAGINING NEW REALITIES

"It is by a sense of possibilities opening before us that we become aware of constrictions that hem us in and of burdens that oppress."

—John Dewey

A NEW HUMANISM FOR AUDIENCES

Audiences are being offered new tools of participation to both enhance and alter their experience of the theatre. Can they also be offered a fundamentally new role in the artistic process itself? Is there a deeper value of humanism that extends the mantle of creativity from the stage to encompass the audience, so that audiences become fuller collaborators in the artistic process?

The internet has changed how we communicate in our culture. Internet communication is two-way—there are no fixed barriers of entry. Anyone can go online and communicate with anyone else; it doesn't matter what you look like or whether you have any particular professional or critical credentials. And there are no fixed boundaries for the content put on the internet. Anyone can upload musings, photos, mash-ups, or original art. People are now becoming active makers of content rather than passive receivers of it.

For the arts, this new mode of communication is creating a fundamental change in expectations of what an artistic experience is and where and how this experience takes place. The picture of a well-dressed audience entering a theatre at eight o'clock, passively watching a play on stage, and then clapping and going home is beginning to feel restrictive and old. Dropping in at an arts center where work from different cultures and disciplines is presented on stages, on the web, and on the streets seems more in tune with our changing times.

Audiences today expect more control over the kinds of art they see and when and where they see them, and many theatres have accommodated this expectation by providing in-depth information about productions ahead of time, developing applications for audience members to use on their phones or other handheld devices during or after performances, and asking audiences for input into season planning and other activities at the theatre. But there is a deeper opportunity for change that goes beyond repackaging the theatrical experience to reconceiving the role of the audience in the act of artistic creation itself.

In his book *Art as Experience*, the American philosopher John Dewey argued that artists and audiences are not only natural but necessary collaborators in the artistic process. Just as artists bring their fullest self to creating art, audiences must bring their fullest selves to experiencing it. It is where art and audiences meet that the act of artistic imagination becomes complete. An unread book, an unseen play, or an unheard symphony doesn't find its fullest expression, its true life, without an audience. The problem, as Dewey saw it, was that too often the work was dull, so it didn't engage the full potential of audiences, or that the idea of art had become so compartmentalized in people that they brought only part of themselves to the experience, truncating their side of the partnership.

The director Peter Brook expresses this in a different way in the book *Conversations with Peter Brook*. He says the best kind of theatrical experience for him as a director is one where he wrestles with a muscular play, but then only goes so far, suggesting much but not telling all, leaving the full act of imagination to the audience.

Both authors recognize the innate potential of an audience to respond to art with imagination and creativity. And both believe in a collaboration that is an act of communion between artists and audience in the very act of artistic expression.

A NEW FREEDOM FOR ARTISTS

The Getty Museum in California recently commissioned Anne Bogart's SITI Company, a long-established ensemble theatre, to create a new interpretation of *The Trojan Women*, Euripides' devastating portrait of war. The company was provided six weeks of rehearsal, tech, and preview time before the play opened for a month's run in the museum's outdoor amphitheater on a hill overlooking the Pacific Ocean. Joining the actors and director for much of this time were the play's composer, costume designer, and lighting designer, as well as experts on history, archeology, and art from the Getty's staff. It was a challenging commission—to explore the meaning of war in our war-torn world—and the artists dug deep into character, form, and staging. Beginning each day with their own form of training, they drew on their years of collaborative work together to build this new piece. The experience was exhilarating and exhausting, but they were able to create a memorable performance.

This is an ideal way for artists to work—rigorously, collaboratively, and with enough time for the artistic process to breathe and the work to come to maturity. But this is a luxury and not the way most artists work in this country. Most theatre artists today work for the traditional theatres that have come to define the field. And it is here that our history has created its most difficult legacy. As successful as these theatres have been in bringing their work to communities all across the country, and as much as they contribute to the economic, educational, and artistic health of these communities, they ultimately created an operating model disadvantageous to artists. The institutions built to support artists have come to dominate them, reversing their role in the theatre and creating the assumption that artists work for institutions rather than the other way around. This assumption has become so entrenched in our thinking that we can't see it any more.

Many of our traditional theatres are genuinely trying to respond to the needs of artists. Serious thought is being given to playwrights, and a number of programs have been developed to include them more closely in the development of new work, such as Arena Stage's American Voices New Play Institute. Some theatres are also breaking down the model of subscription seasons by considering each play a separate project that needs its own audience and then involving artists more closely in these projects. And Theatre Communications Group, the national service organization for nonprofit theatres, has spent over a year asking artists how their relationships with theatre institutions could be improved.

But, as constructive as these efforts are, they all unconsciously accept the imbalance as their starting point. One of the most painful things we have learned in recent years is how difficult it has become for artists to defend themselves or their values in hard times. When budgets get pressed, as they so often do these days, smaller plays, shorter rehearsal periods, and hiring film and TV stars all become accepted strategies for survival. But how can artists create their best work under such compromised conditions? And what about artists' pay? Most artists, even after all these years, still cannot make a living wage in the theatre. When you think about it, it is shocking that the field knowingly accepts this diminished artistry, laying it at the feet of necessity. But necessity is what you define it to be. Millions of dollars continue to be spent on constructing and sustaining new theatre buildings, even under recessionary conditions.

As our field decentralizes and alternative ways of working open up, artists have more choice in how and where they work. Internet art, multimedia art, community art, and the growing number of ensemble companies all provide opportunities for artists to gain control over their own artistry. But the most dramatic change that can happen is for people to recognize that institutions should work for artists, not the other way around. Even without new funding or other outside changes, understanding this would create a revolution in itself. And rather than being an assault on our traditional theatres, such a change in thinking could be a catalyst for opening up new and innovative ways to create theatre—a renaissance from within.

In his book *Concerning the Spiritual in Art,* Wassily Kandinsky said that our best artists are prophets who see ahead of the rest of us and lead us forward, but that, to be a prophet, artists must be free. They must be free to follow where their artistic imaginations lead them, unencumbered by inhibiting attitudes and expectations. We are short on prophets today. Some of our older artists remember a time when artists worked in an environment of more freedom. But many of our best artists now are working on the margins, entering more exciting fields like multimedia art or being socialized into the world of traditional theatre. We must create a more fertile environment for prophets.

A NEW VITALITY FOR THE ART

What about the art? Why is so much of our art small when we live in such big times? Why does so much of it feel old when we live in revolutionary times? Is our imagination so hobbled by the long years of financial constraint that we can't see what to do? Is this why we are producing so much Shakespeare—to fill the desire for bigger, more epic work?

We are currently celebrating the 150th anniversary of our civil war. Some years ago, the Chinese artist Cai Guo-Qiang joined with other artists in an event entitled "The Long March: A Walking Visual Display" in which each artist created a different dialogue with chosen sites along the actual route of Mao's famous Long March of 1934–35. They created a contemporary interaction with that event; in effect, they interrogated it. Wouldn't it be exciting if a group of American artists did the same with our civil war?

Recently, Belarus Free Theatre visited this country and performed their play *Being Harold Pinter*, which combined language from Pinter about violence with the actual words of people being held prisoner or tortured under the repressive Belarus regime. Audiences were electrified by the sense of being part of this brutal current event, particularly since these talented young artists were themselves being persecuted. Although the story was told in the guise of artifice, it was viscerally real. The first work is a big, epic work, the second an intimate, personal one, but both are alive with the relevance of their times.

Just as our artists have been subdued in recent years, so has our artistry. Every era has its full share of mediocre art that is quietly lost in the midst of time. And every era creates entertaining art that doesn't aim to be revolutionary, but remains an important part of the field. But for an art form to retain its vitality, its leading edge must change as its world changes; it must maintain a dialogue with its times.

When we look at our main stages, too often the art feels stuck in the twentieth century. Although we have more video, more technology, and more site-specific work, these are changes in appearance, not in substance. We have plenty of novelty today. What we don't have is breathtaking new work that shatters our imaginations and shows us that, in fact, we can have a powerful new dialogue with the world in which we live.

To make that leap forward, we need to stop accepting that our art is limited by funding and institutional constraints. A great play can be performed on an empty stage or in an empty parking lot, and, today, an audience can be gathered through the internet with just a few clicks of a mouse. We suffer from a lack of imagination and courage, not a lack of funds. Although we think we can cajole audiences with pleasing work, what they really want is more relevant work. Our field is filled with new ideas and visionary artists with energy and ambition, but we repress them within our old assumptions and attitudes. We need to free our art into the vitality of its times.

CHANGING OLD WORLDS TO NEW

"The Giving Pledge is an effort to invite the wealthiest individuals and families in America to commit giving the majority of their wealth to the philanthropic causes and charitable organizations of their choice either during their lifetime or after their death."

—The Giving Pledge

A NEW LOGIC OF FUNDING

Due to the accumulation of wealth in this country, we may be entering the greatest age of individual philanthropy since the time of Mellon, Rockefeller, and Carnegie. Recently, Bill and Melinda Gates and Warren Buffett created an initiative called the Giving Pledge, which asks billionaires to pledge half of their wealth to charity. In meetings with prospective donors, they said, "We live in an exciting time for philanthropy when innovative approaches and advances in technology have redefined what's possible." In expressing their own philosophies of giving, many of the potential donors saw their giving as part of venture philanthropy, a participatory philanthropy that aims to be at the cutting edge of investing in new ways of addressing societal problems such as poverty, healthcare, and education.

So far, almost seventy people have signed the pledge, and *Fortune* magazine estimates that this initiative alone will add up to $300 billion to philanthropy in the coming years. When you add the potential of other wealthy people to give, the transfer of wealth from aging baby boomers and the just-developing potential of internet giving, there are startling possibilities for new philanthropic initiatives. We have always depended on political and voluntary giving, but what we need today is a new logic of funding: self-sustaining funding that is fluid and flexible and can be invested in new ways of working and new kinds of art.

What if three or four of the Giving Pledge billionaires each donated $1 billion to endow a new private arts trust that gave funds directly to artists or groups of artists to choose how they wanted to work, or to new kinds of institutional structures? Such a trust could have the same impact on the field today that the NEA had in its early years. Or what if a group of technology billionaires invested in a revolutionary new web-based arts education program that used video game technology to bring the theatre, dance, music, and poetry of different cultures to millions of students around the world in their own languages at little cost? With a program like this, the internet could become a world platform for arts education. Or what if a group of wealthy people from different countries endowed an international institute of the arts that funded not only new festivals and exchanges of art but the creation of art by artists from different cultures working together? Such an initiative would change the future of global art. These are the kinds of new funding structures we need to underwrite the big changes that can take place in the arts. And they are possible if we can attract even a small part of this new philanthropy.

A NEW DIVERSITY OF STRUCTURES

Just as it is true that new funding is possible, it is also true that we can create new structures with the same imagination and ingenuity as our founders. For example, we could build multimedia cultural centers in our cities where entrepreneurial curators could bring together a wide range of creative work that spanned different art forms and cultures. Perhaps this cultural center would exist in a new kind of open and decentralized architecture that spreads out in different directions with many wings and courtyards. In one wing, theatre, dance, and musical artists might be collaborating with their technological counterparts to create a new *Hamlet* or *La bohème* that would be staged at the center but also streamed to schools, offices, and homes as part of the city's New Classics program. In another wing, master musicians from Japan, Chile, and the United States might be helping talented young people develop their craft while collaborating on a new composition of their own. In a courtyard, senior citizens from different parts of the community might be having a story circle that would lead to a play devised and performed by them. And, in the main atrium of the center, a festival of award-winning theatre and dance work from around the country might be taking place. People would drop in for lunch, or after school or work, or in the evening, always welcome to join the many activities going on, with the understanding that the experience of art is an open and accessible experience that can be part of their lives.

We could build a stronger infrastructure for ensemble companies. Ensemble companies, where artists control their own work, are increasingly the model of choice for new artists entering the field. Some groups like the Rude Mechs, Elevator Repair Service, and Culture Clash have gained considerable recognition in recent years and are starting to be booked by traditional theatres as part of their seasons. And some funders, such as the New England Foundation for the Arts and the Doris Duke Charitable Foundation, are providing new and adventuresome funding for them.

But most ensemble companies remain small, underfunded, and underappreciated, still working on the margins of the field. What if we created new consortiums of ensemble theatres that shared a common overhead structure of fundraising, marketing, and other administrative functions? Such consortiums could create economies of scale for these companies, as well as bring them more recognition. What if four or five of these companies banded together in a new kind of subscription season that toured the country, introducing themselves to new audiences and again raising their visibility? What if potential investors saw ensemble companies as the leading edge for change in the field and decided to invest in them? This might change the whole ecology of the field.

There are also many ways our large, traditional theatres can decentralize and change. What if a major theatre decided to take its hierarchical pyramid structure and flatten and extend it out into the shape of a wheel? At the hub of the wheel would be the artistic and administrative leadership, but all the functions of the theatres would move to the spokes radiating out from this hub. And each spoke would have a high degree of autonomy and would include both artists and non-artists in its mix. Isn't it likely that there would be a new release of imagination, a new agency for artists, and perhaps some exciting new art?

A NEW DIALOGUE OF CHANGE

We also need a new dialogue of change. It is always amazing how eagerly we put provocative dialogue on stage, being incensed if donors or board members or even audiences protest, yet are unable to have honest and provocative conversations among ourselves. We don't seem to respect our own ability to create open dialogue like we respect—and honor—it in our art. We have been having conversations in recent years about many things—about audiences, artists, and the need for new models. But these conversations have usually taken place within certain boundaries and have not challenged the basic assumptions constraining us. We need a new dialogue that is respectful of the past but open to fundamental change, a dialogue that challenges basic assumptions and explores real alternatives, one that is not circumscribed by established institutional thinking and one that is based on generosity and respect, so that everyone feels secure in voicing their concerns and ideas. And we need to recognize that change is hard; old identities and habits of thought get fractured and people lose their grounding as the new takes over from the old. So we need to conduct this dialogue with as much grace and understanding as possible.

A NEW REVOLUTION?

We started with a revolution. But it wasn't just a revolution in structure and funding, or even in geography. It was a revolution in thought. If we can change our thinking, if we can restore our basic values and believe that things can be different, if we have the imagination and tenacity to attract new funding and build new structures, if our theatres aren't too rigid and our artists aren't too socialized to change, if we can ignore the naysayers, if we can dream big and want to create big work, maybe we too will create a revolution, one built on the values of our founders but transformed for today's radically new world.

But we have to start with dreaming, for dreaming isn't about providing blueprints for change. Dreaming is about having the courage our founders had to open up space in our imagination to create alternative realities. That is our challenge today.

JAAN WHITEHEAD

Jaan Whitehead (she/her) is an emeritus trustee and past board chair of SITI Company, an ensemble company founded by Anne Bogart. She has served on the boards of the Acting Company, Arena Stage, Living Stage, the Whole Theatre, Theatre Communications Group, and the National Cultural Alliance. She has also served as executive director of Theatre for a New Audience and as development director of Center Stage. Prior to entering the theatre world, she taught political philosophy at Georgetown University. She has published essays in American Theatre *and* HowlRound *and is the co-editor of* The Art of Governance: Boards in the Performing Arts.

THE NEW WORK OF BUILDING CIVIC PRACTICE

09 JULY 2012

MICHAEL ROHD

A QUESTION

Recently, my father asked me what I'm trying to do with regard to my work in civic practice. I told him: "I think we've got a lot of challenges these days in pretty much every private and public sector in this country, and I think artists are a massive untapped resource that could help in surprising and meaningful ways."

He assumed I meant that by making plays about these challenges, artists could aim the attention of audiences at issues and potential solutions. While I love plays, and sometimes make plays, I told him that wasn't what I meant: "I want to help expand the body of practitioners and advocates who recognize the possibility of, and value in, different kinds of partnerships between artists and members of their community."

My father is a retired lawyer who serves as a volunteer attorney at a legal clinic operated by the University of Maryland School of Law in downtown Baltimore. To try to give a specific example, I asked him about the clinic and what he feels they need to better accomplish their mission. He said they need to get the word out, especially in West Baltimore, about the services they offer and make the case (no pun intended) that they are a free, valuable community resource. I responded by saying: "How would you feel about working with a theatre artist who would partner with you to strategize increasing your relationships and visibility in West Baltimore?"

He asked if I meant fliers, or other marketing strategies. I said I did not.

He asked how, then, might an artist help make the clinic's work more visible and accessible?

RELATIONSHIPS (OF THE NON-FAMILY KIND)

Currently, within institutional theatre organizations, community partnerships are most frequently developed to implement programming that surrounds mainstage productions. That programming exists to deepen dramaturgical reach and impact of the work selected and presented by the artists. Institutions sometimes retain partners beyond singular projects, returning to them for help on other projects when content seems aligned with the partner's constituency or mission. These partnerships are valuable; they can effectively build new relationships around meaningful, shared interests, and they help arts organizations broaden the scope of their presence in their local communities. But they operate in a mode of discourse closer to a monologue than a dialogue. The initiating impulse—the voice that puts out the call, so to speak—is the artist. The non-arts partner has a choice: listen, respond, or not. But rarely does the invitation to conversation, to co-creation, come from the partner.

I think, as artists and organizers involved in a collaborative form that demands, arguably, one skill above all others, we are at a moment where we can put that skill to new use. That skill is listening, and we can radically alter our role in our communities if we employ it with greater intentionality and generosity. Arts organizations do not have to engage with non-arts partners solely through a lens of project-based needs. Partnerships can be relationship-based, and projects can originate from a different type of exchange. Producing new work for/in the theatre does not have to only mean making new plays. It can mean producing new relationships, producing new forms of events and processes, producing new ways of crossing disciplinary and sector boundaries.

INTERSECTIONS

Lately, as an extension of Sojourn Theatre's long-term exploration of relationship-based work, and as part of the Center for Performance and Civic Practice's initial activities, I've begun to define civic practice as activity where a theatre artist employs the assets of his/her craft in response to the needs of non-arts partners as determined through ongoing, relationship-based dialogue. It's the intersection of two sets of content. Let's call them an x-axis and a y-axis.

The x-axis is theatre activity that is not limited to the production of plays, but rather is a set of tools, of assets, that theatre artists have access to because of our experience in producing plays (and performance). We bring these assets to the table, any table, where we are invited.

Some of these tools are:

- The ability to design and lead a process where collaborative activity leads to decision-making and shared investment.

- The ability to conceptualize and execute a public event on a specific timeline.

- The ability to synthesize complex content into meaning that can be articulated and understood.

- The ability to problem-solve.

- The ability to turn diverse stakeholders with varied self-interests into coalitions.

We bring these tools of dramaturgy and process to our own spaces. We can bring them and apply them in other spaces— spaces where artistic expression is not the core mission.

The y-axis is a set of needs, or desired outcomes, that we might encounter at those non-arts-based spaces—if we listen. These desired outcomes offer clear starting impulses for collaborative partnership work. They are:

- Advocacy—help increase visibility and propel mission/message.

- Dialogue—bring diverse groups into meaningful exchange with each other.

- Story-sharing—gather and share narratives from a particular population or around a particular topic.

- Civic application—engage the public and decision-makers together in acts of problem-solving and crafting vision.

- Cross-sector innovation—leverage skills and experience from different fields or disciplines to create and manifest new knowledge.

Articulated in another way, some needs of non-arts partners may be described as:

- Building a framework for dialogue around polarizing issues.

- Acknowledging varied self-interests while building coalitions.

- Developing communications strategies for internal and external stakeholders.

- Remaking how site or space is perceived and experienced.

The x-axis is the tools.

The y-axis is the needs.

Civic practice is what can happen where and when they purposefully intersect.

I am not suggesting that artists should be selflessly in service to whatever outcome any community partner desires. As with any collaboration, values must have some alignment. Conversations must reveal some mutual goals. Activity evolves from a shared, generous curiosity and a co-investment in public work. And at the root of this body of practice is the need to listen, over time, so as to discover how the artist assets and the partner needs may serve each other in surprising moments and previously unimagined forms.

SOME EXAMPLES

There are so many out there—these are a few that get at diversity of initiating impulse, institution, form, and geographic region.

- Appalshop's Thousand Kites is a national dialogue project addressing the criminal justice system.

- Los Angeles Poverty Department's long-time work advocating for and working with homeless collaborators on skid row.

- Ping Chong and Company's Undesirable Elements series, now creating thematically specific story-sharing models based on the needs of partners who contact them, such as their *Secret Survivors* production.

- Marty Pottenger's work as full-time artist-in-residence for the City of Portland, Maine, learning the needs of those at work in municipal government and creating programming with civic application.

- Sojourn Theatre's work with the New River Valley Planning Commission and Virginia Tech in five rural Virginia counties using part of Sojourn's interactive production *BUILT* to make spaces for dialogue and create a public engagement tool with civic application.

- Lookingglass Theatre Company's work in Chicago with Alzheimer's patients and their caregivers using the power of cross-sector innovation to address challenging health and long-term-care issues.

And at universities:

- A theatre graduate student in Illinois working with a Muslim Student Association to develop a performance/installation event focusing on image and cultural identity.

- A theatre graduate student in Maryland working with an LGBTQ center to conceptualize a one-day event that merges spectacle, participation, and construction tasks to raise visibility and make a safe space more welcoming.

DOING THE WORK

Since theatre institutions began to grow education departments decades ago, the term "teaching artist" has become a common title for actors, playwrights, directors, devisers, designers, and other theatre artists who spend some portion of their time, and receive some portion of their income, working with people (most often young people) in a massive variety of learning contexts. Whether they are teaching the skills of the artistic discipline, using integrated performance tactics to deepen other curricular areas, or creating theatre events and workshops to help schools examine and discuss challenging social and cultural subject matter, these teaching artists are using the assets listed on the x-axis above. And they are consummate listeners. The best of them are ever sensitive to the needs of partner organizations and the shifting energies of the individuals with whom they collaborate/teach/guide. In other words, we already have a skilled (and underutilized) legion of artists in our midst who can help pave the way for civic practice as a fieldwide endeavor.

In addition, there are many, many theatre practitioners who have never taught but are hungry for the type of engaged work that civic practice offers them and have the skills to undertake that work meaningfully. University theatre programs across the country are seeing exponential growth in demand for courses that deal with civic engagement, community-based practice, site-based collaborations, and applied theatre. In fact, the field of applied theatre is swiftly gaining traction in this country after years of use overseas, subsuming terms and areas that came before it. The challenge of the trending term "applied" is that it suggests those who use theatre tactics for something other than (though perhaps inclusive of) the creation and presenting of performance are in the service game, while those who make and show are in the art game. But our field needs the strengths of varied impulses and the strategies of all forms to cross-pollinate, spiritually as well as aesthetically. The hybrids at the intersection of civic life and artistic activity offer us, individually and as a community of practitioners, the potential to make our arts organizations truly central to the vitality of community life in new and deeply impactful ways.

We can engage with civic, business, social service, community, health, education, and faith-based partners in ways that are relationship-specific and have as starting impulses not just the content we the arts organizations have chosen for presentation but a broad spectrum of activity that places the assets of creativity and collaboration in service to and in partnership with collaborators old and new. There is capacity-building to do in our field—around skills, partnerships, and leadership. By doing that work, we can, as specific organizations and as a field:

- Build an increased pool of stakeholders and an expanded spectrum of what participation in the arts means.

- Offer new and meaningful opportunities for artists to invest in their communities, practice their art, and build demand for creative public activity.

- Increase demand for the assets that artists bring to community settings beyond the sites where art is traditionally contained and presented.

A RESPONSE

My father asked me: "How could a theatre artist help make the clinic's work more visible and accessible?"

I told him:

With partners in West Baltimore who wanted to act as hosts and believed in the services the clinic offers, a partner artist could work to help shape public conversations and develop interesting, creative ways to bring the clinic and community members in contact with each other. I don't know what form imaginative acts or expressive actions might take in this specific instance. But a theatre artist drawn to this work is accustomed to shared, collaborative goals, has experience in creating inclusive process, and, most importantly, knows what they don't know, and how to know more. By listening.

CONCLUSION

Producing new work does not have to only mean making new plays. And our new work practice can excel not just in the caliber of our expression but in the quality of our listening. If we can accomplish that, we model what civic life today desperately needs: a practice that places dialogue ahead of monologue, imagination at the heart of problem-solving, and listening as equal in value to expression.

MICHAEL ROHD

Michael Rohd (he/him) is an artist for civic imagination with Center for Performance and Civic Practice and a founding ensemble member at Sojourn Theatre. His work as a theatremaker has been seen at sites including Oregon Shakespeare Festival, Steppenwolf Theatre, La Mama, Flint Youth Theatre, and Cleveland Public Theatre. In his work with arts councils, artists, community nonprofits, and municipal agencies around the country, he helps build appetite and capacity for artists to contribute towards institutional and systemic transformation.

RURAL THEATRE IN A DEMOCRACY

01 OCTOBER 2012
DUDLEY COCKE

We know that, in the aggregate, incomes and life expectancies in rural America are significantly lower; infant mortality rates and drug abuse are significantly higher. Presently, there is insufficient attention to such disparities—per capita federal spending remains persistently lower in rural communities, and only 1 percent of private foundation giving in all categories reaches rural not-for-profit organizations. We also know these disparities persist in a grinding recession that has affected middle- and working-class and economically poor people regardless of geography.

I direct Roadside Theater, a part of Appalshop, in the rural central Appalachian coalfields. As one of the nation's handful of rural professional theatres, Roadside has never wanted to be isolated as a special case, nor has it wanted its rural region to be separated from the fortunes and misfortunes of the rest of the country. Roadside's stalwart collaborators over the past thirty years have been actors and musicians in the South Bronx, African American storytellers and musicians in New Orleans, and young and old tradition bearers in Pueblo Zuni, New Mexico. With Pregones Theater, Junebug Productions, and Idiwanan An Chawe, Roadside continues to make new plays—co-productions that are often bilingual and always intended for the entire community.

Rather than make a special case for rural theatre, I wish to make a plea for the democratic arts.

Roadside's regional audience in the mountains of eastern Kentucky, southern West Virginia, northeastern Tennessee, and southwestern Virginia is low income and working- and middle-class people from all walks of life and of all ages. The theatre also tours—so far to communities in forty-three states—reaching an audience whose demographics match those of our regional audience. Six years of national tracking in the 1990s by AMS, an independent research firm, found 73 percent of Roadside's audience earned less than $50,000 a year and 30 percent of those earned $20,000 or less. This demographic is close to the inverse of the national norm for professional theatre, in which 80 percent of the audience comes from the wealthiest 15 percent of the population. A 2002 national poll by the Urban Institute found that "96 percent of respondents said they were 'greatly inspired and moved by art.' However, only 27 percent said that artists contribute 'a lot' to the good of society."[1]

Alexis de Tocqueville begins his 1835 magnum opus, *Democracy in America*, by declaring, "No novelty in the United States struck me more vividly during my stay there than the equality of the conditions." In his chapter "Some Observations on the Theater among Democratic Peoples," he states that "drama, more than any other form of literature, is bound by many close links to the actual state of society," and he goes on to argue that,

> *only in the theatre have the upper classes mingled with the middle and lower classes, and if they have not actually agreed to receive the latters' advice, at least they have allowed it to be given. It has always been in the theatre that the learned and the educated have had the greatest difficulty in making their tastes prevail over that of the people and preventing themselves from being carried away by them. The pit often lays down the law for the boxes.*

de Tocqueville concludes by stating, "An aristocratic theatre may survive for some time in a democracy, sustained by the traditional tastes of some, by vanity, by fashion, or by the genius of an actor. But soon it will fall of its own accord, not overthrown but abandoned."[2]

While today overwhelmingly attended by the wealthiest adults, theatre in the United States once had broad appeal. In the 1820s, New York City's African Company

1   Dudley Cocke, "Class and the Performing Arts: Class Diversity in Community Development," *Roadside Theater*, fall 2008, https://roadside.org/asset/class-and-performing-arts-class-diversity-community-development.

2   Alexis de Tocqueville, *Democracy in America*, trans. George Lawrence, ed. J. P. Mayer (New York: Anchor Books/Doubleday & Company, Inc., 1969).

was presenting *Macbeth* and *Othello* (both popular in Shakespeare's time with rich and poor alike) as well as *The Drama of King Shotaway*, which called for a United States slave rebellion. (As the African Company became increasingly popular with white New Yorkers, the Company's producing director, Mr. Brown, found it necessary to restrict them to one section of the theatre because "some whites did not know how to behave themselves at entertainments designed for ladies and gentlemen of color.")[3]

From 1900 to 1940, the indefatigable Virginia Fábregas—the First Lady of the Mexican Stage—performed for rural and urban Hispanic communities across the United States with a touring company of fifty, including a full orchestra. During the same period, the seeds of the little theatre movement were being sown in upstate New York by Cornell University's Alexander Drummond, who believed every community deserved a theatre to stage its local life. By the 1950s, the little theatre movement had spread across the country, often through partnerships with state agriculture extension agencies. Here is Robert Gard, one of the national leaders in this movement, reflecting on his life's work in 1992 at Cornell University, his alma mater, in what was to be his last public presentation:

> *As I stood thinking, the Great Butternut Valley that was all around me turned golden in the afternoon light. I looked at the hills, and suddenly my spirit was filled and lifted with a clear knowledge. I knew that there must be plays of the people filled with the*

3   William B. Branch, ed., *Black Thunder: An Anthology of Contemporary African American Drama* (New York: Mentor Books, 1992).

spirit of places, and my aimless activities assumed meaning. I felt the conviction then that I have maintained since—that the knowledge and love of place is a large part of the joy in people's lives. There must be plays that grow from all the countrysides of America, fabricated by the people themselves, born of toiling hands and free minds, born of music and love and reason. There must be many great voices singing out the lore and legend of America from a thousand hilltops, and there must be students to listen and to learn, and writers encouraged to use the materials.[4]

From 1935 to 1939, the Federal Theatre Project started to lay out a commons where artists, unbounded by geography, could mix. In the Federal Theatre Project's first two years, it sponsored more than forty-two thousand performances, reaching an audience of more than twenty million Americans in city and hamlet—65 percent of whom were seeing a live play for the first time. On one day alone, 27 October 1936, twenty-two productions of Sinclair Lewis's *It Can't Happen Here* opened simultaneously in seventeen states and in three languages. The Federal Theatre Project's national director, Hallie Flanagan, boiled down the federal agency's mission to "national in scope, regional in emphasis, and democratic in attitude."[5] In her 1940 memoir, *Arena*, Flanagan remains proud of the Federal Theatre Project's public stand against reactionary political currents roiled by geographic, racial, class, and religious prejudice.

---

4   Dudley Cocke, Harry Newman, and Janet Salmons-Rue, *From The Ground Up: Grassroots Theater in Historical and Contemporary Perspective* (Ithaca, NY: Community Based Arts Project/ Cornell University, 1993).

5   Cocke, Newman, and Salmons-Rue, *From The Ground Up.*

After the Second World War, the Black arts movement, inspired by the civil rights movement, took the lead in the vision of theatre of, by, and for the American people by sparking similar arts movements among Chicanos, Appalachians, and Asians. And despite living with the legacy of genocide, Native Americans continue to inspire us all by perpetuating their sacred and secular performance traditions in which entire communities participate.

For these various movements, the central policy issue was how to level the playing field so that all cultures in the United States would have an equal chance to express themselves, to develop, and, inevitably, to cross-pollinate. Despite this shared democratic agenda and a common adversary of monocultural elites, seldom did the different advocates of this policy of cultural equity join as one to press for their cultural rights; rather, each group typically fought alone, mimicking established patterns of social segregation.

Whenever diverse groups did start to pull together in solidarity, the powerful interceded. This was the case in 1939 when Congress (with the aid of the Justice Department and the FBI) closed the Federal Theatre Project; the Project had been too successful advancing theatre that crossed lines of race, place, and class. The 1965 enabling legislation for the National Endowment for the Arts (NEA) states its purpose as: "to support the development and growth of the arts throughout the United States and to provide opportunities for wider appreciation of the arts and the encouragement of excellence." For an analysis of the NEA's fate in the culture wars launched in the 1980s by right-wing power brokers, see "The Unreported Arts Recession of 1997."[6]

6   Dudley Cocke, "The Unreported Arts Recession of 1997," *Roadside Theater*, 5 February 2016,. https://roadside.org/asset/unreported-arts-recession-1997.

It is an axiom of power that who controls the culture controls the story a nation tells itself. So it is especially important that the arts contribute to a national rededication to creating a level playing field across all sectors of society. Will the rural voice be heard in the coming story the nation tells itself about itself? And will that voice rise up with the voices of others presently segregated and muted? That is the promise of art in a twenty-first-century democracy that seeks a more perfect union.

DUDLEY COCKE

 *Dudley Cocke was director of Roadside Theater from 1978 to 2018, and from 2012 to 2014 he simultaneously served as acting director of the Appalachian media center Appalshop, of which Roadside is one branch. Under his direction, Roadside performed its original plays in forty-nine states, with extended runs Off-Broadway in New York City, and represented the United States at international festivals across Europe. In addition to his primary responsibilities at Roadside, which included stage directing and playwriting, he co-founded two national multicultural arts coalitions and served on the boards of three private philanthropies. He received the 2002 Heinz Award for Arts and Humanities.*

WE ARE NOT A MIRROR: THEATRE MUST LEAD WITH WOMEN'S STORIES

24 APRIL 2013
LAUREN GUNDERSON

Here's the thing: theatre should lead culture, not follow it. If the theatre we are making today solely reflects society, then we're failing it. We are not a mirror, we are a lens. We see what's coming, we embody it, we catalyze it, and we make the better future happen because we tell its story first. Or we should.

Unfortunately, with regard to women, their stories, and their valuable lives valued onstage, the American theatre right now is a mirror, not a lens. We look backward (like mirrors do), we look at ourselves (like mirrors do), and we show the world as it is, not as it should be. That doesn't sound like an urgent art form to me. That sounds safe. That sounds easy. That sounds boring.

Generally, a third of the roles go to women actors versus men. Twenty percent of plays produced are by women versus men. Only six women have ever won the Tony for directing.

Now, are we storytelling artists catalyzing a better world, or are we tractors hauling the old guard forward? Are we defining our age or merely maintaining the status quo?

I'm not saying all theatre needs to address this issue, and if it does that it be with serious, frowning faces. Feminism can be fun, funny, heartwarming, thrilling, suspenseful, and poetic. We needn't be righteous to be right. We can still have fun, and entertain, and do the great old plays of yore. But for the love of god, if theatre's stats on women are as bad as the United States Congress's, then we are not doing our art right.[1]

This is happening in London theatre too, as an article from the *Guardian* presents:

> *This failure to represent women, argued the actor, writer and director Stella Duffy, was deeply entwined with society's wider failure to put women's voices on an equal footing with men's. A sense of responsibility to the world was, she said, being ducked – particularly by our larger national stages. In*

1 Women in the United States Congress are at 18.6 percent. Women in the United States Senate are at an all-time high of 20 percent. Boy, those numbers sound familiar.

an impassioned blogpost, she wrote: "When we do not see ourselves on stage we are reminded, yet again, that the people running our world (count the women in the front benches if you are at all unsure) do not notice when we are not there. That they think men (and yes, white, middle-class, middle-aged, able-bodied men at that) are all we need to see."[2]

This wouldn't be as deeply infuriating if the audiences for our work weren't decidedly women. Seventy percent of theatre ticket-buyers are women and at least sixty percent of the audience members in every theatre are women. And yet our women-driven audiences are, over and over again, given men-driven stories, written and directed by men.[3]

WHAT CAN WE DO?

We can ask ourselves these questions while doing season planning:

1   How many roles will we offer to women compared to men?

2   How many plays do we plan to produce that are written by women compared to men?

3   How many of our productions will be directed by women compared to men?

2   Charlotte Higgins, "Women in Theatre: Why Do So Few Make It to the Top?" *Guardian*, 10 December 2012, https://www.theguardian.com/stage/2012/dec/10/women-in-theatre-glass-ceiling.

3   Elizabeth Freestone, Chloe Glover, Ami Sedghi, and Chris Fenn, "Women in Theatre: The Key Statistics – Interactive," *Guardian*, 11 December 2012, https://www.theguardian.com/stage/interactive/2012/dec/11/women-theatre-key-statistics.

4   How many women designers are we hiring compared
    to men?

Then count. *If the numbers don't look fair, it's probably not
fair.* And theatre is better than that.

Some theatres are already proving to be better than that.
I'll use my community in San Francisco as an example.
Shotgun Players in Berkeley is planning an all-women-
written season in 2015; Symmetry Theatre won the 50/50
Applause Award from the International Centre for Women
Playwrights for its work consistently producing plays with
gender parity in casting; TheatreWorks in Silicon Valley
announced a season with *more* roles for women than men,
Crowded Fire reaches parity in almost every category
(women directors, writers, and actors; the theatre's staff
is four women and one man). And, recently, a new group
of excited women theatre practitioners has sprung up
called Yeah, I Said Feminist, started by Fontana Butterfield
Guzman, to rally behind women-positive productions. Good
news, friends. Good news.

And we need good news. Because the world is already
unfair to women in terms of political underrepresentation,
sexual predation, dismissiveness of ability, misogyny, lack
of equal pay, lack of leadership opportunities in business,
not to mention rampant physical and emotional safety in
and out of the home.

Should theatre be on that list too? Hell no. *Theatre should
teach that list a lesson.*

LAUREN GUNDERSON

 *Lauren Gunderson (she/her) is one of the most produced playwrights in America since 2015, topping the list twice including 2019–20. She is a two-time winner of the Steinberg/ATCA New Play Award for* I and You *and* The Book of Will, *the winner of the Lanford Wilson Award and the Otis Guernsey New Voices Award, a finalist for the Susan Smith Blackburn Prize and the John Gassner Award for Playwriting, and a recipient of the Mellon Foundation's* residency with Marin Theatre Company. She studied Southern literature and drama at Emory University and dramatic writing at NYU's Tisch School where she was a Reynolds Fellow in social entrepreneurship. Her play The Catastrophist, about her husband, virologist Nathan Wolfe, premiered digitally in January 2021. She co-authored the Miss Bennet plays with Margot Melcon, and her audioplay The Half-Life of Marie Curie premiered Off-Broadway and at audible.com. Her work is published at Playscripts, Dramatists Play Service, Methuen Drama, and Samuel French. laurengunderson.com.*

MY PARENTS WERE TIGER PEOPLE:

CHRISTOPHER OSCAR PEÑA CHATS ABOUT WRITING RACE WITH A. REY PAMATMAT

19 MAY 2013

A. REY PAMATMAT AND
CHRISTOPHER OSCAR PEÑA

A. Rey Pamatmat: In the lobby for a production of my play *Edith Can Shoot Things and Hit Them* I overheard a woman say, "This play would get done everywhere if the main characters weren't Asian."

Discussing the same play, a young future theatre professional asked, "Why are Kenny and Edith Filipino?" To which I replied, "Why are you white?" And in the year following my apparent need to justify putting Asian American characters on stage, others did their best to keep Asian actors *off* stage by casting white actors in yellow/ brownface (*The Nightingale, The Orphan of Zhao*, and *Pippin: A Bollywood Spectacular* come to mind).

Imagine my surprise when, upon the Flea's announcement of my friend christopher oscar peña's gorgeous play *a cautionary tail*, I felt compelled to ask why his main characters are Chinese American. chris is Latino, and his plays feature characters of his own ethnicity in Icarus Burns or of other Latino descent in *TINY PEOPLE*. All three plays deal with bicultural identity, but in a world that doesn't seem to want Asians onstage, why would a Latino playwright compose a play with two Chinese American leads?

christopher oscar peña: Like you, my initial response is: Why not? This is *America* right? There are two reasons I do it. I grew up in the Bay Area, and San José has the largest population of Vietnamese people outside of Vietnam. There were ninety-nine Nguyen's in my high school class. My best girlfriend was hapa (white-Japanese). The first guy I dated was a Filipino-Spanish mix. I ate lumpia and pho more than tacos, which is what people expect because I'm Latino. Asian Americans are part of my cultural identity and upbringing. To question why I write them is to deny my history.

As American playwrights of color, we are often told what we should be writing, restricting our work to simplistic ideas of race and class politics. As Tanya Saracho and I say, Latino writers are asked to write "rice and beans" plays about immigration, drug cartels, and the working class. That expectation assumes we're all the same, and—most problematically for me—it creates a theatrical culture of inauthenticity. There are amazing Latino playwrights writing about these subjects; they're true and important to them. But when you force me to do that, you're perpetuating a lie.

The second reason I do it is because there are incredible Asian actors who I want to see on stage! Often people in various cities say, "We can't find good Asian actors," or, "We went with the best actor (who happens to be white)." If casting directors can't find good Asian actors, they should quit their jobs (or call me). I write Asian parts because I want to see Jennifer Ikeda, Maureen Sebastian, Peter Kim, Louis Changchien, Mia Katigbak, Rodney To, Jon Norman Schneider, Angel Desai, Ruibo Qian, Angela Lin, Alexis Camins, Dax Valdes, Ching Valdes-Aran, and so many others on stage.

Rey: Do you know of work from Latino colleagues that features non-white or non-Latino characters? I specify Latino because somehow Asian American playwrights easily get away with writing diverse casts in a way that other writers (certainly white writers) don't. I'm thinking, for example, about Qui Nguyen's many Black and LGBT characters; Carla Ching's *Sugar House*, which was written for performers of four different backgrounds; and Lloyd Suh's *Jesus in India*, where the characters were Middle Eastern and Indian. Who else is "getting away with it," and do you have any theories as to why?

chris: Kristoffer Diaz's *The Elaborate Entrance of Chad Deity* and Quiara Alegría Hudes's plays *Water by the*

Spoonful and *The Happiest Song Plays Last* feature well-written, complex characters of African American, Asian, Indian, and Persian descent. In those plays, the main characters—or the people through whose lens we're tracking the play—are Latinos. So maybe the thing that surprises people about my work is that in at least three plays the protagonists are of Asian descent.

Last summer I was part of Two River's Crossing Borders Festival with Tanya Saracho, Andrea Thome, and Carlo Alban. All of our plays featured all Latino characters (*Icarus Burns* is my only all-Latino play), and during a panel the question of what makes a play or a playwright "Latino" came up.

I feel very connected to these exceptional writers (and friends), but I also feel very different from them. Of the four, I'm the youngest. Andrea and I were both born in the United States, but I was born in the Bay Area, a land filled with the children of all types of immigrants who didn't feel different from each other because our differences made us alike. When these playwrights write about immigration or learning English as a second language, the stories are in their DNA, which is why it feels false when someone says I should be doing it. Obviously, I don't know everything about everyone's work, but I think they're writing mostly Latino characters. That's not a bad or good thing. I would never tell them who should be in their plays, but their characters are different from mine.

I'm a huge fan of companies like INTAR and Ma-Yi, which were created to give voice to artists of color. But I wonder whether we need to think of their evolution as race and class evolve. For instance, I have plays with strong Asian roles, but Ma-Yi can't do them, because I'm not Asian. But those plays don't work for INTAR, because featuring their awesome ensemble of Latino actors is important to them. So where do I fit? I dream about a collaboration on one of my plays between those two companies.

This question also makes me think of Naomi Iizuka and Jorge Ignacio Cortiñas. If I'm not mistaken, Jorge's play *Blind Mouth Singing* was either written for Latino actors or wasn't race-specific, but it was produced by NAATCO with an all-Asian company. And it was stunning.

Naomi—my first teacher and the first person to call me a writer—defies being pinned down ethnically in a way that allows her to explore complex ideas and allows more people to experience her plays. I believe her mother is a Spanish woman raised in Queens, her father is Japanese, and she was raised all over world. She navigates between worlds remarkably in her life and work, and we should all be allowed to do it.

So some people do "get away with it" but not as many as I'd like to see.

Rey: Let's go back to something else you said. I love what theatre did for identity politics, but a lot of writers bump up against the strict definitions you're talking about. I'm often confronted by "compliments" that my plays aren't "just" gay plays or "just" Asian American plays. Then, on the flip side, I'm criticized that they aren't gay or Asian "enough." The implication is that my life experience is a limit rather than a gift, when the real limit is others' ideas of what gay or Asian American plays can be. If you could describe your play *a cautionary tail*—keeping the "Latino," "Asian," "gay," or whatever labels away from it, while still embracing its celebration of these things—how would you begin?

chris: I'm going back to Naomi. Dan LeFranc did an interview where he talked about not thinking his childhood was all that interesting, until one day Naomi said something like, "You grew up near Disneyland? What was *that* like?" Suddenly this thing that seemed mundane to Dan empowered him to write his story and to trust his voice.

Again, it's about authenticity. I don't have a problem with labels; I have a problem with being told to have only one and what that one has to be.

There is one identity I wear proudly: I'm a writer in and responding to "my generation." People have a lot to say about us, but it's rare that we get to tell our own story. Our generation grew up with a stronger—though not complete—acceptance of evolving sexualities. Our generation communicates in new ways, which is exciting but also completely terrifying. Our generation grew up with mixed-race kids. Sometimes we're lost or confused, so we're constantly exploring, continually questioning until we see what fits. In my work, that means writing about different people, writing about history and memory, reinventing myth, telling stories from different angles, and changing style, structure, tone.

People need to be okay with labels evolving and redefining themselves. I also wish plays were experienced on their own. The context of the writer's identity is totally exciting… afterward. Let that add to the conversation, not be it.

Rey: I admire that ethnicity is neither the root of *a cautionary tail*'s primary struggle nor is it incidental.

A common misstep when writers cross racial lines is dramaturgical "justification" of their character's background (sometimes offensively), or conversely use of race as a marker without regard to how it shapes character. I've seen playwrights write characters as Latino to indicate that they're poor, or justify underdeveloped women characters by saying they're Asian and de facto mysterious, and hey—this character's cool, because he's Black! Because Black equals cool (don't tell the blerds). How would you describe the central themes of your play, and what about those themes compelled you to write Chinese American leads rather than Honduran, Vietnamese, or Filipino ones?

chris: Originally, this play was a commission by Mark Wing-Davey for NYU Grad Acting. There were three Asian actors in this class, all different ethnicities. He wanted to feature them, so he gave me *Battle Hymn of the Tiger Mom* by Amy Chua and said, "*Go!*" I remember thinking this could go badly and seem racist right away.

So I anchored myself in themes that were true to me, and I realized that the "tiger mom" idea isn't just about Chinese mothers. It's about how an immigrant raises his/her child. My parents were tiger people, so making my leads Asian reaffirmed the commonalities we all share. This play is about how fast the world is moving, how we're all struggling to keep up, and how often we've lost the game before we've even realized we were playing it.

Rey: Finally, let's talk casting. Asian American and Latino performers famously have been plagued by white actors in yellow/brownface taking the few roles available for them. A surprising recent example is New Theater's production of *Around the World in 80 Days* where a white woman will play Aouda, a South Asian—doubly surprising because one of the producers is Asian American. Why does this problem persist? And what can artists do to make people understand how ignorant this practice is?

chris: Honestly, it's too baffling to even process. People are being naively racist or willfully ignorant at best.

a cautionary tail and the Flea itself are important for artists because they embrace our various experiences as people. Our multiethnic cast has an adopted Asian woman who was raised by white parents. We have another Asian woman who emigrated from China. We have a guy who is half Black, half German-Jew. There's a guy who didn't relate to the immigrant experience, until I pointed out that his parents were Brits and he was first-generation. Suddenly he realized that we perceived "immigrant" as Brown. These varied histories add to the conversation and elevate the story we're telling. That's incredibly exciting!

Many of us make work like this and call attention to these things because we believe in the power of theatre. But then these casting issues occur, and it's all so wrong and outdated that theatre feels irrelevant.

As who and what an American is and looks like grows, we want theatre to be part of that conversation. Instead, we look on stage and think, "*That's* the conversation we're having, those are the voices, those are the faces?" It's so far behind we might as well be in dialogue with other art forms that *are* interested in who we are today. Hopefully, the mainstream theatre will figure this out sooner rather than later, because the fact is *we are the mainstream.*

A. REY PAMATMAT

A. Rey Pamatmat *(all pronouns accepted) has written plays including* Edith Can Shoot Things and Hit Them *(Actors Theatre of Louisville), after all the terrible things I do (Milwaukee Rep),* House Rules *(Ma-Yi),* Thunder Above, Deeps Below *(Second Generation),* A Spare Me *(Waterwell), and* DEVIANT. *He is currently working on* Safe, Three Queer Plays, *a cycle that follows the seismic changes in queer America through a gay man of color's romantic and artistic life. Rey is the former co-director of the Ma-Yi Writers Lab and was a PoNY, Hodder, and Princess Grace fellow.*

CHRISTOPHER OSCAR PEÑA

christopher oscar peña *(he/him) has written plays including* The Strangers *(the Clarence Brown Theatre), a cautionary tail (the Flea Theater),* how to make an American Son *(Arizona Theatre Company, Rattlestick Playwrights Theater). He is an artistic associate at Arizona Theatre Company and a member of New Dramatists. In television, he was a writer on the Golden Globe–nominated debut season of the CW show* Jane the Virgin *and the critically acclaimed HBO show* Insecure, *as well as the Starz show* Sweetbitter *and the Freeform series* Motherland: Fort Salem. *He is currently a supervising producer on the ABC show* Promised Land, *where he is also developing an original series.*

A SHRINKING LANDSCAPE: THEATRE CRITICISM IN CHICAGO THEN AND NOW

02 OCTOBER 2013

JOSH SOBEL

The tension—healthy or unhealthy—that has always existed between the artist and the critic is no secret. Having one's creation judged by someone whose role seems to be to dictate the value of said work is a naturally touchy endeavor. Egos flare, defiant stances are taken, fingers point, and artists either breathe sighs of relief or look ahead to the task of rebuilding.

Given the personal stakes at play here, it is no surprise that artists tend to view critics with trepidation and suspicion, if not outright disdain.

This is one of several things that make the Chicago theatre scene a bit remarkable, since many argue that the wealth and depth and scope of work happening every day is due in part to critics. One name in particular comes up again and again: Richard Christiansen, who started at the *Chicago Tribune* in 1978 and was subsequently the paper's chief drama critic until 2002.

But this article is not merely a history lesson, a look back at one of the true greats in dramatic criticism. This is a look at the impact a critic can and does have on an entire community, how critics can nurture that community, and how the shrinking of the critical landscape in Chicago and elsewhere is a much more distressing prospect to our chosen careers than I think artists realize.

***

To attempt to recall Christiansen's immersion into the Chicago theatre scene would require an entire book in itself. Thankfully, Christiansen has already written such a book—*A Theater of Our Own: A History and a Memoir of 1,001 Nights in Chicago*[1] is a must read for any artist or art lover of any town to gain a larger sense of the evolution of a theatrical community, of the value of taking risks, of failing and picking back up, and of unquenchable determination to make one's voice heard.

---

1   Richard Christiansen, *A Theater of Our Own: A History and a Memoir of 1,001 Nights in Chicago* (Evanston, IL: Northwestern University Press, 2004).

In the foreword of the book, stalwart Chicago actor Brian Dennehy sums up what has become Christiansen's legacy: "There was no group so small, no venue so forbidding, that he would not find himself climbing flights of stairs or descending into damp cellars to see what delights or disasters the latest group of young thespians would deliver."

Agree or disagree, it is undeniable that Christiansen paid a great deal of attention to artists outside of the touring houses and Broadway transfers and big-budget spectacles. At the naming ceremony of the Richard Christiansen Theater, Victory Gardens Theater's upstairs studio, I sat in rapt attention as artists such as William Petersen, Rick Cleveland, and others recounted stories of Christiansen first seeing their work in the back rooms of bars and, because the work deserved it, giving them respectful (and at times glowing) reviews.

The thing that seemed to define Christiansen's reviews of the smaller companies was that he never condescended to them in his critique. No matter how scrappy, how low-budget, how tucked away in some warehouse they were, they were not regarded as amateurs; Christiansen always treated and reviewed them as professional productions. As Steve Scott, associate producer of the Goodman Theatre, recalled in a conversation in June, it wasn't necessarily that this was Christiansen's mission, per se. He was just so passionate and articulate about what he saw in these smaller, riskier venues, and thus they were encouraged to keep going. He took young artists seriously—he respected them as equal artists alongside the more established names of the times. This is not to say he loved everything he saw— it would be foolish to expect that of any critic. It was the respect that Christiansen showed that mattered.

When Christiansen began reviewing in Chicago, there were a handful or two of young "storefront" companies, performing in small, makeshift, and/or rented venues, scraping together whatever they could to put on a show. Today, numbers vary but there are anywhere between two hundred and three hundred producing companies of all shapes, sizes, and missions creating work in Chicago. The cause for this expansion is a much-discussed topic, and it often comes back to Steppenwolf's legendary rise—from humble beginnings in a church basement to its current Tony Award–winning, internationally renowned scope. Many young artists fresh out of undergrad come to Chicago with the intention of founding a company and becoming "the next Steppenwolf" (which is a discussion for a different article).

But this analysis leaves out one particularly important factor: the critics who paid attention to Steppenwolf when they were in the church basement, Christiansen included.

This legacy of critics attending the little theatres dotted around the city thrives today. As Christiansen himself has recognized:

> Curious about the tales of opportunities in Chicago, young theatre people in the United States and abroad have migrated to the city, plunging into the stream of activity with the eagerness of those to the city born. They learn that the city's newspaper reviewers will pay attention to productions in the smallest theatres, and they discover that Chicago audiences...are open to new work and new players.

Brett Neveu, a playwright of international reputation who found an artistic home in Chicago, attests to this, recalling (as quoted in *A Theater of Our Own*): "...playwrights I knew, like my friend Rebecca Gilman, kept telling me to come to Chicago. 'You can get produced here,' they said. 'You'll get reviewed here.' That sounded good, and we moved to Chicago."

Since then, Neveu has been commissioned and/or produced at Steppenwolf, the Goodman, A Red Orchid Theatre, American Theater Company, and countless other Chicago companies, as well as abroad at institutions such as the Royal Court. An impressive resume, to say the least.

And it is in this regard—that of the attention paid to the scrappy, small venue risk-takers—that I become concerned for the immediate future.

***

The expansion of the Chicago scene over the last three or so decades is gargantuan, and the task that now faces critics is unenviable. Christiansen agrees: "The problem with writing about theatre in Chicago is that it resists comprehensiveness. There's so much of it, and there's no end to it. In the 1970s, it was possible for one hyperactive person to pretty much cover the beat. That's impossible now."

And yet, valiant efforts have been made to keep up. *The Tribune* does the best it can with shrinking word counts and page real estate, even focusing two of its supporting critics, Kerry Reid and Nina Metz, specifically on the storefront scene. The *Chicago Reader* for a long time was a go-to source of information and opinions on just about every show happening in Chicago, and was a particularly respected resource among artists. In recent years, *Time Out* magazine's Chicago branch (TOC)—led by Christopher Piatt and now by Kris Vire—had emerged as the source that really sought to see and review everything they possibly could. While the reviews were a bit short, in this artist's opinion, they were reliably fair, reliably intelligent, and, as several theatre administrators acknowledged, an invaluable way to stay aware of artists around the city and even scout them for work at larger institutions.

And they really did make a point to see the scene! My first production in Chicago, the world premiere of a new play in the inaugural season of a new company, received an intelligent, balanced (and pretty positive overall) review in *Time Out*. Regardless of the positivity, it was thrilling that *Time Out*—a significant publication with a recognizable brand and no real idea who I was or the playwright was or the company was—came to see our show. My experience is just one story of many. I have encountered countless examples of TOC attending first-time productions by new companies and artists, shining a light on their first work in Chicago. This was a major part of what attracted me to Chicago—Rebecca Gilman's words to Neveu ringing true.

And then, in March of 2013, it was announced that *Time Out Chicago* would be ceasing printed publication, that the majority shareholder in TOC had sold his stock to the parent Time Out Group, which was choosing to go an all-digital route and, later, that a large portion of the staff would no longer be with the publication. The following month I emailed Kris Vire, who remains theatre editor, to ask what sort of impact this would have on *Time Out*'s ability to cover the range of shows it has been able to cover up to this point. While he is still working hard to provide comprehensive coverage, he no longer has the budget he once had for freelance critics, which was a huge part of how he was able to review so much of the beat, particularly the smaller, riskier shows. Since in the prioritization game between storefront theatre and the larger companies, the big guys tend to get the nod, it seems to follow that the number of shows of all shapes and sizes that TOC will be able to cover, and thus the number of new artists and small-venue risk-takers that will be introduced to Chicago through *Time Out*, will be greatly reduced.

***

Audiences pay attention to critics. Reviews help them decide what to see. One hopes that dramatic criticism does more than merely provide a consumer guide; however, one also cannot avoid that aspect of the job. Christiansen writes: "Chicago's artistic and economic strength in the theatre remains anchored in its small and midsize troupes." A recent article on backstage.com agrees that there continues to be a "hotbed of talent" in Chicago storefront theatre.[2]

Without the support, audience reach, and visibility to these smaller groups that established critical resources provide, the game changes significantly. A huge aspect of what has been drawing young, exciting artists to Chicago has shrunk. And if the priorities emerging from this shrinking landscape are aimed toward ensuring reviews for the "biggest" players in the city (in terms of sheer size and budget), are we then moving toward a model similar to that of more commercially driven artistic communities? It is a point of pride in Chicago that small theatre companies have historically carried as much weight and reputation as the big ones. And this is something I believe Chicago artists want to maintain. I certainly do.

2   Suzy Evans, "Chicago's Storefront Theaters Are a Hotbed of Talent," *Backstage*, 23 January 2019, https://www.backstage.com/magazine/article/chicagos-storefront-theaters-hotbed-talent-17562.

While it would be inappropriate to suggest to the critical community that it is the "responsibility" of the critic to seek out the small, the upstarts, the next generation of theatremakers, critics must realize the impact that they *can* have in nurturing a vibrant, bountiful artistic community. The artists build such a community by creating the art. The critics build such a community by paying attention.

In the case of Chicago, the result is a city described as "the current theatre capital of America" in 2004 by the *Guardian*'s Michael Billington.[3] I submit that this was only possible through the attention paid to the "little guys." (And how many of those little guys have gone on to become iconic and household names? Gary Sinise, John Malkovich, William H. Macy, Joan Allen, Jane Lynch, Michael Shannon, Joe Mantegna, Elaine May, William Petersen, Amy Sedaris, Bruce Norris, Tracy Letts, Tanya Saracho.)

And looking at the broader impact of criticism, what is really left once the show, ever ephemeral, is done? Sure, in the age of YouTube and Vimeo there can always be recordings (never the same as the live experience), but in terms of recorded discourse, reviews are our link to, as Christiansen described, "a sense of what it was like when you were there." Or, as *Chicago Reader* critic Albert Williams believes (quoting a former teacher of his), "the best [reviews] were written not just for their own time but for the record." Williams continues:

When people ask me, "Whom do you write for?" I answer, "The future."... In 1966 I was the future—the 15-year-old kid reading Richard Christiansen's

3   Michael Billington, "Off Broadway," *Guardian*, 23 June 2004, https://www.theguardian.com/stage/2004/jun/23/theatre1.

*reviews of Hull House and Second City shows because
I couldn't go to them. The specific words he wrote—
or any critic writes—are less important than the
cumulative excitement they generated over time, the
sense of discovery they engendered, the standards
of excellence they encouraged, and the way all these
things have filtered down through the years.*[4]

I submit that it is this mindset that helped Chicago nearly
ten years ago become the theatre capital of America, and
can help build any artistic community when artists and
critics come together to accept their partnership nurturing
the art. And this is what makes the shrinking critical
landscape feel so personally distressing. I fear losing grasp
of this essential partnership.

Artists will of course persevere. We will find ways to adapt
to the new circumstances. We will find new ways to get
creative in the internet age and build new resources for
visibility and outreach, or perhaps revisit some old ways
(Neo-Futurists founder Greg Allen described to me this past
June how they used to invite people in off the street to see
their weekly "Too Much Light Makes the Baby Go Blind"—
true on-the-ground guerrilla marketing). And I believe
that the critical community will adapt as well, beyond just
starting up more and more blogs.

New models will emerge so that we can have reliable,
trusted sources of artistic criticism that can cover the
vast sea of shows happening in this community. Some
new initiatives have already begun to take shape around
the country, such as Miami's *Artburst*; in this model,

4   Albert Williams, "What Makes a Critic Tick?" *Chicago Reader*, 4 July 2002, http://chicagoreader.
     com/news-politics/what-makes-a-critic-tick.

the Miami-Dade County Department of Cultural Affairs provides a grant to the local Arts and Business Council, which is used to fund a new, independently operated media bureau for the arts that currently covers—and insightfully critiques—a wide range of dance and music in the area, from big-budget companies to more street art–based groups.

However, I think we can only adapt after we have taken complete stock of where we once were, the greater impact over time, and how things have changed over the years. In addition, we, as artists, must acknowledge the larger roles critics are capable of playing in nurturing a theatrical community. It may be a long road ahead in figuring out how to reignite arts criticism across the country in the wake of the ever-evaporating print media and professional journalistic landscape. But it's worth a fight.

JOSH SOBEL

Josh Sobel (he/him) is a director, dramaturg/content developer, and educator specializing in expanded storytelling through pop-influenced, collage-based collaborative approaches. His work has garnered recognition from the Chicago Tribune, Sun-Times, Washington Post, and Time Out, and he was one of Newcity Stage's "Players 2019: The Fifty People Who Really Perform for Chicago." Credits include CalArts CNP, Steppenwolf Theatre, the Eugene O'Neill Theater Center, Haven Chicago, Steep Theatre, Victory Gardens, Flying V, Edinburgh Fringe, and more. He is the executive producer of the upcoming short films "Whole" and "Six Feet Apart," the former artistic director of Haven Chicago, and the recipient of an SDCF Observership. He has a BA from Oberlin College and MFA from CalArts.

I DON'T WANT TO TALK ABOUT INNOVATION: A TALK ABOUT INNOVATION

26 OCTOBER 2013

TODD LONDON

This piece is a revised version of Todd London's address delivered at the National Innovation Summit for Arts + Culture in Denver, 21 October 2013.

I'm reading Dave Eggers' new novel, *The Circle*. It takes place inside a Google-like company by the same name. As the book begins, the Circle's latest hire, Mae, tours the sparkling, communitarian campus, "400 acres of brushed steel and glass." *heaven*, she thinks.

The walkway wound around lemon and orange trees, and its quiet red cobblestones were replaced, occasionally, by tiles with imploring messages of inspiration. "Dream," one said, the word laser-cut into the red stone. "Participate," said another.

There are dozens of these word-bricks, but Eggers just names a few: "Find Community." "Imagine." "Breathe." And yes, you guessed it, "Innovate."

You know where this is going. It's not heaven at all. It's Orwellian hell, Steve Jobs meets L. Ron Hubbard. The people are warm, brilliant, and aglow with a perfectly modulated passion, like those shiny charismatics who dominate the TED Talks. In other words, Eggers' novel describes something like the Platonic ideal of a 24/7 "innovation summit." It's a nightmare.

I'm a writer and I live and work with writers. The stone steps to the old Midtown Manhattan church that houses New Dramatists don't have words etched on them. No one needs to be told to *imagine* or, since they're with us for seven-year residencies, to *find community*. The domed window above the wooden entrance doors does have words, painted in gold: "Dedicated to the Playwright." That's all. We dedicate our service to their efforts and, because art leads change and not the other way around, their work cuts a slow path to the new.

Most of us there—writers, staff, board—swing between incredulity and fury at the rampant spread of this innovation obsession in the arts. So I have to confess: I come to bury innovation, not to praise it.

Here's how the siren call of innovation sounds from our church: It signals another incursion on the arts by corporate culture, directive funders, and those who have drunk the Kool-Aid of high-tech hip and devotional entrepreneurism. It announces the rise of a cult of consultancy, already a solid wing of the funding community. One New York foundation, which formerly gave out sizable general operating support, now requires each grantee to send two senior staffers to spend several mornings at the feet of turnaround-king Michael Kaiser as a prerequisite for payment and any future funding. You follow? They hire a high-paid *macher* to teach us how to fundraise even as they stop funding us.

The world is changing radically and so must we. That's the agenda underlying the innovation mandate. This change agenda is actually a critique, a presumption that arts organizations are calcified, failed. Of course, most of us share this critique and believe it's true of every company but our own. More, it implies that our companies, many five or six decades old, don't know how to adapt.

It's not that we've failed to adapt; we have adapted and adapted, twisting our adaptive muscles into shapes for this funding trend or that initiative, for the new, improved, think it, do it, be it, say it, better believe it world of organizational reorganization until we're blue in the core values. We have lost sight of the ocean, in which we may be sinking, and keep returning to the mechanism of the boat.

Where innovation thinkers see ill-adaptive organizations, I see decades of unsupported art and artists, energy and money thrown at institutional issues, as if this can make the art relevant. I'd suggest it's the funding community that needs to take a deep, humble look at its assumptions and, most urgently, at the human relations and power dynamics of money and expertise. Doctor, please innovate thyself.

Change is no measure of success. Do we do what we say we do? Do we do it well? If we don't, we shouldn't be funded. If we are worthy of funding, we have proved we're capable of self-determination.

So why did New Dramatists attend an "innovation summit," if this is all so wrongheaded, and why did we apply to EmcArts Innovation Lab? It's simple. Funding and learning, in that order. We're as desperate for new funding as the next guy. We've been known to pretzel our priorities to get some. The Lab came with money; the summit with a roomful of important funders. Can we admit this? Both have brought us new colleagues and new insights.

And the summit gave us a chance to talk about artists leading change. To do so in the context of a playwright's laboratory, we have to wrestle with the problem of language. We make home for fifty playwrights in a world of their words. Words discovered and discarded, considered, blown apart, and put back together. Maybe this explains the deep offense I take at the jargon of corporate America that floats the innovation boat.

The freshness of our language reveals the freshness of our thinking. We live with the example of Shakespeare's 1,700 new English words. We live with the awareness that, as the poet Audre Lorde famously wrote, "the master's tools will never dismantle the master's house." And we live with the understanding that, at this moment in history, the master's house is corporate America. Its words are tools that, even uttered with fine intentions and our hearts in our mouths, have one aim: To sell us stuff we don't need. To make a marketplace of our relations.

I teach the history of visionary American theatres to management students at Yale. When we hit the fervent amateur art theatres of the nineteen-teens, the same thing always happens: The students catch fire, infected by grand words: beauty, truth, gift, spirit, play, communion, amateur (from the Latin for "love"), love. Can these chestnuts stand up against our contemporary lexicon: sustainable, adaptive, competencies, sector? We've already sucked the meaning out of that powerhouse word "community." What do we stand for when every website claims the same "core values?"

The summit was not a conference about art. We came together to explore and share organizational-process innovation. But my beauty-truth-gift-spirit-play-communion-amateur-art-heart says enough already. We always talk organization. We've learned the language of strategic thinking and economic impact. We've learned to talk about marketing as though it were community engagement. And now we are challenged to add innovation to the list of empty phrases to live by.

I am grateful to the EmcArts hosts for gathering so many disparate artistic companies together, though I disagree vehemently with the gathering's focus, its leading questions, and the recommendations that inevitably follow. In the weeks leading up to the summit, Richard Evans, EmcArts's president, published an essay in the Grantmakers in the Arts newsletter. He approvingly cites "the first major study of organizational innovation in the not-for-profit sector," in which "the Kellogg Foundation concluded that 'every nonprofit should make innovation part of its core competencies.'"

Since when is it the job of funders to dictate what every nonprofit should do? What is the Foundation's "core competency" that entitles them to tell museums, symphonies, dance and theatre companies what is essential to fulfilling their separate, varied, and sometimes vital missions? Evans then suggests that arts organizations might create capital funds for organizational innovation equal to 20 percent of their operating budgets. Have you ever met a company that actually wants more earmarked capital? For years theatres struggled to build endowments to support the long life of their most essential creative work, to escape the whims of restricted funding. Why in the world would we want a fifth of our budget for mandated newness?

Karina Mangu-Ward, EmcArts's director of activating innovation, seconded Evans' call on HowlRound last week: "We believe that innovation should be considered a core discipline of organization life, along with marketing, administration, fundraising, etc." I'd argue the opposite. Instead of adding another department to our bloated institutions, I'd suggest shrinking those existing departments and bringing more artists in.

Artists innovate every day, because what they make, they make up. How do they innovate? Trial and error, mostly, boring hours alone or with other artists. Years facing their own limitations. The real work of innovation is *theirs, alone or together.* It is organic and ongoing, one bold or tentative foot in front of another. Try to find funding in innovation-land for persistent effort and incremental breakthrough.

Why fetishize innovation? Why not excavation, elaboration, celebration? Not all artistic enterprises, not all historical moments, demand radical departure. More often than not, the new is actually something old, something *other*, that we've previously refused to hear, like all those voices struggling to be heard through the thick white walls of our institutions. But we want our innovations new, even if they're flatuous, a word which, if you don't know, means gassy, inflated, and fatuous. I just innovated it.

There's another crusty word out there: leadership. If art is led by artists, why is the "leader" label applied mostly to us administrators? What would it mean to let them lead? How can we reimagine—innovate if we must—a way forward in which artists curate work, determine who gets funded, and choose the place that will house their work, rather than the other way around?

W. McNeil Lowry, the first great funder of the nation's nonprofit arts, from his perch at Ford, wrote,

> *At its most basic level, art is...about the surge of artistic drive and moral determination.... And philanthropy, in the arts at least, is professionally motivated only when it accepts the artist and the arts on their own terms, and learns from the artist himself at least to recognize the atmosphere in which the artistic process is carried out.[1]*

What an innovative idea: ask artists what they need, what they wish for, what they have. Let that guide practices. Let that guide funding. This is the new thing we've been trying to figure out over the past sixty-five years at New Dramatists—sometimes disastrously and sometimes happily—how to listen and how, with limited means, to make small adjustments with big impact.

1   W. McNiel Lowry, "The Arts and Philanthropy: Motives That Prompt the Philanthropic Act," *GIA Reader* 14, no. 3 (Fall 2003), https://www.giarts.org/article/arts-and-philanthrophy.

Often, it's a matter of words. New Dramatists had a wonderful facilitator in the Innovation Lab, John McCann. In our early discussions with him, board member/alumnus Gordon Dahlquist and then-resident playwright Lucy Thurber turned a simple, pressing question on its head. The staff was asking how to better engage and serve the playwrights. Instead, Lucy and Gordon asked: "What is the writers' responsibility to each other?" Suddenly the ownership and success of the artistic company fell squarely in the laps of the playwrights. Another shift of perspective occurred when playwright Karen Hartman coined the term "host artist" to describe our writers, who mostly think of themselves as guests in the American theatre, waiting to be asked in. In their creative home, they do the inviting. Again, the place became a little more *theirs*.

Playwright Francine Volpe further changed our culture by asking the writers to create a safety net together. She asked each of them to teach one low-cost, two-hour public workshop in their seven years. The money would establish an emergency fund, administered by and for the writers. Within a year they had $4,000 and paid down uncovered medical bills for two New Dramatists.

Our Full Stage program is designed to provide large commissions, extra lab time, and a path to production at partner theatres. During its conception the playwrights again surprised us. The staff suggested teaming up with large theatres with big resources and middling track records with new plays. We would change these theatres' tired ways. But the writers had their own list: they wanted to reward the theatres, including small ones, that already supported their work. They were selecting theatres, instead of the other way around. The theatres, surprisingly, were thrilled to be chosen.

More and more of our writers have opted out of waiting to be read, commissioned, and produced and, instead, formed their own companies—Young Jean Lee, Richard Maxwell, Lisa D'Amour, Qui Nguyen, and Deborah Stein, to name a few. Will their examples embolden others to do the same?

"Ah," the wise ones will say, "this is innovation talking." No. It may fall under innovation's broadest terms, it may be what the deep organizational thinkers are guiding us toward, but it's not what our culture means by it. These small, significant changes are unfundable, unsexy, unseen. They prove the power of real words, not trumped-up ones. They are the call-and-response of artist to artist. They are what can happen when artists lead and we—despite our own brilliant ideas, pressing agendas, and spectacular plans—listen.

TODD LONDON

Todd London's many books include two novels, If You See Him, Let Me Know *and* The World's Room, *and writings about the theatre:* This Is Not My Memoir, *with Andre Gregory;* An Ideal Theater; Outrageous Fortune; The Importance of Staying Earnest; 15 Actors, 20 Years; *and* The Artistic Home. *The inaugural recipient of Theatre Communications Group's Visionary Leadership Award, Todd spent eighteen years as artistic director of New York's New Dramatists and four as executive director of the University of Washington School of Drama. He is the founding director of the Third Bohemia, a national, interdisciplinary retreat for artists.*

WOMEN DIRECTORS: LANGUAGE WORTH REPEATING

05 MARCH 2014

JESS K. SMITH

QUALIFY

My notes were a list of apologies that had fallen out of her mouth without hesitation.

Clear direction, diluted by, "Is that alright?"

Clear direction, undercut by, "Does that even make sense?"

Clear direction, undermined by something as simple as, "Okay?" or, "Sorry."

Here was one of my brightest young directing students and after fifteen minutes of scene work with her peers she hadn't given one direction that wasn't plagued with a qualifier or a question mark at the end, taking away any power she had established in her vision. I looked down my notes and my heart broke a little. It felt overwhelmingly familiar. This type of language plagues rehearsal rooms everywhere, and it's not just in the rooms of young directors. However, it seems to seep into rooms led by women directors far more frequently. It's a language I find myself reverting to much too often. It's a language of fear, a language of accommodation, and a language of insecurity. So why is it such a common language for women directors? Why does it feel appropriate to ask permission to direct? Why must we apologize for asserting an idea or feel like we're somehow imposing on actors with our direction? Why is this our language?

SHRINK

In the fall, a video of an exceptionally articulate Wesleyan University student's poem "Shrinking Women"[1] started popping up on newsfeeds and blog posts everywhere. In her performance at the 2013 College Unions Poetry Slam Invitational, Lily Myers speaks about the culture of women in her family. She stares across the table at her ever-shrinking mother, her ever-expanding father and brother, and she questions what lessons she has been taught and

---

1   "Lily Myers - Shrinking Women," Button Poetry, 18 April 2013, video, 3:33, https://www.youtube.com/watch?v=zQucWXWXp3k.

what traits she has inherited. With powerful lines like, "I have been taught accommodation," "I have been taught to filter," "You have been taught to grow out, I have been taught to grow in," "I have been taught to absorb," you hear the crowd reverberating with recognition. She highlights a disconnect between the expectations and assumptions of men versus women in her family. Men are expected to speak their minds, women are expected to make space and, in doing so, shrink. Although she was referring to her specific family, the fact that women around the world responded to it so emphatically suggests just how familiar her story and lineage is. Like my directing student, she's beginning to identify a history of editing her own power.

What then is the language of power?

DOMINATE

While in New York City, I worked with a number of young actors who had studied and/or worked under the direction of a prolific and internationally acclaimed director. He was known for breaking actors down to rebuild them in his image. Throughout the rehearsal process actors would get hurt, feel manipulated, complain about being taken advantage of, and describe a consistently competitive energy within the company. Actors seemed broken and miserable under his controlling hand. However, the show would open and the result was always the same: incredibly precise, experimental, and heavy-handed.

The director was the star of every production. You could see his hand in each choice and sense his misogynistic worldview in his treatment of all the iconic roles for women. His directing was undeniably bold and not a bit censored. From the process through the product, he had expanded. He had taken all of the space in the room such that even in production, when he was no longer in the room, his voice was still the loudest. And when it was all said and done, something significant would change about the stories the actors would tell. Instead of the torture and pain, the underlying theme turned to gratitude. They were deeply thankful for the chance to work with such a legend, for the chance to be broken down and built back up again, for the chance to fight for his attention and approval.

He never apologized for his direction, his choices, or his words. He has a following. I thought actors respected him *in spite of* his unapologetic approach, but I'm beginning to think that it may be *because of* his unapologetic approach. Perhaps feeling as though they have survived him unifies actors. Perhaps they see it as a taste of the true masters of theatre. Perhaps all of that work and suffering helps to validate their craft and add meaning to their lives. I won't ever fully understand, but when I think about this story, which is one of many, I wonder if I could get away with the same or if actors would simply call me a "bitch." Is this the language of men? Is this the language of power?

ASSIMILATE

She walked into the room, a circle of graduate directing students ready to study her, and she accepted and maybe even inflated with that attention. I was eager to meet her and learn about her journey to becoming one of the most successful American directors of our time. She was confident, she was smart, she was successful, and she infuriated me. I left the room dejected, deflated. From my perspective, she was powerful and successful because she had adopted a model for working that was inherently patriarchal and sexist and, in doing so, she had risen to the top of a male-dominated field. At the top, she wore her reputation as someone "difficult" to work with (aka "a bitch") seemingly with great pride. She had earned the right to be difficult, because she was powerful. She earned the right to be powerful because she adopted the language of power from her male peers. She played their game.

I replayed her visit in my head over and over, and each time I realized I was getting angrier. Each time, she was becoming more and more reflective of a culture I wanted nothing to do with. I was angry because I desperately wanted and expected her, a successful woman director, to be a model for me, but she wasn't. She had accepted someone else's system of power and succeeded within it.

RENEW

I call for a revolution of language. I reject the notion that my options for how to be in a creative process are either nice and accommodating or manipulative and renowned. I believe that the language of accommodation and the language of dominance are both deeply rooted in fear. For the former it's a fear of being considered unlikeable, and for the latter it's a fear of not having control or not owning the best idea. I believe that directing requires great vision, great attention, great awareness, and great humility. It requires egos to be left outside while bold action and outstanding listening enter the room. I am guided by a small piece of text that I return to season after season as a kind of ritual meditation. It's from the foreword of Paul Woodruff's *The Necessity of Theater*. It reads,

> There is an art to watching and being watched, and that is one of the few arts on which all human living depends. If we are unwatched, we diminish and we cannot be entirely as we wish to be. If we never stop to watch, we know only how it feels to be us, never how it feels to be another. Watched too much or in the wrong way, we become frightened. Watching too much, we lose the capacity for action in our own lives. Watching well, together, and being watched well, with limits on both sides, we grow, and grow together.[2]

2 Paul Woodruff, *The Necessity of Theater: The Art of Watching and Being Watched* (New York: Oxford University Press, 2008).

I return to these words because they are a reminder of how I wish to be in the creative process and a foundation for a new language of power to build from. The balance between watching and being watched calls for empathy and action. When I first read the passage, I was surprised by how revelatory this simple text was. The idea of theatre as a place of seeing was not new—it's the origin of the word itself and a starting place for most theatremakers. It was the "If we are unwatched, we diminish and we cannot be entirely as we wish to be" portion that stopped me in my tracks. As a director, as a teacher, as a woman, this felt like an urgent reminder to be visible, to allow my work to be visible, and to allow my language to be heard. This text could easily be adjusted to be about speaking and listening, as opposed to watching and being watched, and be just as powerful and pertinent to a discussion on language.

I am a director. I am a teacher. The way I lead my classrooms and rehearsal rooms needs to model a new language of power—one born out of the idea that you can be both bold and flexible. We should neither soften our vision nor silence our collaborators. We should be the leaders and have the humility to also be led. Instead of feeling threatened by someone other than you contributing a great idea, we should congratulate ourselves for choosing such brilliant collaborators that make the work stronger. A great idea is reflective of strong and clear vision and trust in your collaborators. And the reality is that regardless of whether or not you are a teacher by trade, you will always be a teacher in the example you set, in the words you choose, in the way you work and the priorities you model. So let's speak boldly, let's articulate big huge messy ideas that aren't yet perfected. And let's allow them to take up space, not be brushed to the side and excused for being so presumptuous, but plopped right down into the center of the room. And let's invite our collaborators to articulate great big messy beautiful ideas without asking for permission first or excusing them after. Let's terrify ourselves with just how bold and articulate we can be. Let's create a language worth repeating.

JESS K. SMITH

Jess K. Smith (she/her) is a freelance director, founder and co-artistic director of ARTBARN, intimacy director, and chair and associate professor of theatre arts at the University of Puget Sound. She loves creating work with imaginative interplay between heightened physicality and naturalistic scene work. She has trained with SITI Company and interned with Punchdrunk, Deja Donne, and Seattle Repertory Theatre. Her essay "The Hero in the Human" was published in DEJA DONNE. Dance in Action (Editoria & Spettacolo), and her talk "The Seeing Place" was featured as part of TEDx. She received her MFA in directing at Columbia University under the guidance of Anne Bogart. jessksmith.com.

QUEER NARRATIVES IN THEATRE FOR YOUNG AUDIENCES: A CALL TO ACTION

25 JUNE 2014

LINDZ AMER AND GABRIEL JASON DEAN

Gabriel Jason Dean: To my recent delight, Purple Crayon Players (PCP), a fierce and scrappy student group devoted to staging theatre for young audiences at Northwestern University and in the surrounding community of Evanston, Illinois, produced my play, *The Transition of Doodle Pequeño.*

Through the play's six characters—Doodle, a latchkey fifth grader whose Mexican father has recently been deported; Reno, a fifth-grade boy who loves to rock a ballet tutu; Valencia, an imaginary, sassy, trilingual goat; Baumgartner, Reno's protective grandfather; Marjoram, a neighborhood bully with a secret of her own; and Toph, Marjoram's little brother who's too young to know what he's saying—*The Transition of Doodle Pequeño* is a magic-filled comedy about two boys who become friends in spite of their differences. My hope is that the play examines the consequences of misused and misunderstood language and provides some insight into the lives of Mexican immigrant children and the issues of gender identity and homophobic bullying.

After a successful run of performances on campus at Northwestern, PCP toured their production to three local elementary schools. But they ran into problems when a school cancelled one of the scheduled shows. It's a complex situation to be sure, with multiple points of view, but essentially the cancellation was due to a principal's concerns about how to handle the conversation the play would create. The cancellation resulted from this administrator's fear of "risk," the worry about fielding phone calls from angry parents, and, in my view—after reading the email conversation between the administrator and the production team, accompanied by a negative survey response from a teacher—an unconscious homophobia.

The aim of this article is not to point fingers. Though we were both angry at being censored, the director of the PCP production, Lindz Amer, and I decided to catalyze the incident as an opportunity to have a public conversation both for our own development as artists and as a hopeful contribution to the field of theatre for young audiences

(TYA). We hope this ignites a broader discussion about the popular and problematic phrase "risky play," how we can address homophobia in our field, and how we can ally together to be more inclusive of and to generate new stories with queer characters, narratives, and perspectives.

Lindz Amer: Before we jump into specifics, if you want to talk about why you wrote *Doodle*, that would be a nice way to kick us off.

Gabriel: Always happy to talk about the why of this play. First, what is important to say is that I long for the day when *Doodle* is an irrelevant play. A day, hopefully soon, when the play feels dated and the struggles that Reno, the boy in the tutu, faces seem incomprehensible to audiences. But, until gatekeepers allow the conversation, I think my play will continue to be very necessary.

I wrote *Doodle* for elementary-aged kids because I know from my own childhood, having been the victim of homophobic bullies and then, in turn, becoming the bully—not unlike the journeys of Doodle and Marjoram in the play—that middle school was essentially too late to have this conversation. But, if we can reach children early enough and plant the seeds of acceptance and humanism early on, then there might be hope. Doodle is fun and mostly lighthearted, but underneath it is a very grim reality.

I wrote this play inspired by my friend, Mark, my own Reno. We attended school in Georgia in one of the school systems recently featured in the documentary film *Bully*. I grew up with Mark, watching him suffer at the hands of homophobic bullies, and because I was his friend I was bullied too. At one point I even became a bully to Mark because I thought it might simply be easier to hate him than to love him. But I saw the error of my ways pretty quickly. Mark dropped out of school because it was so bad. He got a GED, went on to become an incredible drag performer in Atlanta, and worked to make abortion and birth control an option for women in countries around the world.

Last year, after years of torment, Mark took his own life. I thought he had made it out. I thought he was the story we never hear. But no, he was so consumed with self-hatred that even as a thirty-something-year-old man with significant accomplishments and successful relationships, he still couldn't see how beautiful he truly was. There were many times I talked Mark out of it growing up and I was devastated that we had lost touch and that he didn't call me just one more time. So the conversation that my sweet play aims to create is a matter of life and death.

I know I don't need to tell you that. I'd love to hear why you chose to produce it and direct it.

Lindz: I think this work is important. This work is necessary. And this work is difficult. There will never be enough plays like *Doodle*. My curiosity surrounding TYA, particularly queer narratives in TYA, piqued in my sophomore year at Northwestern when I took Rives Collins' TYA class. He was able to get us the unpublished script of Sarah Gubbins' *fml: How Carson McCullers Saved My Life*. I read a scene as the "out" character, Jo, while the class sat in a circle surrounding me. I looked up at the end of the scene and Rives' face was red and streaming with tears.

My life would have been incredibly different had this play been presented to me as a teenager. I made myself invisible for years because I was scared of myself, of what others might think, of my parents, of what would happen to me if I were gay, that I would get bullied or beaten up, or that I would become diminished to the label of "that gay girl." I never learned to stand up for myself because I never learned that it was okay to just be me. The fact that I grew up in New York City—possibly the most liberal and diverse place where anyone could be raised—and I still had these reservations leads me to believe that there is something profoundly disturbing about how our culture functions. If I had this much trouble, what are young people in the rest of the country dealing with?

Mark is one of the many who have suffered from the genocide of homophobic discourse. You said something in our earlier conversations that resonated with me about how people always thank you for writing a "brave" play and that the word "brave" always rubs you the wrong way.

Gabriel: Yeah, what's brave about it? It's an act of activism. Maybe that's what scares people. You didn't do this play because you are "brave," right?

Lindz: No. I don't think it's a particularly brave play. It is an honest play. It is so utterly truthful that it is terrifying. Honestly, I was scared to pitch it to PCP. I was scared when I heard I was going to direct it. I was scared reading it over and over again before rehearsals started. Then I brought it to life, and it was exhilarating. I could not be more proud of this production and what we have accomplished, as small as those accomplishments might seem.

Gabriel: It's not small. If you do this play, it means you don't want to continue to live in the world you inherited. You want to have the conversation. You want to tell the story. What you said about *fml* resonates with me too. I wish someone had told me Sarah's or Doodle's story, or one like it, when I was a fifth grader. My life would've been different. I think Mark's would've been different too.

Your accomplishment with this production is not small or insignificant. I guarantee that there is a Reno out there who saw the show and for the first time in his life saw himself onstage. Saw that he was worthy of friendship. I guarantee that there is a Doodle who will be touched by this play and think about how he can become a better friend and ally. I guarantee there is a Marjoram who was so afraid to be herself that she became the bully in order to be safe. I guarantee there was a Toph who didn't yet understand the harm he was doing. And I hope, despite their walls, that there was a Baumgartner among the adults, who saw that Reno shouldn't have to apologize for who he is. Maybe there was even a Valencia, a spirit animal who saw that her magic wasn't necessary if the true magic of friendship was there.

The only thing and the most powerful thing we can do is simple: continue to tell the story. Have the conversations, and those who want to listen, learn, and take part will show up. We can't force it.

Lindz: I absolutely agree. I've known for some time now that the work I do would not be easy, particularly as a queer person, that people would chase me with pitchforks for corrupting their children or pushing a gay agenda. And maybe I am trying to do those things. I am not above admitting that my ultimate goals align with changing the mentality of the next generation to create a more equal and less bigoted world. But with the inevitability of controversy in mind, I never thought I would face it this early in my career.

First hearing about the cancellation was a shock. I've experienced Evanston to be a more progressive school district. I was not prepared for the emotional impact this would have on me. At first I was angry—angry at the schools, angry that I had not done more to make sure this did not happen. But then a profound sadness set in. These gatekeepers have actively kept a room full of students from seeing this story. Because of that, Renos, Doodles, Marjorams, Tophs, Baumgartners, and Valencias suffer.

This play has enormous potential to change lives. But that will not happen if the story is not seen. We cannot accomplish the important work we hope to do if this play is kept from those who need it.

Gabriel: Reading the teacher's comments in the survey responses about inappropriateness and then reading the email trail from the principal was disturbing for me. While the teacher, with anonymity, felt very comfortable—probably because he or she was unaware of it—with his or her own homophobia, the principal, through the email chain and with no anonymity, was very circumspect in the way she addressed what was ultimately homophobia.

Claiming that it is disrespectful to present a play that challenges children's false definitions of the word "gay" is parallel, in my book, to an administrator in 1950s Alabama saying that a play that examined the Black experience and pejorative terms around that experience is disrespectful to students. Disrespectful to whom? Bottom line is that the conversation the play demands makes some people uncomfortable and that discomfort can only occur in a culture plagued by homophobia.

Lindz: The mentality that pervades here is: "We must protect young people from LGBTQ narratives." The fact that the principal at that school later told me, "We don't even teach them about reproduction until the seventh grade," indicates that a corrupting influence is being projected onto plays like *Doodle*. We as artists are classified as corrupters, as an entity to guard against. I wonder how we might address this phobia within discourses between administrators and theatremakers? Administrators and artists should be allies in these endeavors, not enemies.

Gabriel: Exactly. While I'm not surprised, it doesn't make it less heartbreaking. I have had similar conversations with producer types all around the country about this play. Many say, "We love your play, but unfortunately our audience isn't ready for it. We wish they were." Programming from a place of fear will perpetuate fear and, in the case of *Doodle*, not telling the story perpetuates a culture of homophobia. So is the solution to simply not put on plays that might provoke someone to rethink their ideals? Is that what we're left with?

In my experience workshopping this play and in production at UT Austin, the kids are very eager and equipped to have a conversation about acceptance and friendship. And a small—but viciously vocal—number of adults are terrified by it. And who is this play for? Children or their adult gatekeepers? My answer is both. This is our reality. What do we do? We continue to tell the story. Continue to make the story available to students whose gatekeepers say it is disrespectful or its content is not for children. Above our own politics, tell the story. The powers of fiction, myth, laughter, and imagination can transcend narrow-mindedness. They always do.

Like you said, this isn't an easy play. It demands a lot of everyone involved. Did you do any pre- or post-show discussions, contextualization?

Lindz: Yes! When a touring show begins in the fall, PCP sends information out to the drama teachers and PTA contacts. They were given the script and our production study guide, along with an email that, quite transparently, gave a description of the play.

When we got to the schools, we started with a twenty-minute workshop that the cast, our PCP tour managers, and I developed over the course of a month or so. The workshop dealt directly with the use of "gay" in the context of bullying. After the show we would do a short talkback. There were some lovely responses, particularly from the fourth and fifth graders at the first school. When we asked them what they thought the play was about we heard responses like, "friendship," "standing up for people," and "loving others for their differences." I don't think there's anything risky about that.

Gabriel: Let's talk about the word "risky."

Lindz: I actually tend to use the word "radical" more often than "risky." I like that word because of its political connotations and the notion of continual progress. "Risky," especially around kids, can be a scary word. I don't know what people think about "radical" though.

Gabriel: "Radical" is better, I guess, but still it's a term in opposition to something else. It boils down to "risky" as opposed to what? "Risky" as opposed to whose system of values? With that moniker there's always some privileged system in place. You also don't want to say "controversial."

That's barring you from ever being produced as far as TYA goes.

Lindz: It's a cautious mentality. Highly protective.

Gabriel: What I can't understand is how telling a story about two boys who see each other's differences and choose friendship is controversial. Is it a risk because the word "gay" is openly examined in a childlike way in the play? If the word "gay" scares you, I don't want my children being taught by you or coming to your theatre.

In terms of *Doodle*, more than the story it's the conversation that is seen as the risk. But the conversation the play creates is just as important as the play itself. It's act 2. In the published version of the play, Abra Chusid, my dramaturg, and I spent a lot of time crafting engaging pre- and post-show questions for teachers and parents, and the work you did pre and post show to help contextualize what was onstage... What more can we do?

It seems to me like we are handing folks a story, the study guide, and conversation with the artists on a silver platter. So, I keep coming back to my feeling that it is an unconscious—and in some cases conscious—homophobia that is causing the controversy.

Lindz: I wonder about a parent or teacher who doesn't want to have the conversation yet or might feel like this play takes that option away from them. The play forces them to explain something to their child.

Gabriel: Looking at it from a parent's perspective—and I'm starting to have a little bit more of that nowadays as I'm going to be a dad in November... If anything, the incoming little Dean has actually made me more, to use your word, radical. This is a conversation I *want* to have with my child when he or she is ready to have it. What is "gay"? What is "transgender"? Why does this conversation have to be so terrifying?

Lindz: There really isn't a structured understanding about how to talk about these issues with kids. It's been such a quick movement that's happened within the last couple years. Maybe rhetoric hasn't caught up. Especially parents who are heterosexual and of the normative culture. These weren't questions they had when they were kids because it wasn't in the popular discourse. Maybe providing that rhetoric would be helpful. It's in your play. It's a question of language.

Gabriel: It's the central conflict in the play. The play itself grapples with how to talk about these things. To me, the play is not about pushing sexual-identity politics or anything like that. It really is about creating this conversation early on so that the bullying and resistance doesn't happen later.

Lindz: I keep coming back to when the principal told me that they don't even teach the kids about the reproductive system until seventh grade. It's that kind of logic jump that happens when an adult hears the word "gay" said in front of kids. That automatic leap to having to talk about sex. It's not even a question of, "I don't know how to talk about this," it's more, "I don't want to have that conversation about sex yet with my kids because they are not old enough." It's hard for parents to separate those two conversations, one being age appropriate and one not. *Doodle* doesn't talk about sexuality. It talks about gender identity, the contemporary immigrant experience, and the isolation that comes with those experiences.

Gabriel: If you had a child and she or he asks, "What is gay?" How would you answer that question?

Lindz: We did this in our workshop that preceded our touring performances. We defined "gay" as when someone falls in love with someone of the same gender, so when a man falls in love with a man or a woman falls in love with a woman. That's the answer that a kid at our first school tour said to us. Kids get that. Most kids, at that age, don't know what sex is just yet. They don't understand that connotative connection.

Gabriel: Honestly, that was hard for me at first too. Separating sexuality from identity in my child characters. In the early first drafts, I was putting my adult mind onto these characters. There was a moment where Doodle and Reno kissed. It was a sweet moment and I loved it. But it wasn't the right choice for this play and ultimately was a result of my own adult connotations being placed on top of my child characters. *That* play was about sexuality.

Lindz: That would have been a very different play.

Gabriel: We would be having a very different conversation. That play was not for elementary-aged kids. Late middle school, high school maybe. During *Doodle*'s development, we had discussions about the words "tolerance" and "acceptance." I have a strong reaction to the word "tolerance" as well. You're pushing your own views aside and tolerating something else. "Acceptance" is better, but again that is a heteronormative perspective—I have to accept you, it's on my terms.

What I kept coming back to is very simple. How do we become friends? How can we be each other's allies? It goes beyond gender and sexuality. It's friendship. It's about empathy and humanity.

Lindz: The play centralizes the ally's story, establishing Doodle as an ally for Reno. The version of the play where Doodle and Reno kiss would certainly centralize the queer themes. I wonder how a play would be able to centralize a queer storyline for young kids and make it not about sexuality.

Gabriel: I would love to take my child to see that play. I would love to write that play someday. Doodle *was* the boy in the tutu in the first draft. It absolutely centralized the queer narrative. But over the course of developing the play, I found that I wanted to write a queer character, but also to create a story about the journey to becoming an ally. Making Reno the boy in the tutu versus Doodle allowed me to do that. The potential allies see themselves onstage through Doodle, and the queer kids in the audience see themselves onstage through Reno and Marjoram, which is a massive thing.

Lindz: It's a huge thing.

Gabriel: Just to see yourself onstage. Seeing yourself as you really are. To get anecdotal for a second, during the rehearsal process for *Doodle* at UT, directed by the rock star Steven Wilson, the cast was invited to do a music-stand reading for a large crowd of high school–aged theatre students. The theatre was packed with more than four hundred kids. I sat in the midst of them, hoping to eavesdrop on their conversations. At the end, a group of Latino and Latina students approached the actor who played Baumgartner, the inimitable Rudy Ramirez. A male-presenting student with vibrant purple streaks in their hair said to the actor, "I am queer. I am Latina. This is the first time I've ever seen myself onstage. Thank you." I still get chills thinking about it.

Lindz: That is amazing. So how do we ensure kids see this play?

Gabriel: It's up to the gatekeepers to do it. To have the courage to change the conversation. Not to talk about it, but to actually do it. You and I can fight the good fight all day long, bang our drums loudly and proudly, but until we have allies in the gatekeepers, we're going to keep beating our head against a wall. We need them to be willing to start the conversation.

If we continue to relegate stories like *Doodle* to universities, then what we are saying, ultimately, as a field, is that those stories do not belong in the popular discourse. That is profoundly sad and simply not true. To be clear, I'm not making this argument because I'm an ego-driven writer who wants to see his play get on bigger stages. I'm making it because I believe theatre has the power to change lives. To save lives. Because it did mine.

TYA, American theatre: I dare you to commission playwrights to write plays for kids with queer narratives and queer characters. Or do the ones that exist.

It's the theatre companies that have to do it. The onus is on them to say, "We want this work. We want to tell these stories." Let's show the children of today the world we want to see tomorrow.

Lindz: Let's tell the stories that need telling.

LINDZ AMER

Lindz Amer (they/them) creates LGBTQ+ and intersectional social justice media for kids and families. They created their beloved LGBTQ+ family web series Queer Kid Stuff in 2015, which has blossomed into a live performance series, a weekly newsletter, and more! They also write and consult for children's television including their work on the award-winning Blue's Clues & You! "Pride Parade" music video featuring drag queen Nina West. They are currently adapting their viral TED Talk on gender and sexuality for kids into a queer-affirming parenting book. Follow their work through @queerkidstuff and their personal journey through @lindzamer on all social media platforms.

GABRIEL JASON DEAN

Gabriel Jason Dean (he/him) has been dubbed "feisty as hell" by the New Yorker and "a great modern American playwright" by Broadway World. His award-winning work has been done all over the United States and examines the intersections of class, race, sexuality, and nationalism in America. Select fellowships include the Dramatists Guild Fellowship and the Hodder Fellowship from Princeton. He is an assistant professor of theatre and English at Muhlenberg College, an alum of the Civilians R&D Group, and a Usual Suspect at New York Theatre Workshop. He received his MFA from UT Austin. gabrieljasondean.com.

DISPATCH FROM THE YOUTH THEATRE FESTIVAL IN RAMALLAH, PALESTINE—PART TWO

19 JULY 2014

SHEBANA COELHO

It's taken me some time to write about the end of Ashtar Theatre's International Youth Festival. Since the final performances, three Israeli teenagers who had gone missing right when the festival started were discovered dead; Israel blamed Hamas operatives, and a Palestinian teenager from East Jerusalem was kidnapped and killed by Israeli extremists in retaliation.

All this triggered intense demonstrations by both sides, clashes between Palestinians and Israeli police for almost four days in East Jerusalem, and rocket strikes between Israel and Gaza, leading to the current situation in which the death toll in Gaza is rising (as I write this it stands at 274 according to the *Guardian; Ma'an News* cites 298).

In a volatile, war-torn place, things change quickly and recurring issues of conflict, occupation, and survival dominate—all the more reason to have festivals like this and theatres like Ashtar that persist under such circumstances and create transformative experiences.

The final performances and the field trip we took to the Freedom Theatre in the Jenin refugee camp linger vividly.

ON THE ROAD

We drive north through a landscape of olive trees, tapering pines, and valleys with white rock terraces. It is a beautiful day shimmering with heat, cool inside the bus.

We pass Israeli settlements that you can spot from far away, clusters of red-roofed houses side by side, in lines and squares. Settlements are considered illegal under international law—this explains the checkpoint towers and the presence of Israeli security forces. There is a maze of roads that gives settlers direct access to their homes but requires Palestinians to take circuitous routes. We see olive-colored military trucks with thick metal mesh enclosures. "To protect them from stone throwing," says one of the Palestinian students, "the soldiers travel like this." Every time you forget, something reminds you you are in an occupied land. In the Jenin refugee camp, you don't need reminders.

Entering the camp, the first things you see are blue signs of the United Nations Relief and Works Agency for Refugees. The camp is home to sixteen thousand refugees who lost their homes in the *Nakba* (as it is called here)—the Catastrophe—which refers to the period following 1948, when the Arab-Israeli war displaced over seven hundred thousand Palestinians.

The Freedom Theatre, which is inside the camp, was founded in 2006 by Juliano Mer-Khamis, building on the work begun by his mother, Arna, to give children a creative outlet in the late 1980s, during the First Intifada. Arna was born in Israel, married a Palestinian, and devoted her life to Jenin, as documented in the film her son made about her work, *Arna's Children.*

Two of the Ashtar Festival participants, brothers Kamal and Salim, live in the refugee camp and work with the theatre. Kamal has been helping with the children's summer camp, which started a few weeks ago—boys between the ages of nine and fourteen spend the day in storytelling, dancing, and group-building activities.

We are invited to see a performance in progress. "This play," says the director Motaz Malhees, "is about their life and who they want to be. And they have been working on it for a few days now."

On the stage, six boys sit on desks facing away from the audience. They write intently for a few seconds, rise, carry their desks to the side, run around playing games, then take stances on different parts of the stage. They yell about the camp being attacked, run forward, mime throwing stones, huddle again, and form a line center stage.

"This is my dream," one boy says. "I want to be a sailor and sail through the seas and challenge all the waves and everybody." He stands on a chair and salutes. Another circles the group slowly as he talks. "I want to be a cook," he says, "the best cook in the world, a cook who cooks all kinds of food and people will love to eat it."

"I also have a dream," says a third boy. "I want to become a blacksmith—a blacksmith who works with iron—and I will forge a plane and fly it all over the place." In the end, the boys link hands and bow, shy at first and then, as we clap louder, smiling.

Jenin has come to be known for its militant and cultural resistance—in April 2002 it came under siege by the Israeli Defense Forces and in the resulting clashes about fifty Palestinians were killed. Young actors address this issue in the Freedom Theatre promotional video that we also see. Before they started acting, they say, their dream was to die as *shahids*, martyrs.

"But after I started acting," says one, "I began to consider living as a martyr, not dying as one."

FINALLY NOW

It's an hour before curtain on 28 June and I'm standing, amid a steadily growing crowd, in the courtyard of Ramallah's Ottoman Court.

By 8 p.m., there are about one hundred people in the front courtyard of the Ottoman Court waiting for the festival's final performance. The student dancers mingle with the audience then stop abruptly and make small movements, directing the audience to one side of the courtyard and taking their places on the other side. They begin with sudden stillness and continue with sudden movements and fluidity, take the form of a protesting crowd, raise their arms, throw, fall back, retreat, regroup, jump, increase in power, and decrease in force.

In silence, the dancers move towards the audience, motioning them to join in, and for a few seconds, everyone is together, hands linked, stamping their feet in what looks like the traditional Palestinian dance, the *dabke*—when suddenly two uniformed men brusquely interrupt, take two of the dancers by the arm, and haul them up the stairs to the second-floor balcony. Another actor, in the uniform of an Israeli prison guard, stands at the bottom of the stairs, guarding the entrance. The shock is palpable for a second, and then someone giggles, realizing that it is part of the performance. Everyone walks up to the second floor balcony in single file, past the guard who sometimes lets them pass easily, and sometimes not.

Upstairs we wait, crowding the balcony, a mixed audience—women with headscarves, children in shorts, expats, artists, international NGO workers, and government employees. The doors behind the mesh open and guards herd out three boys and one girl, dressed in loose prison garb. The prisoners begin speaking as if to relatives, their voices overlapping, asking if the demonstrations are making any difference, how things are on the outside.

A woman tells her fiancé, "Please, if you want to get married, get married. I don't know how long I'll be here but I'd like to see you happy."

There are over five thousand Palestinian detainees in Israeli prisons, some are political prisoners who have been jailed for years, while others are "administrative detainees" who can, and are, held for up to six months without Israel having to provide a reason. Every six months, their sentence can also be increased.

Abruptly, the lights go out. The prisoners are led back into the rooms. As the door shuts loudly behind them, a muezzin's call for prayer sounds from a mosque nearby. A woman near me wipes her tears and everyone claps.

The event continues with the high farce of a commedia dell'arte performance and an installation piece featuring monologues about beauty, harassment, and self-image.

Later, when I catch up with the young coordinators of the festival, Émile André and Lamis Shalaldeh, they are still reeling. "I wasn't sure how it would turn out," says Lamis, "but really, with this group, with what we did in ten days, it was a miracle." Sixteen-year old Firas adds, "Before the festival, I would call myself very self-centered, but now I feel so open. I got to know so many people, people here in Ramallah I didn't know before, not to mention Norwegians and Germans and Brits and Americans."

In a short video I put together quickly on the last day, the festival participants play around with the festival's theme, "now has passed," with different gestures and deliveries. My favorite is the end, when Waleed and George do a playful sequence in Arabic:

> *"Now is past," says one.*
>
> *"No," says the other, "the past is now."*
>
> *"Actually, now is now."*
>
> *"Ah, ok." They agree, shake hands, and walk out of frame, laughing.*

SHEBANA COELHO

Shebana Coelho (she/her) is a performer and writer, originally from India. She received a CEC Arts Link Award to facilitate creativity workshops with Ashtar Theatre in Palestine. Her solo plays explore the ripple effects of colonization—what oppresses, what liberates—in a felt body sense and combine poetry and dance drawn from flamenco and Indian classical dance/theatre. They include The Good Manners of Colonized Subjects and Once I was a stone, una piedra, ek pathar (presented at the Pan Asian Repertory Theatre, the Arts at Marks Garage, and American Samoa Community College, among others). shebanacoelho.com.

I'LL DISBAND MY ROVING GANG OF THIRTY ASIAN PLAYWRIGHTS WHEN YOU STOP DOING ASIAN PLAYS IN YELLOWFACE*

(*EXCEPTION: DAVID HENRY HWANG'S PLAY *YELLOW FACE*)

06 OCTOBER 2014

MIKE LEW

The Ma-Yi Writers Lab is the largest collective of Asian American playwrights ever assembled. The Lab was founded in 2004 as an offshoot of Ma-Yi Theater, which was itself an offshoot of the Asian American theatre movement; a company formed in 1989 out of the need to tell stories by and about Filipinos at a time when those stories weren't being heard.

Today the Lab comprises the widest possible cross-section of Asian backgrounds: East and South Asian (and biracial), first- and second-generation American (and generations beyond). Collectively our writers have been making a substantial national impact. Recent Labbie achievements include a Helen Merrill Award, a Lanford Wilson Award, a National New Play Network commission, a Leah Ryan prize, a Laurents/Hatcher prize, a Kendeda award, two Princess Grace fellowships, two PoNY fellowships, six Dramatists Guild fellowships, and five New Dramatists residencies.

With such an outpouring of support for our work, it may be tempting to wonder whether an ethnic-specific writers' group is even necessary. Are culturally specific theatre companies outdated? Several years ago I remember (naively) asking Michael John Garcés why he'd earlier chosen to work with ethnic-specific companies like INTAR as opposed to focusing on big theatres all along. He answered—with remarkable patience—that when he was coming up, theatres like INTAR were the only ones that would hire him.

I think that remains true today for many artists of color. Companies like Ma-Yi are giving crucial opportunities to minority artists that big theatres are all too happy to ignore. INTAR is actually a pretty great case study. Over the past few seasons, INTAR has been producing some of the best new plays I've seen *anywhere*, to shockingly little acclaim. Andrea Thome's *Pinkolandia* was pretty much my favorite play of the past five years. Why isn't every major Off-Broadway theatre commissioning her work? José Rivera's *Adoration of the Old Woman* was world-rocking in its form and political complexity. Why isn't someone like that—truly one of America's master writers—being represented on Broadway?

I would posit that when it comes to writers of color, we're being subjected to an anthropological gaze that places our plays under the context of "ethnic work," some kind of category apart from other new plays and judged by a separate criteria. There's this burden of expectation that all we have in us are stories from our homeland. Yet that expectation is increasingly at odds with what we're interested in talking about as writers, or where we're headed as a country. Early in my career I kept encountering well-meaning mentors who encouraged me to "write about my family," which was really code for "write an eighties-style Asian identity play." But I'm third-generation Chinese American. I couldn't write a Chinese immigrant play if I tried.

We recently took in a new class of Ma-Yi Labbies, and during their interviews each writer invariably asked something to the effect of, "So do I have to write about Asian stuff here?" What a relief to be able to tell them that Ma-Yi is a place where Rey Pamatmat can write his Filipino brother/sister play *and* his interdimensional time-travel play; where Qui Nguyen can get a production of his family-history play *and* his Blaxploitation/Samurai mash-up. There's no tenure on membership, so we're able to track each other's output over time and see how each sequential play fits into the constellation of plays that comprise a writer's body of work. It's fascinating to witness the aesthetic diversity each writer brings to the table—the huge range of interests we take on in our work—compared to the much narrower range of plays that gain traction out in the world. Inside the Lab: interdimensional time travel. Outside the Lab: ethnic family dramas only, please.

The anthropological gaze is undoubtedly present in reviews of our work. The humor in Robert O'Hara's play *Bootycandy* was recently compared to *In Living Color*. Dominique Morisseau's *Detroit '67: Good Times*. Tanya Saracho's *Mala Hierba*: a telenovela. The tone of Rey Pamatmat's *Edith Can Shoot Things and Hit Them?* That of "a Tiger Mom-ed kid plonking away at the piano."[1] These aren't allusions we're inviting in our own work based on what's on the page. These are cultural preconceptions being hauled into the theatre and placed upon us. How do you distinguish the singularity of your voice when your voice *isn't really being heard* to begin with? Given the uneasy fellowship between reviewers and producers, how do writers of color ever hope to "break out" if our work is being filtered through a lens of cultural bias?

Recently, there's also been an insidious trend of Orientalism in major productions: plays *set in Asia* or plays that portray *Asian characters* but do not cast Asian actors in the roles. These are instances of figurative or sometimes even literal yellowface. Alongside Asian American Performers Action Coalition (AAPAC) and Signature Theatre, Ma-Yi Writers Lab recently performed an awareness-building event satirizing such productions: *The Orphan of Zhao* in England, *The Nightingale* in San Diego, *Pippin: A Bollywood Spectacular* in Chicago, and *Priscilla, Queen of the Desert* on Broadway. Since then these instances of cultural appropriation and yellowface casting keep popping up. *The Mystery of Edwin Drood* at the Roundabout. *Julius Caesar* in Philadelphia. *The Mikado* in Seattle. All kimonos and kabuki

1   Charles Isherwood, "Louisville Dreaming: Characters Exploring Boundaries," *New York Times*, 4 April 2011, https://www.nytimes.com/2011/04/05/theater/humana-festival-of-new-american-plays-in-louisville.html.

makeup, no Asian actors. It's insensitive. It's neocolonialist. It's as if these productions seek to borrow the trappings of Asian culture while erasing the Asians. I keep coming back to Tanya Barfield's haunting line in her transcendent play *The Call*. To the American couple seeking to adopt a baby from their African immigrant neighbor: "You want a child from Africa but you do not want Africa." *You want Asia but you don't want any Asians.*

What's so crippling about all this is that here I am, wanting to have a nuanced discussion about what an equitable representation of Asian voices in the theatre would look like, and instead I'm put in the position of having to articulate why I think it's unacceptable to have non-Asian actors made up in yellowface, a practice that common decency dictates should have been abandoned decades ago.

When it comes to diversity in the theatre I keep being told, "It's getting better." And it is getting better. It's just that it's not getting better *fast enough*. Check the latest Off-Broadway theatre statistics from AAPAC. Is diversity in the theatre *really* getting better? It's questionable, especially given the segmented way we present race on New York stages despite the racial diversity you can see in the street. Lynn Nottage put it best: "I sometimes think that theater is the last bastion of segregation. When you go to a theater, you see a black play and it's all black people, or a Latin play, and it's all Latinos. When you go to a white play, it's like there are no people of color who live in New York."[2]

2   Dwyer Murphy, "Lynn Nottage: History of Omission," *Guernica*, 1 May 2013, https://www.guernicamag.com/history-of-omission.

What would an equitable representation of people of color actually look like?

- When theatres stop choosing plays based on anthropological expectations and instead treat the experiences of people of color as an extension of their own human experience...

- When our stages reflect the diversity of the cities we live in...

- When we stop thinking about race in terms of segmented populations and treat it as something more complex and polymorphic...

- When we start empowering people of color in management and high-level creative and board positions...

- When theatres and reviewers embrace writers of color for what they have to say and not just the demographics they represent...

That's when we'll have reached a place of genuine inclusion.

But, until then, thank God for places like Ma-Yi (and NAATCO, and Desipina, and 2g). *Of course* they're still necessary.

MIKE LEW

 Mike Lew (he/him) has written plays including tiny father *(Audible)*, Teenage Dick *(Woolly Mammoth, Huntington, Pasadena, Seattle Rep, Donmar, Ma-Yi, O'Neill)*, Tiger Style! *(SCR, Olney, Huntington, La Jolla, Alliance, O'Neill)*, Bike America *(Ma-Yi, Alliance)*, and microcrisis *(Ma-Yi, InterAct)*. He and Rehana Lew Mirza are Mellon playwrights-in-residence at Ma-Yi where they co-wrote the book to Bhangin' It *with composer/lyricist Sam Willmott (La Jolla Playhouse, Richard Rodgers Award, Rhinebeck). Mike is a Dramatists Guild council member, Tony voter, and New Dramatists resident. Honors include Guggenheim, Lark Venturous, and NYFA fellowships, and Kleban, PEN, Lanford Wilson, Helen Merrill, Heideman, and Kendeda awards. He was educated at Juilliard and Yale.*

QUEERING THE ROOM: SOME BEGINNING NOTIONS FOR A QUEER DIRECTING PRACTICE

24 OCTOBER 2014

WILL DAVIS

What does it mean to build a work inside a queer container? What does it mean to queer a rehearsal room or queer a directing practice? I am interested in the experiment of talking about directing from the perspective of my trans identity and seeing what happens when I do. I am certain it informs the way I work, but I've never tried to define how.

I am a trans person in the American theatre. Sometimes I joke that I think there are maybe eight to ten of us in the field and we all seem to know each other. But the point is I am a queer body in a predominantly straight space and it's part of my job to navigate issues of gender and identity alongside the work I do in rehearsal.

I went through a phase in which I outed myself right away to a new group of collaborators. I'd say, "Hello, my name is Will Davis and I use he and him pronouns. If this is confusing to you feel free to grab me at a break and we can check in."

I went through a phase where I said, "Hello, my name is Will Davis. I use he and him pronouns so take a crack at that and, if you have trouble, just go ahead and try again."

These days I am experimenting with not outing myself as trans at all. I say, "Hello, I am Will Davis, and I'm directing this show."

I've had a lot of practice walking into a room of people who have never known a trans person before, and a lot of practice with the moment where what Will Davis looks like on paper and what Will Davis looks like standing in the doorway come crashing together. I have practice owning myself in a room that may not have the language or context to see me as I see myself. And so the internal compass that makes it possible to maintain my sense of Will Davis when no one on the outside can see it is constantly getting a workout—that same compass is also very useful for making theatre.

The four ideas I want to explore in this piece fall under the larger umbrella of building the culture of a rehearsal room.

By culture, I am talking about the values and aesthetics and modes of our working relationships with each other and the material. Though I begin each process differently, I carry a handful of practices with me, show to show, to design a unique working frame for what we're going to accomplish in that room. As directors, we use our own curiosity, taste, style, and artistic impulses to build the particular mode of inquiry for the work. So, in service of building culture with a queered center, here are four core values of my directing process I carry with me:

I. MAKE WORK FROM THE CENTER OF YOUR DESIRE.

The idea of working from the center of your desire has been a big part of my coming out. The very idea that there was a center to find was a radical thought for me for a long time. In my life and in my art, I'd lived a long time at the periphery, waiting for the gravitational pull of someone else's desire or someone else's vision to pull me into action. As I have come to own my identity and pieced together the core values of what it means for me to be a queer person redefining my relationship to gender, I've been able to inch closer and closer to center, and to building a home for my artistic vision.

A great friend of mine once said: our work should look like the people who make it. I often think of that when I stand in a room of new collaborators. In one way, how can the piece *not* look like the people who make it? But in another way, rehearsal is a unique invitation to lift up the particular alchemy of the bodies and minds assembled to build the work. We should encourage the visions of the artists we work with and make space for their impulses with the work. Part of queering the rehearsal requires that I get interested in the taste and style of my collaborators. It feels like my job to find unique ways that the material can be transmitted through the artist instead of projected onto them, and my aim is to build a rehearsal room where there is a rigorous invitation to show up inside the work.

2. THE BEST IDEA IN THE ROOM DOES NOT NEED TO BE YOURS.

When I talk about directing, I talk about inviting the expertise in the room. We often forget that one of the unique principals of coming together to make theatre is that we are coming together. We're placing our individual visions in the same space. To my mind, that means we ought to let those visions sharpen each other and make us all better.

My job is to frame rehearsal with very, very good ideas so that perhaps the best idea might come from a collaborator inside the process. The greatest success to me is when I put a good idea in the room and an actor's eyes light up and they say, "I know!" and then make a choice that refines it into a better idea.

This feels like part of a queer aesthetic because it is an integral part of turning a generative hierarchy on its side—a very queer thing to me. Just because I am on the outside watching does not mean I am always right. I want to cultivate agency and ownership in the performers I work with. They should feel invited to generate material and treated like authentic collaborators. This ups the potential for disagreement, which I think is exciting and valuable. I'm interested in open collaborative relationships and how our varied perspectives can help to sharpen our decision-making.

I am not at all interested in the "right" choice in rehearsal. How could there be such a thing? Instead, I am interested in making a series of choices and seeing where that leads. If you grow up knowing that there are "right" and "wrong" ways to be and somewhere inside you it is alarmingly apparent that you are an example of the "wrong" thing, then the moment you can let go of that "right" and "wrong" binary is the moment you are free. I want to stay curious about how we might best activate the narrative vision, and that means I'm interested in other people's ideas.

3. INVITE BEING SEEN.

This phrase, "invite being seen," is borrowed from the great choreographer Deborah Hay and was first described to me by my mentor Kirk Lynn. To me, the phrase is about practicing presence. It describes an invitation to generate your performance from where you are and invite people to join you there. The best performances are the ones where I am seeing both the character and the actor in action. I'm interested in the moments where both ways of being onstage are activated and I'm invited to live with the performer in that complex moment of identity.

When I talk to actors during a moment in rehearsal when they're not feeling successful, I sometimes say, "I picked you because you were you. I want the *you* in you to perform this role." This feels totally tied into my experience as a queer person moving through the world. The space between who we are and how we perform identity is now a joyful and playful space for me. There was a time when it was harrowing, and I felt helpless trying to navigate the huge chasm between the internal unknown and what I thought was a required external performance of who I was.

It seems to me that it is more interesting to be many things at once. My life has been enriched by the concept that I can get up in the morning and put my gender on. I can choose how I want to perform my gender and my identity as my internal concept of myself shifts. I want to invite the same practice in performance, open up the space for the actor to be more than one thing and attempt to be present for their selves and for the performance in the same moment.

4. LET A THING BE WRONG AS LONG AS POSSIBLE; CULTIVATE A FIERCE LOVE FOR IMPERFECT THINGS. THE GREATEST SKILL A DIRECTOR HAS IS THE TOLERANCE FOR "I DON'T KNOW."

The number of times I've said to myself, *You can't just sit here and not make decisions, you have to get up and walk straight into "I don't know"* is the number of times I have seen my life revolutionized.

The great thing about walking into the unknown is that you have little to no control of the outcome. That's where tolerance comes in, and I have found in my life and in rehearsal that tolerance is the most important value. If I try not to react with fear when I don't know what you are doing, but instead tolerate that it won't go well for a while, I have found that eventually something happens that feels good.

It can be the smallest thing—a cross up left, a line landing right, the beat it took to make the decision to speak—and then suddenly you're in business. Something tells you, *Okay, that seems useful, let's follow that, let's make a series of decisions based on that little detail and through those decisions we'll arrive at a plan.*

This method of working through the unknown and working with a bit of grace with the imperfect is the only way I have managed to arrive at a sense of self in my life. I've had to learn to listen to the impulse inside me that says, *Just cross the threshold, I have no idea why or what will happen but just do it and we'll sort it out on the other side.* That was true when I changed my name, it was true when I started making physical changes to my body, and it is true today.

Working with "I don't know" is all about having a conversation with your limit. It is not a soft or easy place, or a space of giving up. "I don't know" is a call to arms. It says we've taken this idea to its limit, and now we have to get in there and grapple with "I don't know" until the next move becomes clear. It's a place for quickening and a space for new visions and creativity.

As I have learned to do with myself, I sit in rehearsal and fiercely love what isn't working. I try to find the joy in it. It's an exciting moment. Here we are sitting in what feels like a disaster, so let's ask: "What is useful here? Is there something to salvage? Is this the information we need to totally abandon this moment or this concept?" It can be an incredible thing to "break" the play and see what it looks like in pieces. We don't need to be precious; we just need to keep working.

Perhaps this is just what I think good directing is, but it seems to correlate with ideas I encounter in queer spaces. On a basic level, I'm talking about dismantling a binary between the director and the actor, approaching the creative process with a more holistic, come-as-you-are attitude, and activating a less hierarchical frame for good ideas.

Because I spend more of my hours on the planet in rehearsal than I do anywhere else, I am curious about how to operate and animate my values in the work and in the process. It seems to me that trying to talk about a queered rehearsal room results in talking about good collaboration, or at the very least inviting collaborative dialogue. It also seems to be about inviting authentic expression, showing up inside the work, asking others to do the same, and letting the creative process complicate as a result.

WILL DAVIS

Will Davis (he/him) is a transgender director and choreographer focused on physically adventurous new work for the stage. He lives and works in New York City.

DO WHITE PLAYWRIGHTS THINK ABOUT THIS?

27 FEBRUARY 2015

LARISSA FASTHORSE

Afew years ago I won a national playwriting award and decided it was time to find a literary agent. I did a round of meetings in New York and was shocked at how they saw me. I saw myself as a published playwright who had received a second commission at a LORT A theatre and had two well-received equity productions.

Instead I was told, "As a Native American female playwright..." and "You can't ___ because you are a Native American female playwright." Or...

> **Agent:** *As a Native American female playwright you'll never work in LORT. I'd send you to college theatres.*

> **Me:** *But I'm working on my second LORT commission.*

> **Agent:** *Native American female playwrights do best in college theatre.*

> **Me:** *Can't I do both?*

> **Agent:** *Not with me.*

This was a major agent and my first choice. I was thrown. I started to doubt all of my career decisions. Then I met the guy who became—and is still—my agent. He brought my scripts to the meeting—a lovely touch—and never once mentioned "Native American" or "female." He talked about my writing and what kind of artistic life I wanted and how he could support me on that journey.

It turned out well, but on the flight home I asked myself, *Do white playwrights ever have to think about this? Do they ever have an agent spell out their limitations based on their whiteness? Are they told they are not welcome in a whole segment of theatre because they are white? Are they relieved to have a meeting where no one asks them a hundred questions about their whiteness instead of their work?* Don't get me wrong, I'm proud of my ethnic identity and honored to share it, but I've got more going on.

Jump forward to this year: I've been working on the award-winning play with the LORT company. It began as an autobiographical piece and is the hardest story I've ever tried to wrangle. I've typed more on this play than all of my other plays combined. Along the way, the main character's journey became my truth in experiences and obstacles and lessons learned. But that journey no longer matches mine chronologically or geographically. Several real people have combined into one character. Lessons that took years to learn now happen in weeks. Internal battles are externalized. But we finally have something that looks like an engaging play.

On a notes call the director says very carefully, "I'm not sure how being Native American serves the main character now. It seems to be forced into this world in a way that doesn't feel honest to the story." I think about it and have to agree. There is no reason for it to come up in this world. He continues, "If being Native American is important to the character, then there needs to be a better way to bring it into the story. If it's not, maybe you don't need that." I feel like I've walked into a wall. But she's me. She has to be Native American. I'm a Native American female—whoa. He reaches out to me in the silence: "Larissa, you know we don't hire you because you're Native American. We hire you because you're a good writer."

Tears fill my eyes. Despite my supportive agent, as a Native American female playwright I sometimes suspect that the things the trolls say online are true. That I get jobs I don't deserve based on my ethnicity. That I am part of forced gender parity and if the numbers ever get equal I'll be out. That I can't stand on my writing alone.

Then the sincerity of the director's words cascade through my brain and I am euphoric. It's a freedom I've never allowed myself to have, and the limitless possibilities make me giddy. Maybe she'll be ethnic, maybe she won't. I will serve my play and nothing else.

I hang up and instantly panic. I can't un–Native American a character. Do you know how many LORT contracts were available to Native American–specific actors last year? I'm pretty sure it was two and I know who got both of them. (There may have been some lingering productions of *August: Osage County*, but you get the point.) I can't waste this chance to give Native actors jobs and to represent my people. This country has spent hundreds of years trying to erase us and the genocide continues to this day. If I don't write about the Native American experience, am I complicit? Being a Native American female playwright doesn't feel like enough for one play.

I freak out for a few days until I've gone in enough circles that I can see myself from outside myself and finally ask, *Do white playwrights ever think about this? Do they worry about losing jobs for white actors? Do they question if they are writing about enough white issues? Are they expected to be the voice of all white people even when they are just speaking for themselves? Do they fear their play about a girl who wants to be a ballet dancer is responsible for the genocide of their race?*

I see clearly the weird mix of hubris and humility I am living in. Can one play be that important? Should one play be that important? Is my one play really that important? It doesn't mean we won't cast a Native American actress; or, she could be African American or Asian or Hispanic or white or a mix of colors that would look the most like me. So I take the ethnic specificity out and the play is stronger. It's a choice I still struggle with, but it's the right one for this story. Do white playwrights think about this stuff? I don't know, but maybe they should.

LARISSA FASTHORSE

Larissa FastHorse (Sicangu Lakota Nation, she/her) is an award-winning writer and 2020–25 MacArthur Fellow. Her satirical comedy, The Thanksgiving Play *(Playwrights Horizons/Geffen Playhouse), was one of the top ten most-produced plays in America. She is the first Native American playwright in the history of American theatre on that list. Larissa is currently developing new plays with several theatres including Second Stage Theater, Center Theatre Group, the Public Theater, the Guthrie Theater, Seattle Repertory Theatre, and Yale Repertory Theatre. In 2019, Larissa reentered film and television by co-creating a series at Freeform. Since then she has set up projects with Disney Channel, NBC, and DreamWorks, and is writing on a series for Apple+. hoganhorsestudio.com.*

WALKING THE AWKWARDLY HEROIC YET OFTEN DEPRESSING PATH OF NEAR-IMPOSSIBLE CATASTROPHE EVASION THROUGH KICK-ASS POETICS

24 APRIL 2015
ELIZABETH DOUD

I am an out post-post-modern tree-hugging vigilante mermaid and cultural industries agent, and a citizen of the Kickasspora: a new territory of systems change and fused multiplicities where art is *not* a luxury but a necessary tool that we wield in a larger project of remembering, witnessing, reimagining, and celebrating a radical insurgency of love and reverence for this amazing planet we like to call *home*. No, I'm serious. It's not as touchy-feely as it sounds.

It's actually slogging, tough, and paradoxical work that is not for the queasy.

The climate movement is so complex that it needs to be poetic to affect change in consciousness and penetrate the depths of our seemingly impossible current paradigm—and shake it up. Artists who relentlessly create images, texts, operas, music, performances, and films about this issue are infiltrating into spaces that many activist campaigns and government advisories can't reach. We have the tools to hypnotize and beautifully permeate a subconscious. We break hearts and incite laughter one-on-one in intimate spaces of image and visceral transference. We make rituals and allow communities to witness new propositions with an emotional vulnerability that unites us in our humanity, and in our greater universal connectedness.

It is one of the best things we do as a species. Our ability to construct new realities, which shift souls, spark revolutions, and appeal to our higher-order interrelatedness, is so perfect for handling a crisis of this magnitude that it has to play a role in doing what our governments and industries have failed to do.

Making theatre in the age of climate change or the age of the Anthropocene, or dead smack in the middle of what writer Elizabeth Kolbert eloquently unpacks as the "sixth extinction," is what I like to call the radical practice of *walking the awkwardly heroic path of near-impossible catastrophe evasion through poetics*. And it is, I think, one of the hardest jobs out there today.

As a multidisciplinary performing artist, I instinctively shifted towards making work about the larger meta-story of the climate crisis about eight years ago, interested in how vast and complex the micro-narratives and metaphors were. How extremely real and urgent they felt—and still feel—with tentacles reaching into all areas of the human and non-human experience. I'll simply never run out of story... Oh, and I live in Florida. 'Nuff said.

Brief context of our climate change sitch-y-a-shun and the small problem of extinction: Human societies are facing the unprecedented challenges of climate change and the subsequent environmental collapse caused by the extraction of resources from the earth and the rampant processing and consumption of these resources. Communities, industries, cultures, and governments around the world are facing these challenges with responses ranging from urgent proactivity (the minority) to mild or complete denial (the majority).

This crisis has been precipitated by the industrialized systems of capitalism, underpinned by fundamentalist ideologies of a globalized free market and rising neoliberalism. There is an international policy debate on the best ideological path we must take to avoid total extinction, but the overwhelmingly in agreement global scientific research community says we have no more time for discussions. The only solution is a drastic contraction of resource consumption and total reformation of the systems that encourage and support this consumption.

Because the anticipated consequences of the collapse of our economies, societies, and the biosphere in general are so violent, we can postulate that this crisis will test our moral character as nothing before in history. There is a lack of understanding of this massive danger in the human population and less willingness than ever to take action on the part of governments and industries. Naomi Klein has written brilliantly about this in her latest book, *This Changes Everything: Capitalism vs. the Climate.* This is why, when we refer to climate change's causes, we are really pointing to deeply damaged political, economic, and social systems, which need to undergo urgent and radical structural reworking in order to stave off the devastating climate shifts underway.

So, I know exactly why I want to be making this work, yet I feel a tension between wanting to create specific stories for my admittedly limited audiences and feeling the need to leverage my craft for bigger moves in service of the climate—and even larger systems—change movement. I am asking all of my friends, colleagues, and artists I know and meet the following questions:

- What role should artists play to fill this gap in action?

- How can artists create performances/narratives about the climate crisis with a sense of urgency and act efficiently and poetically?

In several informal micro-summits of art-makers and organizers, a series of compelling sub-questions have surfaced, which I think provoke valuable reflection and guidance in our process of making theatre in this context.

- How can we transform the emergencies caused by what author Rob Nixon terms as "slow violence" into narratives and theatrical experiences dramatic enough to arouse public sentiment and ensure sociopolitical intervention? His thesis is that our spectacle-driven attention span has programmed us to overlook and undervalue slower-moving impacts so that we are not reacting to the devastating threats of the climate crisis with the urgency they deserve.

- What is the role of "hope" in the poetics of this issue, and how can we look at it critically as a tool of philosophical manipulation and a needed dramaturgical mechanism? Is hope what we need, or should we replace it with creative intention?

- How can we produce work that has an impact with varied global/local tensions and meet those needs working in collaboration with affected communities?

Besides a low-grade dystopian reverie about the power of arts in the larger climate movement, there are some key points to consider so that we better grasp the myriad complexities and impossibilities that inevitably emerge in the process:

- *Any artistic theme that speaks of the climate crisis or the area of environmental justice is "glocal" or "lobal"— local and global—by definition.* This is often distracting for narrative-makers as we focus on a local story. We might be addressing the plastics pollution on an island in northeastern Brazil and the death of the local fisheries but also know that the planet's oceans are choked with garbage gyres that overshadow, in terms of magnitude, the less-visible or not-so-newsworthy litter on a local beach. From a dramaturgical standpoint, telling the massive global story is not as interesting as the local story—it's vaguer, slower, and has way too many players to have emotional connectivity—but it's inextricably connected to our local narrative and can, if we are crafty, emerge through our careful telling of specific local issues.

- *Any culture project involving a study of the climate crisis or the area of sustainability in the environment is interdisciplinary by definition.* The *trans-multi-intra* triad isn't new to contemporary art-making, so the idea of bringing other disciplines into our creative milieu is by no means revolutionary. However, many artists making theatre about climate change engage with scientists and other non-arts-sector researchers to create a basis for the work, oftentimes wanting to make it more legitimate and fact-based so audiences will be "edified" and moved somehow by the hard data. This can be a trap as audiences report a feeling of fatigue and don't often process hard data emotionally. It's simply too much for us to digest and act on if there is not an emotionally evocative story to wash it down with.

I have been unpacking these two considerations and using them as constant contextualization prompts for my work. They also allude to, and elucidate, useful concepts of interconnectivity of systems, which reminds us that this issue cannot be conceived of within current political, social, ideological, or geographic borders, and that we are dependent on the health of the whole for survival—kind of like a theatre ensemble.

By articulating the complex philosophical reflections at the intersection of climate and culture, creating local-global artistic practices, and forming climate culture–action networks, theatremakers already attracted to this type of performance practice will be better able to express these radical and necessary poetics. I have initiated two projects: Climakaze Miami, which is a platform to create networks that expand my tribe of collaborators regionally and globally, and *The Mermaid Tear Factory*, a performance project that focuses on a specific local catastrophe that needs to be witnessed, unpacked, and processed by the community. It feels like a way to straddle this new territory.

A colleague of mine recently made a statement to me about one of the core operating principles of his organizing and art-making. He called it "outness." He said that he recognizes *outness* as a point of departure for every action he takes. He is involved with queer activism primarily, so the semantics have a particular cultural and political reference: to be "out of the closet" fully so as to dilute the repression of silence and our default conduct of remaining hidden in order to avoid confronting denial and/or being discriminated against.

I wanted to adopt this term for my positioning in the work with culture and the climate. *Outness* in this kind of performance means really digging down and getting clear on what is at stake. We can pick a really late-breaking climate issue for its shock factor, or ride the wave of a certain hipness associated with the breaking politics of the climate movement, but unless we really bare our souls, and confess that these are some of the most heartbreaking and powerful love stories we will ever tell, we won't be tapping our superpowers in the best service of this art-making. We need to be able to say that we are doing this for the love of our miraculous planet and not feel dorky-hippy about it. We need to be fully out tree-hugging, whale-saving theatremakers with the wit and wordsmithery of Beckett and the political savvy of Boal.

I am advocating for a relentless climate *outness*. Not that we should trump other important, sometimes cleverly labeled "special interests" in favor of the often-perceived privileged environmental paradigm shift we are seeking. But we should gently, yet persistently, remind ourselves and others that correcting what has led us to this point of climate collapse will get to the root of economic and social injustices kept in place by the marginalization of oppressed factions and ecologies.

I am hereby an out, zero-waste-wanting, po-po-mo tree-hugging vigilante mermaid theatremaker, and I'm not too cool to say it. I encourage artists and other citizens to mount creative demonstrations that examine this emergency in any way possible. Because we are dealing with the highest level of catastrophe I have been witness to in my lifetime, I'm not afraid to say that I believe it is art's role to sound the siren call to action. Let's do this.

ELIZABETH DOUD

 *Elizabeth Doud (she/her) is a theatre artist, writer, organizer, and educator who works extensively in international exchange and climate arts. She co-created Climakaze Miami with FUNDarte in 2015, an annual climate performance platform, led the Performing Americas Program of the National Performance Network from 2005–18, and holds a PhD in performing arts from the Federal University of Bahia, Brazil. She was a 2017 visiting professor at the Rapoport Center for Human Rights at UT Austin, and received a 2018 Miami Knight Foundation Challenge grant. Her most recent premiere of ecoperformance is entitled* Mermaid Truth or Consequences: A Biodiversity Gameshow. *She is the curator of performance at the Ringling Museum of Art. sirenjones.com.*

OUR DIFFERENCES ARE OUR STRENGTHS: NEURODIVERSITY IN THEATRE

02 MAY 2015

MICKEY ROWE

You may ask yourself, What is an autistic doing working at language-based theatre companies? I often ask myself that question. But I believe that in theatre my "weakness" is one of my strengths.

If you see me walking down the street, I most likely have headphones on. I nearly always wear a blue T-shirt—V-neck, so nothing touches my neck. And I don't wear coats or jackets when it's cold out, which drives my wife crazy. I was late to speak, but I invented my own incredibly detailed sign language to communicate. I had speech therapy all through elementary school and occupational therapy all through middle school.

There is a tension between everything that I am and everything that might be conventional for an actor. This is the same tension that makes incredible theatre. No one wants to see something if it is too comfortable. Every performance should have a tension between what feels easy and what feels risky.

I am also legally blind—autism is often linked with vision or hearing problems—so I can't perform very well in cold readings. If given a few days before an audition, I always memorize sides so I don't read them off the page. I enlarge scripts so they are twice as big, just like all of my textbooks and tests were enlarged in school. I will often secretly record the first readthrough of a play on my cell phone, hidden in my pocket, so that I can learn my lines and study the script by listening; my eyes give out after about fifteen minutes of looking at a page. But because I know this, I get off book damn fast. Often before the first rehearsal.

Autistics use scripts every day. We use scripting for daily situations that we can predict the outcome of, and we stick to those scripts. My job as an autistic is to make you believe that I am coming up with words on the spot, that this is spontaneous, the first time the conversation has ever happened in my life; this is also my job on stage as an actor.

For instance, at a coffee shop:

Me: *Hi, how are you doing today?* (Smile.) *Can I please have a small coffee? Thank you so much!* (If it seems like more conversation is needed.) *Has it been busy today?*
Barista: Any barista response.
Me: *Oh yeah? Is it nicer when it's busy or when it's slow? Have a great rest of your day!*

Always stick to the script. It makes things infinitely easier.

Or playing Edmund in *King Lear*:

Wherefore should I
Stand in the plague of custom, and permit
The curiosity of nations to deprive me...
When my dimensions are as well compact,
My mind as generous, and my shape as true...[?][1]

It's really no different. They're lines I've learned, that I say often, but I'm making you believe they are mine, particular to this specific moment.

These all may seem like reasons why I should never be an actor. But acting is a dichotomy. A tension between what is safe and what is dangerous. What is known and what is unknown. What's mundane and what's exciting.

There is a tension between everything that I am and everything that might be conventional for an actor. This is the same tension that makes incredible theatre. No one wants to see something if it is too comfortable. Every performance should have a tension between what feels

1   William Shakespeare, *King Lear*, ed. G. Blakemore Evans, with the assistance of J. J. M. Tobin, *The Riverside Shakespeare*, 2nd ed. (Boston: Houghton Mifflin Company, 1997).

easy and what feels risky. When a grand piano is gracefully lowered out of a window by a rope onto a flatbed truck, slowly spinning and dangling, the tension in the rope is what everyone is watching. In theatre, the performer is the rope, making the incredible look graceful and easy, making the audience complicit in every thought, every tactical switch. When the rope goes slack, the show is over.

I put my dichotomies to work for me. It's about doing the work and being in control so the audience trusts you to lead them, and then being vulnerable and letting the audience see your soul. The skill, study, and training help create the trust. The challenges make the vulnerability. You need both of them. As an autistic I have felt vulnerable my entire life— to be vulnerable on stage is no biggie.

With autism comes a new way of thinking: a fresh eye, a fresh mind. Literally, a completely different wiring of the brain.

Being in front of an audience of 500 or 2,890 people is very easy for me. The roles are incredibly clear, logical, and laid out. I am on stage; you are sitting in the seats watching me. I am playing a character, and that is what you expect, want, and are paying for. The conversations on stage are scripted, and written much better than the ones in my real life. On the street is where conversations are scary—those roles aren't clear.

Sure, there are lots of things working against me at any given time. For example, one in every sixty-eight Americans is autistic.[2] If all things were equally accessible,

2   "Community Report on Autism 2014," Autism and Developmental Disabilities Monitoring Network, 2014, http://www.cdc.gov/ncbddd/autism/states/comm_report_autism_2014.pdf.

you would expect to see one autistic in sixty-eight employees of any company in the United States. Because small talk is so important in current interviews and auditions, this doesn't happen. But it would happen if things were more accessible. And we can help to make it what we see in the future by acknowledging and realizing that not everyone's brain is wired the same way; by acknowledging neurodiversity exists.

MICKEY ROWE

 *Mickey Rowe (he/him) is the founder and co-executive director of National Disability Theatre. His company has partnered with La Jolla Playhouse in San Diego and the Goodman Theatre in Chicago to create new professional productions written by playwrights with disabilities. He has been featured in the* New York Times, Teen Vogue, Playbill, Huffington Post, *and* Salon *and on PBS, NPR, and CNN, and has keynoted at organizations including Lincoln Center, the Kennedy Center, Yale School of Drama, and the Gershwin Theatre. Mickey was the first autistic actor to play Christopher Boone in the Tony Award–winning play* The Curious Incident of the Dog in the Night-Time. *This also made him the first autistic actor to get to play any autistic character ever professionally. Mickey is a juggler, stilt walker, unicyclist, hat manipulator, acrobat, and more, and is completing his MFA in artistic leadership.*

HOW A SEASON COMES TOGETHER

29 AUGUST 2015

DAVID DOWER

When I first saw the uproar around the Manhattan Theatre Club season announcement, I thought I would just stay on the sidelines and watch it play out. Roundabout had announced a similarly homogenous season earlier and the pushback was fleeting. Other companies around the country had announced similar seasons. This has become something of an annual ritual of announcements followed by denouncements.

But then the *New York Times* quoted artistic director Lynne Meadow responding to the criticism by saying: "I don't deny the fact that this season is anomalous in terms of the percentages of diversity on our stages." She added: "It's just how the season came together."[1]

This comment feels very misleading in how it portrays the role of the artistic team at the center of the season-selection process. It deflects accountability. It denies agency. It paints the picture of an artistic director at the mercy of a confluence of forces that come together to dictate a season. Sometimes, it would be logical to infer, those outside forces just happen to come up all white, all male. "Oh well!" Like lottery numbers or bingo balls. Random. Nothing to be done. No way to avoid it. A season just comes together and, well, there you are.

No. A season is the outcome of a process of many decisions, some small, some large, all ultimately made by the leaders of the institution. A season is a very public expression of the priorities of the institution and of the people accountable for those decisions.

I also take issue with the notion that, in any particular year, a season is "anomalous" and therefore cannot be evaluated outside the context of an institution's historical record. This season, *each* season, is going to play out within the context of the contemporary moment. No matter what we have done in prior seasons, the communication between tonight's performance and today's news is present each time the curtain rises, whether we brought that fact into our planning process with us this time around or not.

1   Laura Collins-Hughes, "Internet Outcry Over Diversity Leads Manhattan Theater Club to Announce Season Details Early," *New York Times*, 20 August 2015, https://www.nytimes.com/2015/08/22/theater/after-outcry-over-diversity-manhattan-theater-club-is-making-a-change.html.

There are hundreds of priorities to balance in the process of planning a season. The decisions we make reveal the hierarchy of those priorities. It is the season, not the mission statement, that expresses what we believe in, what we fight for, what we privilege *right now, in this moment.* A season is an expression of our values, both personally (as leaders) and institutionally. Whether we want to acknowledge it or not, this is the bottom line. A season does not "just come together." It is built on the foundation of our actual values and determined by the ordering of our priorities toward those values.

It struck me, when I read that *Times* quote, that perhaps people didn't have enough perspective on that process to evaluate what was being offered as the explanation for this all-male, all-white announcement at this moment in our culture. So, I offer here, by way of example, the process of how the ArtsEmerson season comes together. I hope other season planners will share their own processes in the comments section. I hope we can start to have a conversation about the thousands of tiny decisions that add up to the result, and how we make those in our organizations.

THE BASELINE.

Like most cultural institutions, at ArtsEmerson there is a baseline set of ideas that helps distinguish what we do from what we don't do. Without some guiding principles, there is simply too much to tackle. Without guiding principles, you wind up defaulting to something like "strong prior relationships," for example, or "things we've heard of," or "things the *New York Times* raved about," or "things that our colleagues had a huge hit with," or "things with money attached," or "things I love."

ArtsEmerson was founded on and operates from four core assumptions:

- We are international in scope. We put the world on stage.

- We are generative in spirit. We look for ways to support the emergence of something new.

- We are additive to the cultural landscape. We program in the artistic gaps in our city and work hard to cultivate an audience for the arts in Boston that has traditionally not actively participated at the major cultural institutions.

- We work in long arcs of relationships with artists. When we find an artist that connects deeply with our community and our values, we support them over time and through multiple projects.

Along with this list of baseline assumptions, we have made a firm commitment to being part of a citywide effort to foster civic transformation around race and class equity through shared experiences of art and public dialogue. This is an initiative we identify as One Boston.

From the very beginning of the process at ArtsEmerson, we analyze the projects that we intend to consider for the various contributions each makes to our baseline. It's like a genome project—we record the component parts of each work and plot the results on our "diversity grid" (see the illustration). There are ten dimensions on which we analyze those projects when they are placed on the list to be considered. They don't land there first because of their contribution to the baseline—*the art leads.* They land there because we are interested in the work itself. But once they enter this planning process, these baseline elements become part of the consideration as well.

This is the ground on which we stand to start the process of planning a season.

STEP ONE: INVESTIGATION.

Like most of my colleagues, I spend a good deal of time during the year scouting work, looking at videos, talking to artists and agents, reading blogs and print reviews, and generally just exploring the world of available work. In my case, as a presenter/producer focused primarily on ensemble work, I don't tend to do as much reading of scripts as many of my counterparts. But the exploration is expansive. And, importantly, I am not alone in this work. P. Carl does the same sort of exploring and brings a whole other set of projects into the room. Rob Orchard, ArtsEmerson's founder, still scouts for us and contributes other projects to the list. Others on staff make suggestions, and many watch DVDs or are asked to see work and report back on it. Our closest audience partners also recommend work that they are hearing about or have seen. By the end of this step there are likely anywhere between forty and fifty titles that we are serious about as a group, for the thirteen to fifteen opportunities in the season.

This list is kept readily available at all times to the whole staff via Basecamp. People can track what is on the list and what is coming off the list. They can look at the videos and write reports that get logged to Basecamp where everyone can read them. It is an open process in that way.

The investigation period also includes extensive listening in our community. What are the issues of importance to us as a city? What are the conversations taking place in the world that haven't yet found voice in our city? We say we put the world on stage, so where have we not paid sufficient attention recently? What are the artistic gaps when looking at the programming at other institutions, as well as at our most recent seasons?

The list, at this point, is an expression of our interests—it reveals what's on our minds and in our conversations. Priorities have been at play here already. It is emanating from our baseline, from our values.

STEP TWO: A GATHERING, A WINNOWING.

As the calendar advances, certain projects need commitments in order to stay in the conversation with us. Their planning timelines mean they cannot keep open a space for us on the off chance that their project remains standing at the end of our whole process. If we feel ready to commit, we move to contracting and scheduling conversations. If we don't, we have to let them go. A decision point. A priority check. "Privilege this one?" "Let it ride longer and risk losing it?" "Let it go outright?" Some projects fall apart at this stage for other reasons. We can't make the schedule work. The money won't work. The theatres are the wrong dimensions. We can't have live flame on the stage. Things like that. These, too, are decision points. These are our priorities being sorted out, our values being acted upon.

STEP THREE: ASSESSMENT. WHERE ARE WE?

At this point, there are a certain number of projects we've now privileged in the process and they are inked into our calendar and our budget. Those artists are building their plans based on these commitments. We begin a process of assessing where we stand with respect to our overall hopes and dreams for this season we are planning. By now we can see how much balance there is in the projects we've already committed to, which priorities are well met, and which aren't. Is the work all Eurocentric so far? Is it heavily male? Is there a balance in terms of form? Is our generative spirit being expressed? We interrogate the list for what it tells us about where we are in relation to our values.

STEP FOUR: ADJUSTMENT. WHAT DO WE DO ABOUT IT?

Here is the point where the push against what's easy, or what would "just come together," gets fully engaged at ArtsEmerson.

Remember, we have a list of more titles than we can possibly do in one season. So now we turn to this list to fill out the remaining opportunities in such a way that it tells our full story.

If we find, for instance, that we've committed to a bunch of projects led by men, we have to look at the list of remaining projects (all of which we're already excited about) for projects that help us express our value of gender diversity. If we find we've committed to known titles, we must look to our list to prioritize the new and emerging works or forms. If we find that there are timely projects that absolutely need to be programmed now in order to connect to the cultural moment in our city, those move up in priority. There are many, many permutations of this sort of calculus of the planning process. Drafts of seasons are drawn up and circulated. Members of the staff debate the balance reflected in these drafts using our values as the guide. We share aspects of it with community partners to test our own assumptions about the relevance and impact of the choices.

It has happened that we've had to go back on a commitment in order to make the space to fill a gap. In that case we attempt to move the commitment to the next season so we don't abandon the artist entirely. In one case we kept the time and money commitment but turned it to a workshop for a new work rather than a presentation of the piece we'd planned. This was not comfortable for the artist. It was not comfortable for us. But it was the only solution we could find for balancing the season in harmony with our values.

STEP FIVE: ANNOUNCE IT.

That's skipping a few steps, in truth. We have to budget it. We have to get far enough in our talks with the artists that we can all agree it is ready to be announced. We discuss the season with the whole staff. We discuss it with our community partners. We discuss it with the press. And, at some point, we go public with it. Just to say, there are multiple points along the way where stakeholders can, and do, raise questions or point out blind spots. The list did not "just come together," and it is not "just announced."

ANALYZING THE 2015–16 SEASON: THE DIVERSITY GRID

So, here's a look at the specifics of the 2015–16 ArtsEmerson season and how it came together to express our values and tell our story.

Here is what the planning grid looked like when we were ready to announce. You see there are ten columns where we are evaluating each project against our values. We are aiming for balance across the whole spectrum of our priorities. We do not need every project to hit on every dimension. But you'll see when you look at it that the colored boxes appear in every column multiple times and that, overall, there is a rough balance between the number of colored boxes and the number of colorless boxes. This is the outcome from the list of forty-five projects that we started with in step four of the process.

Title	Country	Culture	Generative	Form	Venue	One Boston	Gender	Family	Arc	X Factor
Ernest Shackelton Loves Me	US	Euro	New work	Music Theater	Paramount		F/M		New	Shackelton
Mr. Joy/ Emergency	US	African American	New Production	Solo	Black Box?	Yes	M	Older	Arc	
An Audience With Meow Meow	US/UK	Euro	New Work	Music Theater	Majestic	Yes	F		New	Celeb
Chopin Without Piano	Poland	Euro	First US Tour	Music Theater	Paramount	Yes	M/F	*	New	Student Collab
Carmen/ Midsummer	South Africa	African	No/Yes	Music Theater	Majestic	Yes	M/F	*	Ongoing	Happy Audiences from Flute
Octoroon w/ Company One	US	African American	Recent Work/New Production	Play	Black Box	Yes	M	No	Ongoing	Local Company
Twelfth Night	UK	Euro		Shakespeare Redux	Paramount		M	*	New	Triad
Three Sisters/ Maly	Russia	Euro		Play	Majestic	Yes	M			Russian Community
Historia De Amor	Chile	Latino	New Work	Multimedia	Majestic	Yes	M/F		New	Film Elements
*The Wong Kids	US	Asian American	Recent Work	Play For Young People	Paramount	Yes	M	*	New	MaYi
Cuban Revolutionary	US/ Cuba	Latino		Solo	Black Box	Yes	F	No	New/ LTC	
Beckett	UK	Euro	Classic	Solo	Paramount	No	M	No	New	
Premeditation	US	Latino	New work	Ensemble Play	Paramount	Yes	F/M		New/ LTC	Comedy

KEY:

Country: What country did the work originate in?

Culture: What is the culture of origin in this work?

Generative: Is there a generative component to the project?

Form: What is the form this project takes?

Venue: Which space is it suited for?

One Boston: Does this project create opportunities to foster the race/class equity conversation?

Gender: What is the gender composition of the artistic leadership of the project?

Family: Is the piece suitable for a family audience?

Arc: Is there a relationship already building with this company at ArtsEmerson?

X Factor: Is there an intangible element here that is helpful in understanding its place in our season?

Every theatre has a process for season planning. This is just the one at ArtsEmerson. The engine of every one of these processes is a series of decisions along a timeline. Every decision is informed by our priorities. And, in the end, the accumulation of these small negotiations with our personal and institutional priorities reveals the values underlying those decisions. We may not like what is revealed about ourselves or our institution. It may disappoint our audience, our colleagues, or our artists when they see our values on display. But we were not victims. We were not passive. We were not capricious. We were not surprised.

DAVID DOWER

David Dower (he/him) began his journey as a theatre producer in San Francisco, where he founded Z Space and produced more than fifty productions over a twenty-year span. David led Z Space for twelve years before assuming the role of associate artistic director at Arena Stage in Washington, DC. In six seasons there he oversaw the production of three Tony-winning shows (33 Variations, Next to Normal, and Edward Albee's Who's Afraid of Virginia Woolf) and the development of three shows that ultimately earned the Pulitzer Prize for Drama (Next to Normal, Fun Home, and Sweat). David then became artistic director at ArtsEmerson in Boston, where he presented several seasons of international theatre in four venues in the city's theatre district. He returned to San Francisco at the end of 2020 to assume the role of executive producer for the 7 Fingers United States operations and lead the Club Fugazi project. David is a founder of HowlRound Theatre Commons.

ON THE MERITS OF YELLOWFACE: WHY CASTING THE "BEST" ACTOR FOR THE ROLE IS ACTUALLY JUST A SELECTION OF BIAS IN A RACIST SYSTEM

09 OCTOBER 2015

NELSON T. EUSEBIO III

In the backlash of yellowface casting in *The Mikado*, a long-held argument has resurfaced, one that is both patently false and dangerous. That argument is the one for meritocracy—that regardless of race we must protect and advocate for the integrity of the art. That argument is this: a part should go to the best actor for the role.

Define "best." Best as in most qualified? The person with the most credits? That's not a great measurement.

We could measure "best" by technical measurements: height, singing ability, body type, etc.

Let's go with this: the best actor is the one who best fits what the creative team wants.

So it's up to the creative team to decide who is best. As a director, let me tell you the God's honest truth: If all those things are equal (or close), I'm going with the person I know. Or the person who's worked with people I know.

An actor can give an amazing audition and change my mind. But the bias of experience is that if I'm directing, I'm counting on this person to be able to deliver when they get on stage or set. And how do I know they will? Most likely because I've seen them do it before—either in the audition, in another show, or because I've worked with them.

That's my bias as a director. I'm sure I have others, as do many people who cast shows. But that's my point: the best is subjective. In Joy Meads' exceptional article in *American Theatre* magazine, she examines the deeply held biases that are ingrained in our society, even those of us who consider ourselves open-minded:

> *None of us is immune. "Bias is as natural to the human condition as breathing," Ross says. And, crucially, research has shown that we sometimes bear unconscious bias against our will, and even when it conflicts with our conscious values and beliefs. Indeed, researchers have found unconscious bias in people who believe deeply in racial and gender equality.*[1]

1   Joy Meads, "What Lies Beneath: The Truth About Unconscious Bias," *American Theatre*, 21 September 2015, https://www.americantheatre.org/2015/09/21/what-lies-beneath-the-truth-about-unconscious-bias.

We like to think that our field functions as a meritocracy. That if you are talented, work hard, and get a few lucky breaks, you will have a career. But that is not true, especially if you are a woman or a person of color.

The most clear bias in our white supremacist society is that white is universal, better, more preferred. And why not? History is written by the winners, and history books tell us that white people created America, invented theatre, and created *The Mikado*. The people casting are most likely white.

So how do we pick the best actor? Talent is required, yes. Work ethic, sure. But the last and most key one is this: you have to fit into the big-ass blind spot of meritocracy called "bias."

Every human being has different tastes and biases. When we pretend that theatre is a meritocracy where the best actor gets the job, and that people who don't get jobs are less talented, then we continue to enforce the idea that theatre is some magical utopia where bias (which we like to call "taste") doesn't exist.

What is theatre if not a meritocracy? When we complain that our field is not a meritocracy, one of our most popular arguments is: it's about the power of your network, i.e. who you know. It becomes a system in which those who have access to resources are far more likely to succeed than those who do not. That access takes many forms: education/ training, networks, gender, etc.

I can hear the actors protest: "But I'm good and talented, that's why I work."

Actually, as many actors—especially those of color—can tell you, that's *not* why you work. You work because you seem familiar to those behind the table, because often those people are white. If you're not trained and talented you don't get into the room. But if you're trained and talented and white, you have an advantage. Why? Because all major media—the news, the movies your directors grew up on, the television you've been watching—tells us that the primacy of the American narrative is the experience of the white, cisgender, able-bodied male. He can portray an Indian, an Asian, or whatever else the story calls for him to be. We like to call it "universal." So that bias exists in all of us, even those of us who exist outside of that narrative.

To quote Viola Davis: "The only thing that separates women of color from anyone else is opportunity."[2] Opportunity is not just being in the room to audition; it's being truly considered for the role based on the totality of your artistry, including race. Opportunity requires people to see through their biases and take a chance.

But this is theatre, right? Where we can have fun, play pretend, etc. So why can't white people pretend to be Asian?

Because we have the actors to play the roles. Because it reinforces stereotypes. Because of so many reasons, but mostly because it takes away the humanity of an entire community. Theatre is better than that; it's an art form that *aspires*. It should be a place where we aspire for a better world and inspire others to create it. If it can't do that, then can we at least reflect the world we live in now?

2   "Viola Davis Gives Powerful Speech About Diversity and Opportunity | Emmys 2015," Television Academy, 21 September 2015, video, 2:42, https://www.youtube.com/watch?v=OSpQfvd_zkE.

To the people wondering about why these jobs just don't go to the best actor: Put some representatives of the culture being portrayed in charge and let them decide who the best person to represent them is. And respect it, because white people *never* have to worry about representation on stage.

And to those who want to continue to perpetrate yellowface on the American stage: You have every right to do that. Just know that with that choice, with the revelation of that bias, there are communities that you are damaging, you are reenacting racist practices, and there will be people who stand against you.

It has nothing to do with who the best actor is. And everything to do with who the better person is.

NELSON T. EUSEBIO III

Nelson T. Eusebio III (he/him) is a Filipino American director, producer, and award-winning filmmaker. He is the associate artistic director of Kansas City Repertory Theatre. He has directed and developed work at theatres throughout the country. Nelson was a resident artist at Ensemble Studio Theatre, Target Margin Theater Institute, and Mabou Mines. He is a member of SDC, LCT Directors Lab, and the Rhodopi International Theatre Collective. Nelson was a participant of the NEA/TCG Career Development Program and a recipient of the Killian Directing Fellowship. He also served as the artistic director of Leviathan Lab, LoNyLa, and Creative Destruction. He is a participant in the SPARK Leadership program and received his MFA in directing at Yale School of Drama. Nelson notably served as a United States marine. nelsoneusebio.com.

AD III: FROSH BITES— ELEVENTY-ONE NUGGETS FOR BEING A SUCCESSFUL AND ETHICAL ARTISTIC DIRECTOR

02 FEBRUARY 2016

JACK REULER

HUMAN

1. Lead with generosity.

2. Know your place and role on the privilege-inequity-responsibility continuum. *Diversity, inclusion, and equity are nonnegotiable.*

3. Your role with board and staff—the buck stops with you. There is no "Mommy." *It is always good and important to surround yourself with talented, smart, responsible people to advise and support you, some of whom you may report to, but the final call is almost always yours to make.*

4. Dream as though you'll live forever. Live as though you'll die today.

5. Be an active listener and trust your instincts.

6. Know the rules well—break them often.

7. Don't lead a transactional life. *My father preached, "Do good and disappear," meaning that one does what one does for another person or organization or industry or society without conditions and doesn't keep track of those niceties or favors or acts of generosity in hopes of reciprocation. By doing it repeatedly for a long time, the rewards are many and come back in a myriad ways. It has never failed to be true.*

8. Don't get addicted to stress. *While many perseverate over avoiding, reducing, or managing stress, for a leader it can be a seductive aphrodisiac that allows one to feel alive, needed, pleased, and vital, even if they feel burdened by it.*

9. When you're certain that you're most right is when you're often most alone.

10. People die. Know how to speak in *feelings* embodied by words.

11. Hurt-people hurt people.

12. It is not enough to know right from wrong. It is important to right that which is wrong.

13. While it is important to align with community—geographic, professional, ethnic, etc.—it is also important to create community.

14. The world may segment your career into whippersnapper/wunderkind, has-been, and sage while you're doing exactly the same thing or getting better at it.

15. Facilitating the dreams of others is the most rewarding work of all.

16. There is no "they." *All people, but especially those with a public profile, find themselves worrying what "they" will think, an amorphous undefined body of humanity that will have a collective opinion of an action, decision, or appearance. It's just not true, and when it is, it passes very quickly.*

17. Do what you can do really well.

18. It's nice to be important, but it's more important to be nice.

19. Be careful not to think you don't have control issues when you're in control. Assess that when you don't control something.

20. Adhere to the following adages:

    • Watch your thoughts, for they become words. Choose your words, for they become actions. Understand your actions, for they become habits. Study your habits, for they will become your character. Develop your character, for it becomes your destiny.

    • Be the master of your will and the slave of your conscience.

- Do all the good you can, by all the means you can, in all the places that you can, at all the times you can, to all the people you can, for as long as you ever can.

- Start doing what's necessary, then what's possible, and suddenly you're doing the impossible.

- The best preparation for tomorrow is to do today's work superbly well.

ARTISTIC

21. Nurture talent without compromising excellence. *There is a myth in the cosmos that creating opportunity for young, early career, cross-discipline, less experienced, or any type of marginalized artists mandates acceptance of diminished quality. It's simply not true. Both can be accomplished simultaneously.*

22. Be imperialistic—your theatre's talent and material appearing at theatres everywhere is good for your theatre. *When other arts organizations clamor to utilize talent that you have developed and inadvertently screw you for the chance to work with them, be flattered. You're doing something right. That talent will eventually, if not immediately, return and perhaps even be appreciative.*

23. Trust your taste—eschew validation. *All too often decision-makers look to see where or with whom someone has worked/performed as a determinant of quality rather than trusting her/his own eyes, ears,*

and judgment. Similarly, awards are frequently used to verify the quality/value of someone or something. Try to avoid such behavior.

24. If you aren't the best theatre in America, what do you need to do to become that?

25. Size doesn't matter—don't think small size, midsize, or large based on budget or number of seats or any indicator, but think in terms of "right size": those that do what they want to do at the caliber they want to do it with the resources they have.

26. Befriend literary managers, dramaturgs, and writers— they know where the ideas are hidden.

27. Audiences don't care about "hard"—they care about "good." *Sometimes while we're producing, it's easy to become convinced that amazing technology, multiple languages, remarkable casting, and other extraordinary challenges will be appreciated for sheer ambition. They will not. Theatre is a meritocracy. It is virtuosity that earns kudos.*

28. "Can't" isn't in our vocabulary. *Be in constant conversation with your limits.*

29. "Good enough" is never acceptable.

30. Mission. Mission. Mission. Mission must be glue.

31. A mission is something to be achieved.

32. Representing and realizing the mission and providing vision define the job.

33. Absolute excellence is non-negotiable. *A falsehood circulates that the "right to fail" is a birthright of non-*

profitdom. It is not. Bad theatre is unhealthy for not just theatre, but all live events. The longevity of the art form will be reliant on the reduction and elimination of bad theatre. That "bad" is in your hands. If you think it's not absolute virtuosity, then don't show it to an audience, please.

34. The art of an artistic director is producing. *An artistic director's work as a leader is judged by mission realization and providing vision and balanced budgets, but the art of an artistic director is gauged by that person's producing skills—assembling stellar talent to accomplish amazing art in a healthy atmosphere on a realistic budget (income and expenses) in pursuit of a successful conspiracy for artists, mission, venue, and audiences.*

35. When casting with a freelance director, your opportunity is to nominate and veto, but not elect. *The director's mantra regarding casting is (and should be), "Be good or perish." As artistic director, you may tell a freelance director that certain roles are cast... before that director accepts the job. After that, you may invite countless actors in to audition and you may, with justification, veto a director's choice. Coerce, cajole, and persuade all you like, but that director, within those parameters, has final say.*

36. Go to plays. How do you know what's good if you don't see what's better and worse?

37. Your favorite or best show is always your next one.

38. Trust the material. *If you've chosen good work to offer your stakeholders and have a lapse of faith in the*

people charged with executing, trust that you've got great taste and the material will prevail. It is sometimes unbelievable what can be accomplished in the final day or days.

39. Aspire to the crossroads of virtuosity and authenticity.

40. See, learn, do, teach. *Ushering the next generation of theatre leaders into the field is a responsibility of the job.*

41. Make work. Make world.

42. The artistic director of a nonprofit theatre does not ask audiences what they want to see and program that. They lead audiences to see that which they don't yet know they want to see.

43. Theatre is not a democracy.

44. Talent over type. Chemistry trumps both.

45. What people say in the nine days before an opening doesn't count. *During tech and the final stretch before opening, people say and do things that they otherwise might not do or say. Have a short memory and don't hold it against them.*

MANAGEMENT/DECISION-MAKING

46. Avoid power imbalances—treat each freelancer like it is your privilege to work with them and treat each funder as a partner.

47. Manage expectations—avoid surprises.

48. Be selective about opportunities to be trained, to sit on panels, to be the voice of the field or community. *There are an infinite number of learning, judging, and teaching sessions to which you'll be invited— sometimes with compensation, but often without credit or pay. Be careful not to seize so many that you don't have time to do your core job.*

49. No matter how attracted to, enamored of, or in love with someone you are, if that person is or may ever be an employee, contractor, or vendor, do not act upon your feelings. *Know it now. Don't learn it the hard way.*

50. Think simultaneously of the organization, community (however defined), and the field.

51. "No" is a complete sentence.

52. The competition of live theatre is not other live theatre or even other live events.

53. Deal so good, they couldn't say yes. *Sometimes, for some people, nothing is ever enough. It usually has nothing to do with you or the specific situation. It can be that person's frustration with the field and its treatment of freelancers, past unfair treatment of that individual, the cost of childcare, or that the dog pooped on the pillow. While rare, recognize it and move on.*

54. What does compromise mean to you? *For some, compromise is the devil's tool, leading invariably to a diluted result and insisting on mediocrity. For others, it is the result of good diplomacy. Case by case, both can be true, but know its influence on your psyche.*

55. The media are equals, not pawns or adversaries. *The ecosystem of a theatre community is comprised, generally, of theatremakers, those who see theatre, those who write about the theatre that is made, and those who read what is written. It may often be unfair, but over duration it is unfair equally in both directions: your best work is poorly received by those writers as often as your worst work is unduly praised.*

56. Honor and encourage honesty, self-criticism, and dissent.

57. Plan, implement, analyze, replan. (Strategic plan. Communication plan. Marketing plan. Fundraising plan.)

58. There is never enough time for strategic planning. Tough shit. Do it and do it well.

59. The formula for good management: provide *information* with ample *time*, proper *resources* (human and financial), articulated *expectations*, *support* from the top and bottom, and *hold accountable*.

60. Spend as much time and attention finding audience as you do to making the programming, whether it's mainstage, workshops, residencies.

61. Employees who work inspired by mission outperform those who perform for compensation.

62. Try not to let others' crises become your emergency.

63. Retention of audience is overrated but retention of staff is undervalued.

64. Aspire to be the parent of the future and not the child of the past.

65. Avoid dual reporting. *In structures in which two people report to the board, it yields the board as "Mommy," called upon to iron out disagreements between staff leaders. Eventually board recruitment is jeopardized and board function diluted. Similarly, no employee should be the direct report of more than one person lest troubles ensue.*

66. Leaders eat last.

67. Responsibility without authority can be unfair.

68. Even though you are officially management, be pro-labor. The unions are your friends, even when it doesn't appear so.

69. Ask for help before you need to be rescued.

70. "You can make a killing in the theatre, but not a living." *The rewards of making a career in the professional theatre are not financial, but they are substantial. This oft-cited phrase is usually used in connection with commercial theatre, but it is, to me, about a fulfilled soul.*

71. Answer the question, "What is capacity?" (Don't let yourself be flagellated by, "We don't have the capacity.")

72. Eschew institutional models.

73. Disallow the phrase beginning with, "It'd be easier if..."

74. Use your vacation.

75. Know what branding is and live the brand 24/7.

76. Don't fuck with people's money, ever. *You may need to hold vendors and utilities and rent and an endless list of payables at bay, but manage cash flow such that the freelance employees and contractors get paid when contractual obligations commit to said payments. When necessary, communicate frequently and specifically about relevant issues and the anticipated timing of their resolution. The consequences of mishandling missed compensation take a long, long time to reverse.*

77. There is no downside to transparency.

78. Solving complex problems is profoundly rewarding.

79. Work/life balance may just be for everyone else. It's okay to accept and honor that.

80. Don't let your gag reflex show when a full-time staff member says, "That's not my job" when times are difficult.

81. Follow the data. *It has been said that "the best indicator of future behavior it to examine past behavior." It is also true that a futurist is not someone with a crystal ball, but someone who recognizes trends and stays ahead of them. Analyze data of all kinds all the time— of your organization, of the field, of the community, of society, of the cosmos. It only lets you down if you a) don't track it, or b) assess it poorly. Analysis is an undeniable avenue to a successful tomorrow.*

82. Learn when to do nothing. Visualize.

83. Learn to write from the heart, not head.

84. Always listen and listen hard. *Things may be said privately and publicly about you, your organization, your work, and more. These things may offend you. You may vehemently disagree with them. They may simply be inaccurate. Never stop listening and you will continually get wiser and smarter about what you are doing. Disregarding what is being said may be the road to your undoing.*

85. Avoid the word "innovate." It cycles in and out of fashion, cycling out suddenly and without warning, rendering you unintentionally passé.

86. Don't be passé.

87. Think of contracts as one-way agreements and be pleasantly surprised when they're not. *When you offer anyone a contract for anything and they accept, you stop looking. Yet for some (maybe even for many) that contract is a placeholder and they keep looking for a "better job," feeling absolutely justified when letting you know that the better opportunity has been accepted, nullifying the earlier mutual legal agreement. But woe to the artistic director that would ever sign someone to a contract and then give that person notice because a greater talent had been identified who would work for less and accepted an offer. Accept the double standard, unfair though it may be.*

88. Embrace risk. Move swiftly. Capitalize risk.

89. "Don't tell me a question." *People will ask a question for which they will accept only one answer, which indicates that a question is not really being asked. They are rarely prepared for the consequences of any alternate answer.*

90. In the eyes of others, an "expert" is always someone from out of town.

91. It is far more important to be respected than liked. *The job description of an artistic director inherently includes making subjective judgments on the quality of others' work and choosing to utilize those persons' abilities. Those decisions are met with scrutiny and opinion. That comes with the territory. Treating people with kindness and dignity and honor while making the organization or project your best friend and doing absolute right by that organization or project will garner respect that, in the big picture and long run, endears you to those who choose to judge. Being liked as an ambition can, sadly, lead to mediocrity that can dilute respect.*

92. Don't comment publicly on your thoughts of another artistic director's choices or decisions.

93. Loyalty is an unparalleled virtue.

94. Talent complements tenacity. Talent without tenacity is flaccid.

95. You will attend innumerable meetings in your career as artistic director. Be prepared, not just present, for every one.

96. Never take for granted the amount of free food and free travel that comes with the job. It's awesome!

97. You will learn about things you never imagined would be part of being an artistic director: a plethora of government regulations, insurance minutiae, building codes, political ramifications, and so much more.

Educate yourself and know them thoroughly until you're virtually scholarly on the needed topic. No one will sympathize with ignorance and you will find that a little knowledge can be, indeed, dangerous.

98. Go to the dot!

Go directly to any problem. Don't circumnavigate it in hopes that it will resolve itself on its own.

99. Be public and specific in praise of people who deserve gratitude and appreciation.

100. People often imagine that the people they really like and admire are really good at what they claim to do. It can be difficult to dissuade them of that notion.

101. Lead a culture in which gender is not binary.

FINANCIAL

102. Be very involved with fundraising and budget management. Know the budget better than anyone. Your numbers aren't numbers—they are people and things and activities with a narrative.

103. Don't follow the money. *Try to never rationalize that something is good for the organization for which money is possibly available. It is a tempting trap that is often unhealthy in the long run and for the field. Would you have chosen to pursue that course of action had those dollars not revealed themselves? Ask and answer that question honestly and know that staff and board may declare it a missed opportunity.*

104. Constantly be successfully on top of projected year-end (PYE) and cash flow and you will thrive. *For theatres of all sizes (and probably for any business of any type of any size), knowing that the end of the year will reveal income equal to or exceeding expenses and that cash flow can always be managed to be positive allows fiscal health. Be vigilant and know this to be true 365 days a year.*

105. Use restricted funds for only their appointed purposes. *In the nonprofit world, cash is not king. The road to ruination for many nonprofits is spending dollars that have been designated (usually by a funder/donor) for a specific activity, for an identified time period, or for a geographic area on general operations with the internal promise to pay them back.*

106. Value is on a continuum of quality and cost.

107. Don't let programming be considered variable costs. *When financial times are tight, staffs and boards needing to fill budgetary gaps may view programming—the very delivery system of mission, vision, purpose, and quality—as the most vulnerable cells in the budget to be adjusted. Resist this and share the burden across numerous, if not all, administrative,*

financial, and programmatic areas. The majority
of dollars come into the organization because of
programming and an institution's ability to accomplish
that to which it aspires.

108. Don't acknowledge the game. *People in the field often
offer sage advice on "how the game is played" so that
you can be informed and succeed at the game. If you
don't acknowledge that there is a game to be played,
you get to invent your own way to navigate the field
and its players that can very often serve you better
than the rules of an amorphous, undefined, nameless
game.*

109. When things look bleak, ask yourself not what the
community would feel like without your organization,
but what the community would feel like without
theatre! Then work an extra ten hours that day and
right the ship.

110. Lead change management.

VISION	+	SKILLS	+	INCENTIVE	+	RESOURCES	+	ACTION PLAN	=	**CHANGE**
		SKILLS	+	INCENTIVE	+	RESOURCES	+	ACTION PLAN	=	CONFUSION
VISION	+			INCENTIVE	+	RESOURCES	+	ACTION PLAN	=	ANXIETY
VISION	+	SKILLS	+			RESOURCES	+	ACTION PLAN	=	RESISTANCE
VISION	+	SKILLS	+	INCENTIVE	+			ACTION PLAN	=	FRUSTRATION
VISION	+	SKILLS	+	INCENTIVE	+	RESOURCES	+		=	TREADMILL

Adapted from a model originally created by M. Lippitt (1987) for "The Managing Complex Change
Model" and found at Erin "Folletto" Casali, "A Framework for Thinking About Systems Change," *Intense
Minimalism,* 9 May 2015, https://intenseminimalism.com/2015/a-framework-for-thinking-about-
systems-change.

111. Know your grade. As I entered high school, my sister gave me this sage advice:

The freshman knows not that he knows not.

The sophomore knows that she knows not.

The junior knows not that he knows.

The senior knows that he knows.

For each decision you make, be aware of what grade you're in regarding that decision-making.

ELEVENTY-ONE

Years ago a St. Paul kindergartener named Reuler was asked to demonstrate that he could count. As he got into three digits, he counted one hundred eight, one hundred nine, eleventy, eleventy-one... at which time he was stopped by his teacher and corrected, being told that it is, correctly, one hundred ten and one hundred eleven. The five-year-old responded, "If 81 is eighty-one and 91 is ninety-one, then 111 is eleventy-one!" and held his ground. While that may have, in another time, led to a diagnosis of oppositional defiance disorder, that young contrarian became determined to live a life in which things aren't always what they appear to be or what others name them to be. My fascination with the symmetry of numbers remains to this day and so having 111 (eleventy-one) nuggets that I have gleaned through decades of leading a regional theatre in America will, hopefully, save years of discovery through trial and error for new artistic directors.

JACK REULER

Jack Reuler (he/him) founded the Mixed Blood Theatre Company at the age of twenty-two, served as its artistic director until 2022, and is now its artistic director emeritus. Mixed Blood promotes successful pluralism, using theatre as a vehicle for artistry, entertainment, education, and effecting social change. He is a founder and co-president of the National New Play Network. Theatre Communications Group presented Jack with its Peter Zeisler Award for exemplifying pioneering practices in theatre, dedication to the freedom of expression, and being unafraid to take risks in the advancement of the art form. He was presented with the Ivey Award for Lifetime Achievement. He has also accepted Actors' Equity's first Rosetta LeNoire Award for "celebrating the universality of the human experience on the American stage." Jack was named to Esquire magazine's first "Register of People Under Forty Who Are Changing America" and received Macalester College's Distinguished Citizen Award, the City's Minneapolis Award, and MCTC's Martin Luther King Humanitarian Award.

WHY *HAMILTON* IS NOT THE REVOLUTION YOU THINK IT IS

23 FEBRUARY 2016

JAMES MCMASTER

Since opening on Broadway earlier this year, Lin-Manuel Miranda has received seemingly unlimited praise for his hip-hop-infused mega-musical *Hamilton*, which tells the story of the eponymous American founding father. More specifically, from the *New York Times* to the Oval Office, many have lauded the piece for its apparently progressive positions: some have commented on *Hamilton*'s feminist interventions, while others have raved about the racial diversity of its cast. Even a critic at the conservative-leaning Wall Street Journal called *Hamilton* revolutionary. Why?

In another HowlRound piece,[1] Jonathan Mandell identified the musical's groundbreaking character through its difference: different history, different casting, and a different American musical in general. But, politically speaking, how different is *Hamilton* really? More to the point, what is the function of difference within *Hamilton*? Is *Hamilton* as revolutionary as so many seem to suggest it is? I don't think so for a number of reasons.

HAMILTON'S (MORE THAN QUESTIONABLE) FEMINISM

I am startled when I come across critics who speak in unqualified terms of *Hamilton*'s feminist merits. The female characters simply do not get enough stage time and, when they do appear onstage, their desires, fears, hopes, plans, and narratives exist only in relation to Alexander, the man at the center of Miranda's musical. I'm not even sure *Hamilton* passes the Bechdel test, the bare minimum for feminine representation in popular culture. It's arguable. (To pass, two women need to speak to each other about something other than a man.)

Even the show's most overtly feminist interventions fall short of satisfying. By way of example, consider Angelica Schuyler's crowd-pleasing revisionary recitation of the

---

1   See Jonathan Mandell, "*Hamilton*: Five Ways Lin-Manuel Miranda's Hip-Hopped History Musical Breaks New Ground," *HowlRound Theatre Commons*, 5 March 2015, https://howlround.com/hamilton.

Declaration of Independence in the song, "The Schuyler Sisters":

"We hold these truths to be self-evident
that all men are created equal."
But when I meet Thomas Jefferson,
I'ma compel him to include women in the sequel!

Unfortunately, these lyrics are then followed by: "Look around, look around at how lucky we are to be alive right now" after the song's melody returns us to Jefferson's famous words. Though one could argue that this line exhibits the sisters' excitement to be living in revolutionary times, such a lyrical celebration merely and tellingly displaces a reiteration of the show's most overt feminist critique of that same revolution. Namely, the beneficiaries of the revolution—and thus equality in the new nation— were always explicitly stated: white, land-owning men.

One could rationalize Miranda's gender-related creative choices with ye olde historical accuracy argument: "Well, this is just how things were back then! Can't argue with history!" But it's hard to accept such an explanation when Black and Brown men populate the stage, a historically *inaccurate* depiction of our founding fathers. Given all of the cross-racial casting, why was gender-bent casting beyond the musical's imagination? Though Miranda does offer an admirable amplification of Eliza Schuyler's historical contributions, this move is both too little and too late for this male-dominated musical. Where were the duets *between* women *about* women? Why choose to tell *this* story?

THE PROBLEM OF THE BOOTSTRAPS IMMIGRATION NARRATIVE

One gets the sense that Miranda saw a prime opportunity to tell the tale of "another immigrant comin' up from the bottom," a story that epitomizes the American dream. This is the narrative we get in the show's opening moments:

> *The ten-dollar founding father*
> *Without a father*
> *Got a lot farther*
> *By working a lot harder*
> *By being a lot smarter*
> *By being a self-starter*
> *By fourteen, they placed him*
> *in charge of a trading charter.*

This is a bootstraps immigration narrative. The message? *Work exceptionally hard and you too can "rise up" up and out of the struggles of your station.* Indeed, *Hamilton* seems to want to present an *exceptionally* successful immigrant (Alexander Hamilton) as a model of historical precedent and possibility for contemporary immigration discourse in the United States. The problem? The assertions here, that Hamilton worked harder and was smarter, true or not, imply that other immigrants who have not experienced success in their new nation are somehow at fault. They either do not work hard enough or, simply, are not smart enough. Such logic neglects and obscures the material obstacles and violences (structural racism, predatory capitalism, long-burned bridges to citizenship) imposed on racialized immigrants within the United States in order to celebrate the (false) promise of the American dream and the nation-state. This is the familiar and fallacious narrative that founds the logic of mainstream, immigration-unfriendly politicians on the right (Trump's wall) and on the left (Obama's exceptional Dreamers) in the contemporary moment. Given this, one wonders whether Miranda miscalculated the political implications of Alexander Hamilton's narrative when he chose *this* story to tell. After all, the musical's ability to uphold Hamilton as a good American immigrant is premised on its neglect of Hamilton's own support for the Alien and Sedition Acts of 1798, which augmented the new nation's ability to surveil and deport its residents while making it more difficult to become a naturalized citizen and to vote.

It's puzzling, to say the least, that Miranda would propagate this typical bootstraps narrative after producing such a triumphant, complicated portrait of diasporic life with *In the Heights*. *In the Heights* depicts first- and second-generation Americans of Puerto Rican, Dominican, and Latin American descent trying to survive and thrive in contemporary Manhattan. The characters each have different relationships to the English language, to money, to education, to opportunity, and to the United States. Contra *Hamilton*, *In the Heights* presents a complex tapestry of minoritized experiences. While *Hamilton* celebrates settler-colonists as patriots for stabilizing stolen land into a new nation, *In the Heights* is a *critique* of the violence of gentrification—an ongoing urban process of displacing Black and Brown people from their homes, colonization by another name.

THE MISPLACED REVOLUTION OF HAMILTON'S RACIAL DIVERSITY

As I write, the Black Lives Matter movement continues to "rise up" against the essential anti-Blackness of the United States. Progressive audiences seem to want to read *Hamilton*, complete with its multiracial ensemble, as a production that is politically copacetic with this contemporary racial revolution. However, in *Hamilton*, the fact that the white men who founded the United States— colonizers all, slaveholders some—are played by men of color actually obfuscates histories of racialized violence in the United States. Case in point: during "Cabinet Battle #1," when the talented Daveed Diggs argues as Thomas Jefferson for the security of the South's slaveholding economy, the actor's Blackness visually distances his performance of racism from Jefferson's whiteness, enabling a (largely white) audience to forget the degree to which they are implicated in the violent, anti-Black histories of the United States.

Remember who actually gets to witness *Hamilton* in the flesh. The exorbitantly high ticket prices coupled with the perpetually sold-out status of the production prohibit most working-class people of color from attending the show. Given that the production's audience, then, is overwhelmingly white and upper middle class, one wonders about the reception of the show's racial performance. How many one-percenters walk away from *Hamilton* thinking they are on the right side of history simply because they exchanged hundreds of dollars for the opportunity to sit through a racialized song and dance? My guess: too many.

Rather than aligning with the critiques leveled against the United States by contemporary leftist social movements such as Black Lives Matter, *Hamilton*'s valorization of the revolution of 1776 merely indulges in the fiction of a small, innocent, and oppressed group of young (implicitly white) men fighting for freedom against tyranny. Such a narrative resonates much too loudly with contemporary *conservative* social movements that wax nostalgic for white male "militias" armed against the threat of outsiders and government overreach, "militias" like the one that recently overtook a federal building in Oregon. While *Hamilton* makes an effort to outline its protagonist's abolitionist investments and to track the status of slavery in its performance of history, the show's narrative—made palatable and profitable both by these referential concessions and by the neoliberal imperative of racial diversity in casting—ultimately amounts to a valorization of the United States nation-state and it's juridical and financial systems, systems Alexander Hamilton helped to establish, and systems that have always functioned to the detriment of Black and Brown bodies despite what the musical might have us feel.

"NEVER BE SATISFIED"

I'm aware: I'm being too hard on *Hamilton*. It's unlikely that I would hold Jason Robert Brown or Stephen Sondheim to such high political standards. But if I'm too hard on *Hamilton* it's for two reasons: 1) a polemic is called for; critical engagement with the show's politics has been sparse at best, and 2)

Lin-Manuel Miranda is the best chance we've got in the musical theatre. To the former point, I and others who have risked critiquing *Hamilton* in public forums have often been dismissed or denigrated for doing so. *Hamilton* has received rave reviews almost categorically. I agree with much of this praise—the book, the score, the choreography, the direction, the lighting: it's all genius artistry. I also yield that a Broadway production that puts so many performers of color to work does constitute a victory. This should be celebrated, but *this is not enough*. We cannot afford to position *Hamilton* above critique. The critic, perhaps ironically, must be like Hamilton himself, or, better yet, like Angelica Schuyler. The critic must "never be satisfied." We can and should demand the best from Miranda and from all of our most brilliant cultural producers. We can and should demand that the musical theatre stage the revolution we need, that the musical theatre materialize and make irresistible, with its unique magic, the just world that we all deserve.

JAMES MCMASTER

James McMaster (he/him) is assistant professor of gender and women's studies and Asian American studies at the University of Wisconsin–Madison where he is also affiliated with the program in interdisciplinary theatre studies.

WHY I'M BREAKING UP WITH ARISTOTLE

22 APRIL 2016
CHANTAL BILODEAU

It's me, of course, not him. After all, Aristotle and his posse of ancient Greeks gave us many of the elements that have become the foundation of Western civilization. They gave us human rights, democracy, and the Olympics. They gave us philosophy, significant advances in mathematics, and medicine. And they gave us dramatic structure, the golden principle behind all of Western dramatic literature.

That's a lot to admire, I know. But I'm still breaking up with him.

The thing is, our relationship has run its course. Given the new challenges brought on by a rapidly changing world and our inability to communicate effectively around them, and given the fact that I feel he doesn't really *see* me as a woman, it's best we go our separate ways. I have no doubt he'll continue to be influential in my life—we had many good years together and I will forever value the lessons I learned from him—but in the end he's too controlling and I need to break free.

To be completely honest, I've been feeling a growing discomfort for quite some time. It wasn't exactly boredom, and we were not fighting either, but we didn't seem to fit anymore. Round hole, square peg type of thing. And then, not too long ago, I came across Josephine Green's presentation "The Power of Abundance."[1] Boom. Suddenly it all became clear.

The idea is this: Though Aristotle and his pals gave us all the good things mentioned above, they also subtly imparted their worldview and its attending values to us. Not that there's anything wrong with that. That worldview has allowed human civilization to thrive for over twenty-five hundred years. But in the context of a world that is now massively different from ancient Greece—more populated and exponentially more connected—that worldview has become a liability rather than an asset.

1   "Chairs Present Series: Prof. Ezio Manzini Chair of Design for Social Innovation and Josephine Green," UAL Post-Grad Community, 5 February 2015, featuring a talk by Josephine Green titled "The Power of Abundance," video, 18:16, https://www.youtube.com/watch?v=u9h6kE531tk.

On the most basic level, ancient Greeks were ruled by a bunch of unpredictable gods whose whims directly affected every aspect of human affairs. Largely ignorant of the natural forces shaping life on Earth, people assigned power and knowledge to these supernatural beings and lived under their capricious rule. Then, as empirical knowledge developed through the study of science, some of the powers previously assigned to gods became better understood and a single Almighty God replaced the jolly bunch. The Almighty God prevailed until the industrial revolution when our increased resources and self-reliance moved us away from the divine and into the arms of mega-corporations.

Though these represent big shifts in how we conceive the world and our place in it, the underlying assumption—that power is at the top and everybody below is subservient—has remained unchanged. In fact, it is so deeply embedded in our culture that most of the time we don't notice it.

The simplest way to illustrate this concept is with a pyramid. Power and wealth live at the top, in the hands of a minority, while the majority exists at the bottom to support the top. This is how religions are organized, how monarchies thrived, and how today's capitalist system functions. But as Green points out in her presentation, the pyramid model is not an absolute truth. It's a worldview. Or, put another way, it's a function of the stories we tell ourselves about who we are. It should come as no surprise then that the structure we use to build our societies, and the structure we use to shape our stories, are one and the same. Aristotle's theory of dramatic writing, later modified by German playwright and novelist Gustav Freytag, is a pyramid. Rising action on one side, climax at the top, and falling action on the other side.

This form of storytelling flourished at a time where man needed to conquer in order to survive. Life was hard; nature, a hostile force to be reckoned with; and other nations, a constant threat. Subjugating nature was a matter of life or death, while subjugating the masses was a way to secure power and resources and to build a sense of security. As this worldview and the stories used to keep it alive were passed down generations, they were (and still are) used to justify a slew of abusive behaviors such as feudalism, colonialism, slavery, genocide, violence against women and children, economic injustices, the plundering of natural resources, etc. In addition, Aristotle excluded a very important point of view from his theory. The festival of Dionysus, where ancient Greek theatre began, was for men only. Aristotle's "core data" was in fact stories written by men, for men, and about men.

How can a dramatic theory developed in these conditions represent the world we live in today and the world we are striving to create? We're living through an unprecedented transition in human history where we're slowly shifting from a hierarchical worldview to a heterarchical worldview. New technologies and social digital media have created a complex world and, in the process, flattened the pyramid into what Green calls a pancake, with relationships organized laterally instead of vertically. Given this new paradigm, is it ethical to embrace a dramatic form that was designed to justify inequality and violence? Can we, writers, say something new, something of value, if we don't break free from that mold? If we don't find a way to write ourselves out of the pyramid?

My friend Koffi Kwahulé knows this problem intimately. An African playwright born and raised in Côte d'Ivoire,

Koffi spoke his tribal language at home and was taught French—a legacy of French colonization—in school. He was also taught playwriting according to the classical French tradition. But, like most of his contemporaries, he realized that the experience of colonialism can't be expressed using the language and forms of the colonizer. Koffi had to find a way to appropriate the French language and make it sing a different song. He had to develop a dramatic form that would express his own unique experience. Over the next thirty years he developed a unique aesthetic, akin to jazz music; in the words of NYU professor Judith Miller, "Kwahulé intends his theatre—with its stylistic nods to jazz, through its riffs, refrains, and repetitions, through references to composers and musical numbers—to capture both something of the pain of contemporary existential despair and the exuberant energy of improvisation." Borrowing from a form developed by African American slaves struggling to maintain their cultural identity, Koffi reconceives jazz music to express the pain of French colonialism and, by extension, the pain of oppression.

The idea is not new. Many playwrights—including Beckett, Churchill, Pinter, and Kushner, just to name a few—have played with form. But they did so in isolation and it could be argued that their concern was mainly aesthetic. In contrast, what we need today is a conscious use of dramatic structure in service of societal change. The hierarchical pyramidal worldview is based on values that promote competition, control, and a sense of scarcity—there isn't enough to go around. And since we have to fight for everything, there will always be winners and losers. The heterarchical worldview, on the other hand, promotes innovation, collaboration, and creativity. It works with the assumption of abundance—there *is* enough. We just need to learn to look for it and distribute it more equitably.

Moreover, writing plays where scenes have a neat cause-and-effect relationship in the internet age, where ideas emerge through associations and where biomimicry is replacing old mechanical principles, seems archaic. And with quantum physics telling us that two realities can exist at the same time and that an observed behavior is forever changed by the act of observation, shouldn't we explore all the possible realms of existence and consciousness rather than stick to a thin sliver of observable reality? Humans are not the center of the universe anymore. Time is no longer linear. Our species could go extinct. These are profound ideas that should inform how we structure our stories.

I've seen some exciting plays recently that grapple with these concepts. And these plays have both nothing to do with climate change and everything to do with climate change. None of them addresses the topic directly. But embedded in their structure is an attempt to break down the many pyramids that rob us of power and agency, and to view humanity as part of a vast web of life. *O, Earth* by Casey Llewellyn, *Smokefall* by Noah Haidle, and CollaborationTown's *Family Play (1979 to Present)* all possess a new sensibility that positions us within a larger and more compassionate frame. These playwrights are seizing the moment; they're sensing what's floating in the ether and responding to it. They're creating the sustainable culture of tomorrow.

In her book *This Changes Everything*, Naomi Klein argues that we can't fix climate change using the economic system that created the problem in the first place. In *The Heart of*

Sustainability, Andres R. Edwards explains that we can't create a sustainable future unless we change the culture of shortsightedness that's ushering us to the brink of catastrophe. If we are to change our culture and the stories that create culture, it follows that we also need to change how we tell those stories. Just like for Klein, there can be no lasting solution to climate change without a shift away from the pyramid of free-market capitalism; for us writers, there can be no formulating a new vision for humanity without a shift away from the Aristotelian pyramid of classical dramatic structure.

So this is it. For better or for worse, I'm breaking up with Aristotle. I don't harbor any bad feelings towards him; I did love him. For a long time, our relationship was fun, passionate, and intellectually stimulating. But then things changed.

Maybe I grew and he didn't. Or maybe it was always meant to end this way, with us going down our separate paths. It's the end of an era, that's for sure. But it's also the dawn of a new age. Though it's not easy to leave the comfort of the known and knowable, I'm excited at the possibilities that lie ahead, at the chance to craft stories that are in line with my values and my vision of what the world is and can be. I'm excited to do my part and to bring all of me in that effort. I think I've earned the right to.

So long, Aristotle. It was swell.

Oh, and happy Earth Day.

CHANTAL BILODEAU

Chantal Bilodeau (she/her) is a Montreal-born, New York–based playwright and translator. As artistic director of the Arctic Cycle, she has been instrumental in getting the theatre and educational communities, as well as audiences in the United States and abroad, to engage in climate action through live events, talks, publications, workshops, national and international convenings, and a worldwide distributed theatre festival. She is writing a series of eight plays that look at the social and environmental changes taking place in the eight Arctic states. In 2019, she was named one of "8 Trailblazers Who Are Changing the Climate Conversation" by Audubon magazine.

DOUBLE EDGE THEATRE'S LATIN AMERICAN CYCLE BUILDS BRIDGES ACROSS MASSACHUSETTS

20 OCTOBER 2016

JOSH PLATT

Over the course of the past decade or so, the annual summer spectacle at Double Edge Theatre has become increasingly important to the company's identity. The spectacle is a promenade piece that moves through the outdoor and indoor spaces on the company's farm in Western Massachusetts where the company trains, teaches, develops work, grows vegetables, and cares for livestock.

Double Edge often conceives their work in cycles, and this year's spectacle became part of a Latin American Cycle. In addition to the midsummer run of *Cada Luna Azul / Once a Blue Moon* at the farm, the company collaborated with the Hyde Park Task Force in Jamaica Plain, Massachusetts at the beginning of the summer to stage a free version of the piece, including a parade, as a celebration of Boston's official recognition of the neighborhood as the city's Latin Quarter. In late September the company put up yet another version of the piece in Springfield, Massachusetts' Forest Park, in partnership with Springfield Public Schools and the Community Music School of Springfield, and presented by Springfield City Mosaic. Both pieces featured a supporting cast of middle schoolers who trained with the ensemble and performed alongside them as actors, acrobats, and musicians.

Most theatre tourists cross through the Pioneer Valley from east to west, Boston to the Berkshires, or else up from New York to the Berkshires and then east. But the shift in landscape, culture, and politics along the north-south axis is the defining feature of our region. A meme of Massachusetts regional stereotypes circulated recently. The northern Valley, where the Double Edge farm is located, was indeed labeled "Hippie farmers." The central Valley was labeled "Hippie students," in recognition of the presence of a five-college consortium. The southern Valley, where Springfield and the city of Holyoke are located, was labeled "Blight & Basketball." The Basketball Hall of Fame is a major Springfield landmark, and "Blight" is the stereotype. I grew up in the northern Valley, and as an upper-middle-class white kid I was raised to think of Springfield and Holyoke as foreign territory. Although I've worked in Springfield and Holyoke, some part of me still struggles to see the Pioneer Valley as one place, and I think this is not an uncommon problem.

These divisions may begin in the distribution of wealth and power, but they come to reside in the imagination. The economic relationship between Western Massachusetts and Boston has also been difficult at times—suffice it to say that the meme calls Boston "the Hub of the Universe." So Double Edge hasn't just been touring and retooling a show over the past year. The company has been attempting to build imaginative bridges across the state.

If Boston is the Hub, Jamaica Plain is one of its spokes—a so-called "streetcar suburb" of Boston and a historically Latinx neighborhood, which in recent years has been gradually gentrifying. The performance started and ended on the steps of a church recently purchased by the Hyde Square Task Force as their new home base, with core ensemble member Carlos Uriona inviting us to join him on a journey into memories of his village, the half-magical *Agua Santa* (Living Water), and also teaching (or reminding) us that the origin of the name of Jamaica Plain before the colonizers arrived had almost the same meaning as Agua Santa. Meanwhile, across the street—unnoticed by many audience members—two British colonizers went through an absurd loop as they tried to build something invisible with only one brick. Uriona invited us into the church, where the first sequence took place.

Actors and students wore bird costumes in loud colors, some flapping around and some suspended on low silks strung up along each buttress. Behind us, on a balcony over the door to the church, two musicians sang, hushing the audience. A wild cackling man swung out on a zip line over our heads.

There was an early-twentieth-century nightclub in the apse, and a few young people rapped about neighborhood pride and freedom on the altar, directly opposite the door. And I remember three of the younger girls continuing to play their scene, doing chores and gossiping, long after the dialogue had ended and the action had shifted elsewhere. Throughout the sequence, Uriona floated around through the audience on a set of stairs, followed and guided by Stacy Klein, the founding co–artistic director of Double Edge and director of the multiple incarnations of the show.

We followed the performers, some of them on stilts, in a parade down the blocked-off street to the proud rhythm of a song that I've come to think of as the Agua Santa anthem. They led us to a park where freestanding windows were staggered across the concrete. Small fountains sprang up around the actors as the colonizer villain fell over the fence backwards. (I realized at some point that of course I myself was a gentrifying colonizer in Jamaica Plain, fully supporting the Whole Foods that now stands where a Latinx market once did. There were many of us in the audience, and the piece let us off the hook lightly.) The actors had a dancing curtain call in a fenced-in area behind the fountains. The fence reduplicated the work of the windows; space works differently in cities. The design and staging had tapped into the differences between urban and rural spaces by treating the city as an extension of the farm, feeling out the poetic logic of the landscape.

A few months later, I went to the Double Edge farm in Ashfield to see *Cada Luna Azul / Once a Blue Moon*. The show was a celebration of the communion between artists and audience. Uriona's monologues, spotted with spontaneous embellishments, were completely disarming ("Why do I say this? Well with me it's never just one thing...."), and when we moved from station to station it was often as part of a small parade of performers on stilts, musicians, and dancers. We were with them and they were with us right from the start. Each stopping point offered a piece of story, and at some multiple stories would overlay one another, as at Señorita's, a café/nightclub/rooming house run by the Señorita (Jennifer Johnson). As we traveled around the farm with the ensemble, they gently laid multiple layers of history over one another, as though the history of an entire continent was flowing together with Uriona's personal memory. A nymph of pre-Columbian South America based on Isabel Allende's *Eva Luna*, played by Milena Dabova, danced through the same world as Adam Bright's nineteenth-century British colonizer. At one point we found ourselves with a nervous husband-to-be (Matthew Glassman) at a Latin American Jewish wedding, and not long afterward the historical trauma of the "disappeared" and civil unrest in Argentina quietly drifted past.

The magnificent sequence in the barn that followed transcended story. We were seated on the upper level surrounding a playing space beneath us. The people of Agua Santa danced and made music together across time and space below us, while musicians and singers on our level laid down the anthem. The space was eventually submerged under floating blue fabric as Bright shouted with joy—he was diverting the river! The narrative link between his success here and ambition earlier wasn't clear, but the piece swept us along. For a brief moment, before they were drowned or washed away by the diverted river, the people of Agua Santa became beings coextensive with the land itself, like Luna.

The triumphant diversion of the flood was not our final destination. In the final scene, we were led to the edge of the farm's pond. Bright clambered up a tall contraption in order to complete the diversion of the river and we were still with him as he achieved his goal. Gradually we saw an exodus of the people of Agua Santa through the forest behind the pond and in rowboats across the pond as they gathered up their meager possessions. Uriona spoke tenderly of the nature of memory. The piece ended with a rowboat coming ashore to where we were standing with survivors of the flood aboard. His memories had come home—to us.

It's obvious how deeply Double Edge is invested in exploring the relationship between theatrical storytelling and a sense of place. I would hesitate to call this "site-specific theatre," because the raw stuff of the piece came from a long and perpetually revisited devising process, sculpted by Klein, and ultimately resolved into a script written by Glassman, the other co-artistic director. *Cada Luna Azul / Once a Blue Moon* has been part of the company's life for at least two years. The meandering style of Alejandro Jodorowsky's magical realist memoir *Where the Bird Sings Best* may be partly responsible for the narrative fluidity that made it possible to successfully transpose the same show to three different landscapes for audiences of significantly different sizes.

Hundreds of people attended the two performances around the pond in Springfield's Forest Park—even larger crowds than the ensemble expected, based on the structure of some staging areas. At this final production, as in the other performances, Uriona shared a thought in his concluding speech: for him, "returning to memory is a form of protest." He explained each time that when he returns to his memories, he alters and renews them through his imagination. For him, this act serves as a form of resistance to the present. I understand him—and Glassman, the author of the text—to mean that the search for lost time can be more than a solitary stay against one's mortality. The revitalization of personal memory through performance can disrupt the imagination's self-protective habit of dividing up the world. Double Edge's ambition to create a "living culture" is unapologetically utopian, and the *Cada Luna Azul / Once a Blue Moon* sequence put aesthetic utopianism into action.

JOSH PLATT

Josh Platt (he/him) is a theatremaker and writer. He holds degrees from Yale University and Emerson College, and he lives in Turners Falls/Great Falls, Massachusetts.

A CALL FOR EQUAL SUPPORT IN THEATRICAL DESIGN

23 NOVEMBER 2016

ELSA HILTNER

Technical theatre is comprised of designing and constructing. In some areas of design, those roles are separated and separately compensated. Set and lighting designers overwhelmingly have a technical director and master electrician hired by the company to execute a designer's plan, even at smaller, non-equity, and storefront theatres. In contrast, costume designers are left to their own devices at all but the largest institutions.

Without the support of a technician, costume designers have their hands in each step of bringing the design to the stage—measuring actors, drafting patterns, building costumes, shopping, coordinating rentals, fittings, completing alterations, writing up laundry instructions, coordinating understudy costumes, returns, budgets, the occasional mid-run maintenance, and strike. The stitchers and assistants they work with are usually interviewed and hired by the costume designer and are paid from the designer's fee, or occasionally the costume budget if there's room.

Costume design is also the only area of technical theatre in which women make up the majority. Based on three years of numbers she compiled, Porsche McGovern notes that 76.5 percent of set designers and 80 percent of lighting designers are male, while only 30 percent of costume designers are male in the League of Resident Theatres (LORT). I argue that much of this division of labor (or lack thereof) is based on institutionalized gender bias within theatre and our society. This inequity stems from our culture's gendered views on who makes clothing, how much their time is worth, and the often skewed understanding of what skills are required to design and build a costume, let alone an entire show. This imbalance compounds inequities between male and female designers. It relegates costume designers, mostly women, to artisans, while set and lighting designers, mostly men, remain purely artists. This enables set and lighting designers to focus purely on their design, while costume designers must be both designer and technician. It means that a costume designer cannot design as many shows per year as a set or lighting designer can, and therefore earns less. It also affects the kinds of theatre we make and the types of voices theatre gives voice to.

And, finally, it harms the collaborative dynamic within a production team and influences theatre designer diversity.

On the surface, the allocation of support and resources within a theatre company is based on the design discipline. Female set designers are offered the same resources as male set designers within an institution, as are male and female costume designers. But this is where our culture's gendered views on garment work come into play. For most of Western history, paid garment work was seen as men's work. While women made garments in the home, men held the vast majority of paid positions as tailors and patternmakers up until industrialization in the nineteenth century. When the modern garment factory was born at the end of the nineteenth century, women were brought in as stitchers, a source of cheap and dependent labor.

More than a hundred years later, the labor of garment work is still effectively women's work and is incorrectly considered, much like modern agricultural labor, to be unskilled, disposable, and worth minimal compensation. In the age of a globalized garment industry and the five-dollar Old Navy T-shirt, garment work is performed by women with few rights and resources, women who are not deemed worthy of a living wage and have little voice with which to lobby their case. Anyone who has ever completed a garment, let alone patterned one, knows that garment construction is, in fact, highly skilled labor. Yet I see a direct correlation between how much any stitcher's skills are valued and the market rate for mass-produced clothing.

Given our gendered views on who makes clothing and how much their time is worth, it is telling that in the female-dominated, garment-based field of costume design, designers are expected to act not only as designer, but also (still) as laborer. We should move beyond these outmoded expectations. If and when designers choose to construct their designs, the time and labor that go into each process should be compensated fairly, just like any other area of theatrical design. Between design disciplines, as between genders, support should be equal and resources should be commensurate.

As companies, theatres have done little to question how often set and lighting designers only work with hired technicians. It serves their bottom line not to. Statistics show that women are more likely to take on uncompensated work than men. For better or worse, it's a tactic used by ambitious women who need to maneuver in our culture's (and, dare I say, theatre's) male-dominated system. Women are also much less likely to ask for increased compensation or assistance. In many ways it's a rigged system in which women who don't take on extra work are penalized for seeming uncooperative, while women who ask for increased compensation are often deemed entitled. Theatre companies benefit greatly from this free labor.

Artistic directors, production managers, and designers alike have also done little to reassess the expectation that some, but not all, designers are both designer and technician. We have grown accustomed to the roles we all play. The familiarity makes them seem natural, ubiquity makes them seem fair. Yet if a set designer were expected to design and build a set at a midsize theatre they would likely balk. Conversely, when a costume designer says that they don't build their designs, it's viewed as overly demanding or as a sign of incompetency.

As a costume designer, I am also guilty of maintaining the role of costume designer–technician. By being willing and able to do some work that I am not paid for, I am maintaining a norm that limits costume designers to people who are privileged enough to take on extra work without compensation. When I build the costumes I design, I make it harder for costume designers to request assistance and gain an equal footing. The thousands of unreimbursed miles I have driven for shows every year are another barrier I have helped build. When I complete alterations or return mid-run to repair a shoe, I am limiting who can afford to work as a costume designer. I have often seen this donated time as the crux of making art that I deeply care about and that has my name attached to it. (Not to mention the price I have to pay to "make it.")

Like any art form, the process of making theatre can't be separated from the final product. As creators of art, we benefit from collaborating with people with diverse viewpoints and backgrounds. We create better and more fulfilling work when our concepts are challenged and new ideas are brought into the room. Theatre is a response to the times, a place where people can gather and "hold up the mirror." In order to make our art relevant and more reflective of our diverse society, we need to promote diversity backstage as well as on stage. Designers of all disciplines will be more diverse if we support them equally. And theatre will be better for it.

As collaborative artists who come together to solve problems in the most creative and technical ways, I am confident that we can balance this load. My goal is for theatres that hire technical directors, carpenters, and master electricians to hire technicians for their other designers. The smallest of our theatres, which rely on volunteers to build their sets or cable their lights, should coordinate the same resources for other designers. Changes like this happen over time, so I would like to start the conversation and begin moving forward now.

From my perspective as a costume designer, there are some small, easy steps that could be implemented relatively quickly at any theatre, including small storefronts. All theatres should reimburse production-errand mileage and add a budget line for costume builds or alterations. If a storefront can hire a technical director, they can afford to budget for these items as well.

If they have not done so already, midsize to larger theatres should also add an assistant and maintenance/costume-build position for each production that suits the size, scale, and style of the production. This is a larger budget item within a season and may take longer to fully implement, but goals should be set and planned now as budgets and grants are being prepared for upcoming seasons.

I also encourage companies to look at how they can support their props, video, and sound designers, among others, and create a long-term plan so that all designers have commensurate resources, equal support, and therefore comparable worth.

We are all affected when resources are divided unequally. The current imbalance restrains creativity and collaboration, and limits the impact of our art. It's a dynamic that favors privilege and therefore restricts designer diversity. And, as it is rooted in societal gender bias, it compounds gender inequities. We need to work consciously to correct that bias. The current system is a product of its history. We must move beyond our history and actively work to equally support all designers.

ELSA HILTNER

Elsa Hiltner (she/her) is a pay-equity organizer and has extensively researched, written, and activated on pay equity within the arts. She is a co-founder of On Our Team and the creator of the Pay Equity Standards, a system for establishing and publicly recognizing pay equity within an organization. Her essays and data-driven resources on labor and pay equity have inspired systemic change in the theatre industry. Elsa has a background as a theatrical costume designer, is a pay-equity consultant, and is a company member of Collaboraction. In 2021, she was honored with the Michael Merritt Arts Advocate Award. elsahiltner.com.

ONE QUEEN'S HIGHLY PERSONAL/SUBJECTIVE REACTION TO TAYLOR MAC'S *A 24-DECADE HISTORY OF POPULAR MUSIC*

15 DECEMBER 2016
ROB ONORATO

1. All efforts to recapture the experience are failures.

2. Failure is a virtue. Sarah Garton Stanley: "Once you've failed to be male enough or punctual enough or whatever the criteria you've been proven to have failed against, then you can just exist."

3. Having acknowledged that, we can move on.

4.   At about 12:17 p.m. on Saturday, 8 October 2016, the lights dimmed in St. Ann's Warehouse, under the Manhattan Bridge. At once, as one, six hundred queers and friends of judy erupted into applause; a twenty-four-piece orchestra began to play; and Taylor Mac made a fabulous, triumphant entrance from the back of the house and began a performance art concert that did not stop until after 12:00 p.m. the next afternoon.

5.   "This show is long!" bellows Time with her head stuck in a clock nailed to the wall at the top of *The Lily's Revenge*, previously judy's longest and most spectacular project, at five hours, with a cast of around thirty-five. I cut rehearsal and took a guy to see *Lily* in 2012, when it was at Harvard; at dinner after the show, he had *nothing* at all to say about it. He looked like he'd been through combat. We didn't last.

6.   —judy is Taylor's pronoun. Camp genuflection to Garland, the goddess of midcentury fagdom (though why forget Collins, Holliday, Kaye, Kuhn, Chicago?), but also a rather brilliant linguistic logjam, forcing you to accommodate the spaciousness and ridiculousness of a two-syllable pronoun.

7.   This essay is also long.

8.   Like gay sex in the 1980s, enormously lengthy works of theatre are not safe enterprises. They can't be. These near-mythic colossal ones come along rarely, and it's even more rare that one can clear the time to succumb completely to the experience. For as long as you're in the room with them, they demand your attention. There's nowhere to hide: the show just *keeps happening*. It'll exhaust you. It'll frustrate

you. It'll threaten to devour you whole and leave nothing behind, and you might even gladly acquiesce, because you're going to pieces anyway either from bliss or boredom. (Thoreau: "The cost of a thing is the amount of what I will call life which is required to be exchanged for it."[1]) You will want it to end. You will never want it to end. It may seem like it will, indeed, never end. It ends. You as an audience member at a marathon show are much more *necessary* than at a two-hour-and-twenty-minute realistic four-hander with a unit set. In *Great Lengths*, his study of contemporary marathon theatre from *Nicholas Nickleby* to Forced Entertainment and everywhere in between, Jonathan Kalb proposes that any lengthy work of performance that purports to be "theatre," regardless of its venue or form or adherence to narrative, shares DNA with endurance performance art (Marina Abramović, Tehching Hsieh): both are "deeply and riskily concerned with the experience of the *body* in time and space"[2] [emphasis mine].

9.   At the top of the third hour, Taylor, having changed into the third outfit (there was a different Machine Dazzle ensemble for each hour/decade), appeared on a ledge in front of a curtain twenty feet in the air, extreme house left. The look: a bloom of wine corks on wires as a wig; lacy gloves; and a crocheted trash-dress covered in sex toys. This would be a decade of drinking songs. Taylor started to tell a story about a frat party judy had been invited to once after a

---

1   Henry David Thoreau, *Walden; or, Life in the Woods* (Boston: Ticknor and Fields, 1854).
2   Jonathan Kalb, *Great Lengths: Seven Works of Marathon Theater* (Ann Arbor: University of Michigan Press, 2011).

performance at Dartmouth. The party—in particular, its fetid basement—had reminded judy of a particular relic of gay history. "In New York in the seventies and eighties," judy said, even though judy wasn't there (though neither was I—no matter, it's in the *queer archive*: "not simply a repository...a theory of cultural relevance, a construction of collective memory, and a complex record of queer activity"—Jack Halberstam[3]), "there used to be a bar called the *Mineshaft*." Pause for effect. (The whoop you heard here, if you were in the room, was me.) "And in the men's room of the Mineshaft," judy told us, "they didn't have urinals; they just had a naked man in a bathtub." Pause for reaction. We reacted. judy, chuckling: "Half of the room just said, 'Yeah, sure, whatever, fine,' and the other half said, 'No. *Noooo...*'" Nervous laughter. Then judy said: "They want you to think we're all Ellen, but we queers are some *kinky motherfuckers*." Loud cheers and dissembling, again especially from me. Then judy stepped down from the ledge, and the band played on, and the history of America continued, the Mineshaft and its men's room and all.

10. In case you weren't there—whether for the marathon, the eight different three-hour concerts Taylor gave at St. Ann's leading up to the marathon, or any of the dozens of work-in-progress performances judy gave around the world during the six-plus years it took to develop the full show—*A 24-Decade History of Popular Music* is a twenty-four-hour performance art concert in which Taylor Mac, along with scores of

3   J. Jack Halberstam, *In a Queer Time and Place: Transgender Bodies, Subcultural Lives* (New York: New York University Press, 2005).

musicians and two dozen "Dandy Minions," performs the evolution of popular song in America from 1776 to 2016. There is an agenda to the set list: judy intends to wrest control of the narrative back from the dominant modes of power (often patriarchal and racist), which have suppressed Others in the United States for the past 240 years (and earlier, and in the present). Each decade gets an hour, and often a unifying theme: 1846–56 imagined a smackdown between Stephen Foster and Walt Whitman for the title of the Father of American Song (Foster didn't stand a chance: we pummeled his effigy, a game audience member, with ping-pong balls, while alt-stripper royalty James Tigger! Ferguson mashed his jock in the poor [lucky?] guy's face); 1876–86 inverted Gilbert and Sullivan's *Mikado* and reset it on Mars to remove any traces of cultural appropriation and orientalism (this act was *bizarre*: vocoders and blacklight spaceships and the refrain of "Tit-Willow" chanted *ad infinitum delirium*); 1976–86 was a backroom sex party. From the first song to the last, Taylor incorporates the audience into the show through oftentimes radical strategies of participation, many of which, delightfully, tip into the erotic. (One thing we queers tend to do at least to some degree when we get in a room together: we cruise.) From 1816 to 1826, we were all blindfolded (to celebrate the invention of braille) and invited to participate in a series of hobbled seduction rituals with our neighbors; ninety years later, in the middle of the night, a stranger spooned me onstage (an experience I shared with most of the men in the audience: we were away from home in World War I!) while Taylor sang "Make Me a Pallet On Your Floor";

by morning I found myself completely broken down, slow dancing with an attractive bear, sobbing into his shoulder, it was the 1970s (my emotional Achilles' heel) and the entire room was the gay prom we never had, I *sobbed* and he held me and I held him and later he told me I was the first man he'd ever danced with—

11. It was a *radical faerie realness ritual sacrifice.*

12. "Everything you're feeling is appropriate!" Taylor said over and over.

13. A twenty-four-hour show—a twenty-four-hour impermanent collapsible community of majority-queers—is long enough ("*finally*," breathes the size queen) to contain a different show for every single person in the audience. A queer friend of mine says that one of their main objectives as a performer is to give a gift to a single person in the audience, at least, at any given moment—and everyone else benefits through witnessing that ritual of generosity. judy gave us a gift every few seconds and we were all there for all of them.

14. I am ruined, as I said, for all other theatre that isn't made by Taylor Mac now. I've been biting the bars of that gilded cage for ages now—how *stale* and unnecessary realism is compared to what we can *really* do on stage—and *A 24-Decade* once and for all burned the fourth wall to the ground. If you don't acknowledge me as an audience member—all of *us* in the room as a community brought together for a vital, wonderful purpose—I don't have time for your glorified television show. But people still make and want to see that stuff. Guess I'm just queer to the

hilt—but not alone: "Sometimes in the theatre," Taylor lamented around hour five, "if you want to do anything other than straight realism, it's like trying to have sex with someone who wants to put on ten condoms."

15. Gay and queer theatremakers of the world: Are you tired of the near-total infestation of queer theatre by the pernicious forces of realism, of *their* realism? Theatre is and has always been our province and tool for subversion. We cannot let our artists toil in realism! "Unscrew the locks from the doors! / Unscrew the doors themselves from their jambs!"[4] (Whitman knew, queen that he was, all the way back in 1855.) We cannot let our regional theatres (and their audiences and their donors) dictate what stories gay and queer and trans playwrights can tell. *We must make queer art on our own terms.*

16. Not just that: We need to show up for each other. We need queer collectivity *now*, just like we needed it on 28 June 1969, and at every ACT UP demonstration, and at every ball and zap and Black Party and tea dance and march, march, march. There is something very powerful that occurs when queer people gather together and make a room full of themselves: our right to exist, and our individual weirdnesses, curiosities, and inversions, can no longer be denied. We charge each other up. We may be "Preaching to the Converted" (as David Román and Tim Miller write in their seminal 1995 essay), sure, but "to dismiss queer performance as preaching to the converted presupposes that we, the converted, no longer need occasions, events, and

4   Walt Whitman, "Song of Myself," *Leaves of Grass* (New York: 1855).

rituals where members of our community profess and perform to us their beliefs so that we in the assembled crowd can take these performances and incorporate their insights into our own continuing struggle to live in a deeply homophobic world." Because I saw male-adjacent people wear makeup and dresses and skirts made of gay porn and chip bags (and, in other queer spaces at other times, leather and rubber and uniforms and nothing at all), I learned that not only could I wear the same things and sing the same special songs, but that doing so might set me free, make me whole, help me—us—survive.

17. It is so important to me that this show was about sex, that it spoke about it, spoke sex to power. You are powerful because you have sex—queer sex, anonymous sex, endless sex, backroom sex, sex in a tent, in the shower, in prison, in the bushes, in your house in the suburbs, in the tenements, on the roof, safe sex, unsafe sex, in the dressing room, in the lobby, in the bathroom, in the streets.

18. "I *love* anonymous sex," judy merrily chirped around 1976. Then judy sang "Heroes," the David Bowie classic, as a disco number. Those who have gay sex in public (as Taylor has and presumably still does, especially at the Cock, one of New York City's [rather paltry, but beggars can't be choosers] twenty-first-century answers to the Mineshaft) and talk about it are, judy suggested, heroes. This is especially true for those vanguard queers who *invented new ways of living* (and fucking), for the first time relatively out of the shadows, for that all-too-brief decade of total sexual freedom.

19. If we do not remember queer history (and remember it in all its glory: messy, sloppy, inchoate, glamorous, scrappy, trash-strewn, aching, weeping, defiant), proto-gay children growing up in a post-gay-marriage world will think that that has always been the case, and it hasn't. We have always been kinky motherfuckers—and not just in the bedroom; in our art, too. To forget this, or "clean this up," is to behave as if history never happened, or has nothing to teach us. Taylor showed us that history is cumulative, that patterns of oppression repeat, and reify, and resist all but the most united fronts of community-based retaliation.

20. "No family is safe when I sashay," warns the singer Perfume Genius in "Queen," his twenty-first-century anthem for rebel queers. If you're not sashaying—working your sparkly self through all the halls of the world—you're not taking enough advantage of your queerness. Popular culture threatens to eradicate your queerness, to parlay whipped-up horror at "Masculine Women and Feminine Men" into suppression of difference. Remember that when the Angel pounds on his ceiling, Prior hollers back: "I am a gay man and I am used to pressure, to trouble."[5] It's an amulet, not a liability.

21. The first song making fun of dandies in the show is, of course, "Yankee Doodle," forty-five minutes in; the latest, in the 1970s (as gay lib starts to make wobbly this united front against limp wrists) is a gossamer rearrangement of a foul Ted Nugent song, "Snakeskin

5   Tony Kushner, *Angels in America: A Gay Fantasia on National Themes* (New York: Theatre Communications Group, 1992).

Cowboys." This is baked into our culture, this opprobrium for male people who toe the line of weary gender roles. We as gays can even perpetuate it: we did it in the seventies ("No fats, no fems," whined the Clones) and we're still doing it today (gotta be "masc," maybe even "straight-acting"). And to *defy* this—to fling those wrists every which way and claim your queendom—is a powerful, powerful thing, mary.

22. I want to clarify the kind of power I'm talking about here: not power on *their* terms, not the power to subjugate, strong-arm, bully, oppress, or bury. That kind of power, chained to capitalism, colonialism, imperialism, necessitates that when one body becomes more powerful, the bodies in opposition become less so. *Queer power*—which encompasses radicalism in gender, sexuality, mode of sex, style, class, occupation, size, color, art form—operates on a principle of *abundance*. It multiplies; it never subtracts. There is no limit to the number of queer bodies that can claim power. This power, too, is *not* the power to subjugate, strong-arm, bully, oppress, or bury, but the precise opposite: the power, through cultivation and performance of and pride in identity, to exalt, support, recognize, name, and love that which the brute forces aforementioned would rather bulldoze right through.

23. And the sheer variety of different genders and gender expressions in that room! There were glitterbears—great big bearded fairies in caftans. There was a daddy in leather suspenders. A butch woman in a yarness. All kinds of masculine women. Stem-to-stern drag queens. Genderfuckers, androgynes. Young gays, still growing.

Straight couples, game for anything—they, too, are queer, at least these ones; they are absolutely in the club, I promise (I spent the Civil War with a sweet pair: he wore a satin cape and she borrowed my lipstick to draw on a mustache—all the female people had to be soldiers in drag). And to top it all off: Taylor Mac, whose clothes (by Machine Dazzle, a true genius) telegraphed neither male- nor femaleness, masculinity nor femininity, but judy's chosen gender, which is *performer*.

24. ... So. This is the show I saw:

25. A communal, intelligent, erotic, participatory, spectacular performance art concert, a highly subjective history of these rarely United States and the songs we played and sang, danced and fucked to; a marathon survey dedicated to destroying through exposure the racism, patriarchy, supremacy, and fascism suppressing the fabulosity of all our country's different beleaguered Others over the years. Notable among these Othernesses—since this is nearly the very first time I have witnessed (and been included in) this very specific theatrical agenda—is the shadow history of effeminate men in America: dandies, poofs, nellies, faggots, queers; their reclamation as people who are 1) sexual, sexy, etc.; 2) fabulous, beloved *because of* their gender play/fusion/failure/fuckery; 3) perhaps, as Taylor sang in Patti Smith's "Birdland," *not human*, because being human is pretty boring.

26. And besides that, it was just the best party I've ever been to, and the most bliss I have ever, ever felt. I mean—I got misty during the *first song* because I was just so happy to be there, in that room, with six

hundred tender comrades and something so big it could alter the course of (our) history.

27. "We do not need to ask permission to participate in the creativity of our own survival," Taylor reminded us, all of us, in the early morning hours, Sunday morning, *church*; we've by now come through over two hundred years of time, emerging from the backroom, love has torn us apart but we're building *each other* back together, weary, unrested, split open, basking in the light of Taylor's split-open performerhood, "I want to reach people through my falling apart," very near the end of the whole thing, which would only be the beginning of the rest of our lives as queer disciples, daughters of judy, celebrants, not-humans, fuckers-of-form, artists all, who, now, knew what we needed to do and *could* do with art and our queer performer selves to reach the people, who, as Taylor sang, and Patti before judy, *have the power.*

ROB ONORATO

Rob Onorato is a gay artist. He loves thinking about community, tranquility, what's beautiful about history and the past, and radical approaches to form. He grew up in New England and New York, which still feel like home, even though he's spent his twenties in Chicago. He's contributed essays to HowlRound *since its early years, and he's written a few plays and monologues, too; they're called* Flapjack, The Lizards, *and* Night of a Million Barbras. *He loves the Grateful Dead and the Great American Songbook in equal measure, and he hopes to someday wind up in Provincetown, Massachusetts.*

DIVERSITY FOR DUMMIES

25 MARCH 2017

RALPH B. PEÑA

The first thing to say about this quickstart manual is that I'm a dummy myself. In all the years I've grappled with diversity, the one constant has been recalibration. What was diverse ten years ago is privileged today, and today's diversity models will become obsolete in the coming years. Historically disenfranchised groups are just now finding their voices after decades, even centuries, of silence. Diversity requires periodic check-ins, assessment, and retuning.

I think it's fair to say that the theatre community is committed to the ideals of diversity. This guide will focus on implementation, which can be trickier. And while every exercise in diversity must include gender, physical abilities, and age (to name just a few), this guide will focus on ethnic diversity.

Here are a few ways you can check on your theatre's diversity smarts.

IT'S NOT REALLY ABOUT NUMBERS— BUT LOOK AT THEM ANYWAY

Diversity is not a numbers game, but a quick look at your digits can be telling. How many people of color work in your back office? How many artists of color perform on your stages? Divide those numbers by your total employees, and the total number of artists you employed for the season. What number do you get?

Compare that number to your community's demographics. Don't use your ticket subscriber base, use the population of the geographic area in which you operate. Don't gerrymander or redistrict your sample area. Is your diversity percentage a close approximation of your area's ethnic diversity? If not, why not?

Here's a sample comparison between New York City's 2010 ethnic demographics and a hypothetical theatre company's organizational and season programming numbers. The total columns at the bottom and the far right have a story to tell. It may not be the full story, but it deserves close investigation.

SAMPLE 2010 Census	
White	33.30%
Black	25.50%
Am. Indian/Alaska Native	0.70%
Asian	12.50%
Hispanic/Latino	28.00%
TOTAL	100.00%

Roles	White	Black	Amer. Indian	Asian	Latino/ Hispanic	TOTAL	White as % of Total
Managers	2					2	100%
Staff	4	1		1		6	67%
Performers	25	5		3	5	38	66%
Playwrights	3	2			1	6	50%
Directors	4	1			1	6	67%
Designers	12	4		5	4	25	48%
Technical	8	5		3	5	21	38%
Consultants	2					2	100%
All Others	2				2	4	50%
TOTAL	62	18	0	12	18	110	
% of Total	56%	16%	0%	11%	16%	100%	

If your theatre has been around ten or twenty years, take a look back to see how your organization and programming lines up with the demographic changes in your community over time. That may tell another story.

Don't lump all peoples of color into one category. One ethnic group is not a surrogate for the other. In other words, just because you hired four Black actors for the season, you're not off the hook from hiring performers of other ethnicities.

You can look up your city's data on the United States Census Bureau.

WHO'S IN CHARGE?

Let's look at agency and the power to make decisions.

Look at your organization's hierarchy. Who are the top decision-makers? Who has the power to advance a play into production? For many theatre organizations, one person holds this power.

Who are the other gatekeepers in your organization? This includes your literary managers, casting directors, and associate producers. Oftentimes, they are the sentries who give or deny access to your theatre. Is diversity a part of their operational objectives? Are they empowered to open your theatre's doors to artists of color?

Putting managers of color in these positions is important—as important as providing them with the training and work environment to succeed.

White men run a majority of theatres in the United States and that needs to change. Not because white men are incapable of empathy or because they don't have a sense for what's right or wrong—we need diverse leaders because it drives innovation, adaptability, and organizational smarts. Diverse thinking is crucial in navigating a world in flux and, ultimately, in how the theatre responds to its changing environs.

WHO'S ON STAGE?

I have heard artistic directors and managing directors boast of how diverse their organization is. "Our back office is a veritable Rainbow Coalition!"

But wait. Aren't you running a theatre? How diverse are the faces you put on stage? What opportunities are there to diversity your casting practices?

Are you color conscious when you choose a play? How white is Thornton Wilder's Grover's Corners? What about Shakespeare's Elsinore? How about Tobias and Agnes's household in *A Delicate Balance*? Is ethnicity a marker of historical accuracy? There are many arguments for and against "authenticity," which we won't parse here. What's important is that you're aware of the implications of your decisions and how they affect who gets on stage.

This might be a good time to touch on the implicit canard in the term "colorblind casting." It is not meant to provide cover for casting white actors in roles written for performers of color. It is not meant to allow a theatre to cast a white actor as Martin Luther King, Jr., by invoking the "what's good for the goose" argument, or the "if we're truly after equality, then *any* actor can play *any* role." Why not? Because colorblind casting is intended to correct a gross inequity in American theatre, where more than 75 percent of all roles go to white actors. Calling on the goose/gander equation doesn't work because *inequality* is the current norm. A tit for tat proposal only works when all parties are on equal footing, so that for every tit, the corresponding tat is intended to rebalance the equation.

WHO'S WATCHING?

Do you have a subscriber base? How does it break down ethnically? Why? Does your pricing exclude certain communities? How about your marketing outreach? What has shaped your audience makeup over time?

Here's a big hurdle for some theatres. When the audience watching is overwhelmingly white, why should a theatre care about choosing plays that are not? For the majority of theatres that find themselves in this position, there's a good chance they've already proven to themselves that their audiences are delighted by diverse programming. Theatre audiences are voyeurs at heart and relish being able to look into lives other than their own.

But there's a more important and compelling reason to present a multiplicity of perspectives to our audiences: empathy. Forces that underscore differences and divisions shape our world today. Theatre can propose a compelling alternative by putting a human face on "the other" and stressing the truism that we are more alike than we are different. If we do this often enough, theatre can be an agent for change.

Note that I inserted a caveat in that last sentence. "If we do this often enough..." One-offs won't do it. I can't tell you how many times I've heard this refrain, "We did an Asian play, but Asian audiences didn't come." You can't expect to mobilize a community that you've ignored in the past. You have to engage, and engage again, and again. And again. You have to earn its trust.

This is true for audiences and communities of all colors.

IT'S GOING TO COST YOU

Diversity requires dedicated resources. You have to invest in it.

As a business proposition, it's a no-brainer. According to the United States Census, just "over half–50.2%–of U.S. babies younger than 1 year old were racial or ethnic minorities. In sheer numbers, there were 1,995,102 minority babies compared with 1,982,936 non-Hispanic white infants."[1]

This is what drove Google to increase its workforce diversity initiative budget from $115 million in 2014 to $150 million in 2015.

No theatre has $150 million to spend on a diversity initiative, but a close and honest look at your organization will likely reveal practices that should be made more inclusive. But let's talk about the scary stuff: box office/earned revenue.

Theatres are terrified of losing income because they took a chance on a play their audiences are not familiar with, or "can't relate to." A sea of empty seats is a scary sight, but as I said previously, you can't expect them to come if you've never put in the work. It's also wrongheaded to put up a play featuring Asian American actors and assume the Asian American community will come rushing to your doors. Don't blame the community if they don't know you.

This is where the investment opportunities come in.

Put more muscle into your outreach programs. Consider *going* to communities of color and presenting work *there*. Not everyone can come to you. Make the first move, and keep making moves. Earning trust takes time and tenacity.

---

1   D'Vera Cohn, "It's Official: Minority Babies Are the Majority Among the Nation's Infants, but Only Just," Pew Research Center, 23 June 2016, https://www.pewresearch.org/fact-tank/2016/06/23/its-official-minority-babies-are-the-majority-among-the-nations-infants-but-only-just.

Prepare for the possibility of reduced box office revenue. This may not happen. In some cases, the opposite could be true—a box office bonanza. But there are risks in choosing unknown artists—that is, artists not familiar to your theatre patrons. These are the risks you have to take, not once but multiple times, until your audiences no longer think of diversity as a concession and begin to accept it as the norm.

Cast a wider net. Diversity is not low-hanging fruit that you can pick and enjoy without much effort. You have to work at it. Sometimes you won't get enough actors of color to respond to your casting call. Maybe no plays by writers of color crossed your desk for consideration this season. Don't give up. Go out and get them. Call your colleagues and ask for referrals. Partner with community organizations to get the word out. Make noise and let the world know you want it.

LAST WORD

This guide is meant to stop theatres from paying lip service to diversity. Giving a playwright of color five workshops without ever producing the play may earn you the heterogeneity badge, but it falls way short of making your theatre an exemplar of diversity.

You have to try harder than that.

RALPH B. PEÑA

Ralph B. Peña is a founding member and the current producing artistic director of Ma-Yi Theatre Company, a leading professional Off-Broadway theatre based in New York City focused on developing and producing new works by Asian American playwrights. Recent directing credits include the world premieres of Lloyd Suh's The Chinese Lady, Hansol Jung's Among the Dead, and A. Rey Pamatmat's House Rules for Ma-Yi; a new translation of The Orphan of Zhao for Fordham Theatre; Nicolas Pichay's Macho Dancer: A Musical for the Virgin Labfest 11; Lloyd Suh's The Wong Kids in the Secret of the Space, Chupacabra, Go! (Off-Broadway Alliance Award), Joshua Conkel's Curmudgeons in Love (EST Marathon), and Mike Lew's microcrisis (Youngblood, Ma-Yi). Ralph is the recipient of an Obie Award for his work on The Romance of Magno Rubio and is a member of the Ensemble Studio Theatre and the Ma-Yi Writers Lab.

A COLLECTIVE CALL AGAINST CRITICAL BIAS

26 JUNE 2017
CRITICAL MASS

Much ado has been made of the fact that Paula Vogel and Lynn Nottage, two Pulitzer Prize–winning dramatists, finally cracked the glass ceiling this season. These theatre veterans made their long-awaited Broadway debuts, with *Indecent* and *Sweat*, which both garnered Tony Award nominations for Best Play. Surprisingly little attention was paid, however, to the announcement that these productions—the only new works by women on the Great White Way this year—would close early, in large part because they were doomed by the male critical establishment.

Both productions were slated for early termination on 25 June, but *Indecent* received a daring last-minute reprieve by producer Daryl Roth, who, inspired by an upsurge in ticket sales, will keep the show open through 6 August (for a total of just sixteen weeks). In the wake of their closing notices, Vogel and Nottage took to social media to confront the critics. Vogel fired the first shot on Twitter, singling out Ben Brantley and Jesse Green of the *New York Times* for helping usher women off stage while ensuring the longevity of straight white men, namely Lucas Hnath (*A Doll's House, Part 2*) and J. T. Rogers, whose *Oslo* won the Tony, along with almost every other prize this year.

Paula Vogel @VogelPaula · Jun 14
Brantley&Green 2-0. Nottage&Vogel 0-2. Lynn, they help close us down,&gifted str8 white guys run: ourplayswill last.B&G#footnotesinhistory.

   ◯ 28   ⟲ 197   ♡ 478   ✉

Nottage retweeted Vogel's post with the heading "The patriarchy flexing their muscles to prove their power" to underscore the profound gender disparity among the critical establishment, which is most noticeable among first-string critics at major outlets.

Lynn Nottage @Lynnbrooklyn · Jun 14
The patriarchy flexing their muscles to prove their power.

> **Paula Vogel** @VogelPaula
> Brantley&Green 2-0. Nottage&Vogel 0-2. Lynn, they help close us down,&gifted str8 white guys run: ourplayswill last.B&G#footnotesinhistory.
>
>   ◯ 2   ⟲ 50   ♡ 127   ✉

Subsequent tweets by Vogel make it clear that she welcomes criticism, and even appreciates "well written pans" of her work. What she objects to is a market manipulation that dismisses women and POC (people of color). The complaint is not personal. In other words, it is structural. Individual critics are "not the enemy," Vogel notes; there needs to be more dialogue: "We need a better way."

Paula Vogel @VogelPaula · Jun 15
Btw I like well written pans of my plays (John Simon!) NYT was not a pan. Is there a manipulation of marketplace that dismisses women&POC?

1   11   58

Paula Vogel @VogelPaula · Jun 15
I respect Ben Brantley. I served on a pulitzer jury w/him. He is not the enemy. hope to have more thoughtful dialogue. We need a better way.

4   16   139

A better way involves a consideration of resource allocation, or what Vogel calls "Basic math." Let's compare the annual budget of the Off-Broadway theatres where this season's Tony-nominated plays were developed. The Vineyard Theatre (*Indecent*) operates on a shoestring budget of a mere $3 million per year. Then, the Public Theater (*Sweat*) has more than ten times this amount ($40 million), though it funds many more projects on multiple stages, including the free Shakespeare in the Park program. Lincoln Center (*Oslo*) commands a staggering coffer of $70 million, catering to a much more affluent audience. *A Doll's House, Part 2*, bankrolled by producer Scott Rudin's seemingly bottomless war chest, went straight to Broadway. While bigger budgets often result in higher production values and star-studded casts, they don't guarantee better plays. We need a more expansive and informed notion of how critics come to decide what is "good," and a more honest conversation about why "good" is often associated with plays by and about white men.

AN OLD PROBLEM MADE URGENT

As female artists and academics, we know that the tension between minority playwrights and critics is not a new problem. It's a very old problem, one made newly urgent by biased reviews of productions by women and playmakers of color this season. We have dedicated our careers, in large part, to dismantling discriminatory structures and practices in theatre, and the criticism this year is so blatantly prejudicial that we felt compelled to collectively author an editorial that both documents the problem and puts it in a historical context.

Take, for example, a full-page feature on Vogel and Nottage in the *New York Times* titled, "Two Female Playwrights Arrive on Broadway. What Took So Long?"[1] The profile surveys a number of "theories about why their earlier plays never reached Broadway, from basic sexism to content, scale, or timing," yet ignores the single most obvious factor: the paper's own unbalanced evaluations of women's work.

Despite the shower of accolades for both *Sweat* and *Indecent*, reception by the *New York Times* and the East

---

1   Michael Paulson, "Two Female Playwrights Arrive on Broadway. What Took So Long?," *New York Times*, 22 March 2017, https://www.nytimes.com/2017/03/22/theater/lynn-nottage-paula-vogel-broadway.html.

Coast male critical establishment has been tepid at best. These plays, which tackle profound social, political, and ethical questions about racism and immigration, have been repeatedly and resoundingly lambasted for being too ambitious and too serious—accusations never leveled at work by men.

Brantley calls Nottage's play a "bracingly topical portrait" of a vibrant multiethnic, working-class community fractured by industrial layoffs, which he faults for being "an old fashioned... socially conscious" drama that is "too conscientiously assembled."[2] Jesse Green, tapped by the *Times* to replace Charles Isherwood (who raved about the Off-Broadway runs of *Sweat* and *Indecent*), begins his *Vulture* review with an apology. While *Sweat* "is a lot of great things," he decrees, "...[w]hat it isn't, I'm sorry to say, is a great play." His reason: Nottage does too much research, attenuating the story's "power in the very process of forcing the facts into drama." Green dubs *Sweat* "gripping but disappointing."[3]

He also damns with faint praise Vogel's *Indecent*, a metatheatrical exploration of Sholem Asch's scandalous 1906 Yiddish drama, *God of Vengeance*, which featured the first lesbian kiss on Broadway. Green calls Vogel's sweeping epic "the most ambitious" history play of the season, "and in all ways the least convincing." Once again, Green apologizes for his critique. "I say that with sorrow and surprise— and yet not too much surprise," he adds, noting that the

2   Ben Brantley, "Review: 'Sweat' Imagines the Local Bar as a Caldron," *New York Times*, 27 March 2017, https://www.nytimes.com/2017/03/26/theater/sweat-review-broadway.html.

3   Jesse Green, "Theater Review: Lynn Nottage's *Sweat* Tells But Doesn't Show," *Vulture*, 26 March 2017, https://www.vulture.com/2017/03/theater-lynn-nottages-sweat-tells-but-doesnt-show.html.

transition to Broadway simply amplified the faults he found with the Off-Broadway production.[4] The not-so-subtle subtext of Green's reviews: Keep it simple, ladies. Leave the big themes to the men.

FEMALE VOICES, RARE AND BELEAGUERED

Attempts to circumscribe women playwrights are not restricted to the *Times*. Edward Rothstein, writing for the *Wall Street Journal*, accuses Vogel of distorting "Asch, Yiddish theatre, and history," when in actuality he is the one who distorts all of those things in his review, which is astonishingly indifferent to the actual events on stage.[5] Rothstein writes as if Asch's *God of Vengeance* was not, in fact, a schematic melodrama, or that Yiddish theatre did not critique hypocritical piety, and that immigrants did not return from the United States to Europe, when history proves thousands upon thousands did so. Most of all, Rothstein objects to a playwright—a female playwright—using her imagination and dramatic skills to create a play based on the past, telling a compelling history that speaks to the present moment. With Linda Winer's resignation from *Newsday*, there are very few first-string female critics in the country. When a rare female critic's voice is heard, she is prone to be attacked more frequently than her male

4   Jesse Green, "Theater Review: A Holocaust Meta-History, in Paula Vogel's *Indecent*," *Vulture*, 18 April, 2017, https://www.vulture.com/2017/04/theater-a-holocaust-meta-history-in-paula-vogels-indecent.html.

5   Edward Rothstein, "'Indecent' Review: Based on a Not-So-True Story," *Wall Street Journal*, 19 April 2017, https://www.wsj.com/articles/indecent-review-based-on-a-not-so-true-story-1492635617.

peers. Jack Viertel, artistic director of New York City Center Encores!, issued a scathing rejoinder to Laura Collins-Hughes for raising questions about racial representation in the revival of *Big River* (the Tony Award–winning musical adaptation of Mark Twain's *The Adventures of Huck Finn*), in what was an essentially positive review. Viertel said nothing about Jesse Green's critique, which made a similar point as Collins-Hughes. We can hardly imagine a situation in which Viertel would publicly humiliate a male critic, but we can point to a number of situations in which women and people of color are accused of harboring "myopic notions about...the place of racial and gender diversity" in the arts.[6]

Notably, both productions of *Sweat* and *Indecent* are helmed by female directors. Kate Whoriskey made her Broadway debut in 2010 with *The Miracle Worker*. Rebecca Taichman, Vogel's co-creator, took home the Tony Award for *Indecent*. The fact that Taichman was so visibly shaken when the award was announced is no wonder. It was her first Broadway show, and she is only the seventh woman in the history of the award to take home the prize (fourteen women since 2000 have been nominated in the directing category, compared to sixty-two men). An even rarer breed of artists, female directors have not fared well with the critical establishment, especially this year. Consider Hilton Als' attack on Leigh Silverman's production of *Sweet Charity*.[7] Als is often the most open-minded and culturally astute of the gatekeepers, but he, too, has slapped female artists' hands for the sin, in his view, of trying to reach too

6   Robert Viagas, "NY Times Responds to Producer's Complaint About *Big River* Review," *Playbill*, 13 February 2017, https://www.playbill.com/article/ny-times-responds-to-producers-complaint-about-big-river-review.

7   Hilton Als, "A Strangely Muted 'Sweet Charity,'" *New Yorker*, 27 November 2016, https://www.newyorker.com/magazine/2016/12/05/a-strangely-muted-sweet-charity.

high. In his condemnation of Silverman, he writes that her "problem is that she's too serious about theatre" because "she wants her shows to count—to have a moral purpose." Like Brantley, Green, and Rothstein, he doesn't object to female artists' failure to live up to high ideals (fair game for a critic), but to their very ambition.

FITS AND STARTS TOWARD GENDER AND RACIAL EQUITY

Critical endorsements directly impact ticket sales and the length of a show's run, in addition to making or breaking a playwright's opportunity for future work. Women and people of color have about the same chance of seeing their plays produced today as they did before they had the right to vote. Racial and gender disparity is a chronic problem in the American theatre, from play selection and development to casting and production. Approximately 75 percent of the plays produced in this country have white male authors, and the numbers are even higher for Broadway, which is not everyone's aspiration but it is where the greatest critical attention is focused and where the prestige, power, and money reside.

According to "The Count," a detailed and ongoing study of not-for-profit regional theatres that asks "Who is Being Produced in America," female-authored productions hover at 22 percent, with women of color writing just over 3 percent of all staged plays.[8] The International Centre for Women Playwrights (ICWP)[9] reports that the global outlook is equally bleak: less than 25 percent of the plays produced across the world have female authors. The situation is so dire that the ICWP bestows a prize, the 50/50 Applause Award, for theatres that produce seasons in which half (or more) of the shows are written by women.

Progress toward gender and racial equity has not come in a steady arc, but rather in fits and starts. This year marked only the fourth time in history when two women were nominated for Tony Awards for Best Play (1956, 1960, 2002, and 2017). In fact, in the seven decades that this prize has been given, forty-six of those years have included only male dramatists. Nottage and Vogel are only the ninth and tenth women, since 2000, to be nominated for Best Play.

While there are a number of awards honoring female playmakers (e.g. the Susan Smith Blackburn Prize, the Jane Chambers Playwriting Award, the Wendy Wasserstein Prize, and the Lilly Awards), as well as ample archives of plays by women (including the Kilroys List), we cannot hope to achieve parity in the theatre without a greater variety of critical voices. The American Theatre Critics Association supports women critics nationally and oversees several awards including the Primus Prize focused exclusively on female playwrights. Organizations like the Drama Desk support women in its ranks and demonstrate parity in staffing their board, nominating, and other committees. Yet the desired outcome of supported female critical voices

8   Suzy Evans, "The Gender Parity Count Ticks Up—Slightly," *American Theatre*, 20 July 2015, https://www.americantheatre.org/2015/07/20/the-gender-parity-count-ticks-up-slightly.
9   "The International Centre for Women Playwrights – Home," International Centre for Women Playwrights, accessed 7 February 2022, https://womenplaywrights.org.

in print and online outlets is as much aspiration as reality. In the ever-shrinking world of arts journalism, we call on news outlets to hire critics who reflect the diversity of the world in which we live.

CRITICAL MASS

Critical Mass, a group of artists, academics, and theatre advocates, came together in the summer of 2017 to collectively author this essay and raise awareness about Paula Vogel's Indecent and Lynn Nottage's Sweat on Broadway amid a conversation about critical bias toward women playwrights and playwrights of color. This essay was co-authored and co-signed by Gwendolyn Alker, Robin Bernstein, Meghan Brodie, Jocelyn L. Buckner, Charlotte M. Canning, Soyica Colbert, Jessica Del Vecchio, Jill Dolan, Miriam Felton-Dansky, Lisa A. Freeman, Donatella Galella, Holly Hughes, Susan Jonas, Joan Lipkin, Lisa Merrill, Jennifer-Scott Mobley, Priscilla Page, Jennifer Parker-Starbuck, Maya Roth, Martha Wade Steketee, Willa Taylor, Lisa B. Thompson, Sara Warner, and Stacy Wolf.

TEENAGE GIRLS ON STAGE: YOUNG WOMEN WHO DO THINGS

13 OCTOBER 2017
HELEN SCHULTZ

Oh to experience the world of a teenage girl in ninety minutes (disclosure: I wish my teenage years had only lasted ninety minutes). When I sat in the Duke on 42nd in New York City, next to the green, green Astroturf and girls in shorts dribbling soccer balls, I found myself back at sixteen—no more acne or braces, but with a distinct sense of longing for a time that felt both limitless and impossibly constricting.

Sarah DeLappe's *The Wolves* has—naturally—excited audiences from Vassar to Playwrights Realm to, now, Lincoln Center. And it deserves it: *The Wolves* is a beautiful, funny, weird, lovely play and I cried when I first read it, I cried when I saw it Off-Broadway, and I'll cry when I see it at Lincoln Center.

But something else about *The Wolves* struck me as I first read it: it was about girls. Girls! Ever since I'd cracked open a teenage monologue book when I was auditioning for the school play, I've found it impossible to find plays about girls. Sure, you have your myriad *Little Women* adaptations and I guess *Annie* is a tween, but where are the plays about teenage girls?

So I took to Facebook. I posed the question to my friends, asking them to shout out as many plays about teenage girls by women as they could think of. *The Wolves* was joined by *Dry Land*, last season's favorite about two friends on a swim team, featuring a medically induced abortion.

But otherwise? A lot of head-scratching. (Granted, these are produced plays I'm counting. Unproduced plays—and unrepresented plays—took up a wide swath of the list at the end of this essay.)

My Kilroys List Jr. was very short—just thirty-one plays total. And, rest assured, I surround myself with people who enjoy sitting at home with plays as a way of life. If anyone could compile this list, it was the 1,069 dramaturgy nerds I call my Facebook friends.

Now, as an agent and dramaturg, I see this question as a matter of great importance to our theatrical ecosystem. If we take our New Play Map (thanks, HowlRound!), how much of it will contain plays by women about young women? The Lilly Awards' the Count tells us that 22 percent of the plays on stage would be written by women.[1] And the Kilroys would tell you that, despite a huge amount of female writers graduating from prestigious grad schools and snagging agents, they still can release an extensive list of unproduced plays.[2] And, in looking at catalogues for this season on Off-Broadway *and* on Broadway, I could only scrounge up two (brilliant, thrilling) plays by women about young women: *The African Mean Girls Play* by Jocelyn Bioh and… *The Wolves*. (Honorable mention to Michael Crowley's *The Rape of the Sabine Women, by Grace B. Matthias*, which is, perhaps, one of the most sympathetic portrayals of a young woman by a man that I've ever read.)

What gives? According to the Broadway League's 2015 study, over 1.45 million teenagers saw a Broadway show in the 2014–15 season, and 67 percent of theatregoers were female. (Their average age? Forty-four, just old enough to be raising a teen.)[3] That's not counting Off-Broadway, LORT theatres, college conservatories, high schools, your friend's backyard, community theatre…. If my memory serves me and my intern applications keep coming up overwhelmingly female, I would argue that teenage girls are some of the most ardent theatregoers around. So why don't we have more stories about them? And why, oh why, are more theatres not choosing to put teenage women at the center of their stories following the success of *The Wolves*?

1   "The Count 1.0.," Lillys, accessed 4 February 2022, https://the-lillys.org/the-count-1.
2   "The List 2017: The Top 9%," Kilroys, 12 May 2017, https://thekilroys.org/list-2017.
3   "Research Reports," Broadway League, accessed 24 January 2022, https://www.broadwayleague.com/research/research-reports.

It's not that teenage girls haven't been on stage, per se. After all, many male coming-of-age stories feature a young woman prominently (think Kenneth Lonergan's *This Is Our Youth* or Anna Jordan's *Yen*), as do Shakespearean classics like *Romeo and Juliet* and *Hamlet*. But rarely do we see women at the center of their own stories rather than as objects of desire—or victims of violence (one could write a whole series on bodily harm done to young girls on stage and our culture's fascination with sexual violence).

But to focus on the inner lives of teenage girls—to portray them as subject rather than object—is something that seems to have evaded us. While the Judy Blumes of the novelistic world were born, something stayed dormant in the theatre community. "Agency is something I want to see more of in plays about women," Playwrights Horizons literary manager Sarah Lunnie told me over drinks as we pondered my list. I wanted it too: women who do things, not have things done to them. Did this seem too much to ask?

Maybe it's the idea that only certain people can inhabit the world of drama. After all, before Willy Loman, we weren't much interested in the everyman—let alone the everywoman. Theatre has often been reserved for the rich and proud and high in stature: if the 2016 election shows us anything, it's that these seats aren't open to even the most privileged of women. Indeed, when looking at the plays that *do* pass the teenage-girls test, it's worth noting that most take place in the suburban, primary white, and decidedly upper-middle-class sphere. Is this surprising considering the high price tag of most MFA programs and the demographic makeup of most audiences? Well, no. But it is worth saying that male characters have their Sam Hunters and David Lindsay-Abaires, writers who focus on lower-income male characters. Female teens seem to have... no one. Aside from Kirsten Greenidge's *Milk Like Sugar*, the majority of the list I compiled portrayed women in positions of relative financial security. And, as in the rest of stories represented on stage, the list was overwhelmingly white—*Milk Like Sugar*, *BFE* by Julia Cho, and *Our Lady of Kibeho* by Katori Hall were the only plays by women of color. None of the plays on the list were written by trans women.

To be a teenage girl is to be blisteringly vulnerable—to talk about periods, first kisses, crushes, sexual awakenings, fantasies, dying your hair in the sink, going shopping at Forever 21, crashing your mom's car. Teenage girls are difficult and intense and awkward and unapologetically female. And perhaps, I wonder, that's why we won't put these stories onstage. After all, male theatre critics are slow to take to plays that play girlish. "I didn't care for the show the first time I saw it. Female empowerment is fine for daytime television, but it's flesh-crawling in a musical," wrote Michael Riedel of teen-centric *The Color Purple*'s revival in 2015.[4]

And the darkest thought remains: there's much cause to think that our society may just have a seething hatred of teenage girls—point-blank. There are the capital "M" Misogynistic things: the Steubenville rape case; cuts in funding for the Teen Pregnancy Prevention Program, which works with organizations across the United States to implement evidence-based, proven programming; the erasure of Title IX protections by the Trump administration; a lack of sex education with a focus on issues of consent and

---

4   Michael Riedel, "Jennifer Hudson to Make Long-Awaited Broadway Debut in 'Color Purple,'" *NY Post*, 9 January 2015, https://nypost.com/2015/01/09/jennifer-hudson-to-make-long-awaited-broadway-debut-in-color-purple.

female pleasure. There are the slyer, more creakingly sexist things: internalized misogyny; the way we dismiss young women's emotions as irrational or dishonest or dangerous; how we tell girls to hide their tampons in their bags, their opinions in their throats, and their anger in their stomachs.

But, in my more optimistic moments, I think we do not have these plays because we are only just beginning. I think the most optimistic way to look is forward—and I think we must do so to create change. We will know trans girls and undocumented girls and girls who are not skinny and girls who are not "nice" and girls who like girls and girls who don't particularly like anyone and girls who are unlikable and gross and mean and horrible.

On good days, I am excited for this future season of bustling teenage brilliance to come. On bad days, I wonder if we are too late for someone—if we've left too many young girls out in the cold and exiled them out of the theatre. I don't want to think of that scenario, but think about it we must if we're going to take full responsibility for our power as gatekeepers.

For me, perhaps the most exciting part of The Wolves was when the lights came up on a jumble of female bodies—different shapes, queer bodies, Brown bodies, athletic bodies, bodies that looked like my friends' bodies, and bodies that looked like my body. It was exhilarating to see myself at sixteen on stage. I hope to have this experience again soon—one I wish I had known when I was a teenage girl.

LIST*

1. *The Wolves* by Sarah DeLappe

2. *Milk Like Sugar* by Kirsten Greenidge

3. *Dry Land* by Ruby Rae Spiegel

4. *I'll Never Love Again* by Clare Barron

5. *Chimichangas and Zoloft* by Fernanda Coppel

6. *Our Lady of Kibeho* by Katori Hall

7. *How to Make Friends and Then Kill Them* by Halley Feiffer

8. *All the Roads Home* by Jen Silverman

9. *Dance Nation* by Clare Barron

10. *BFE* by Julia Cho

11. *tender of you too* by Anya Richkind

12. *The Children's Hour* by Lillian Hellman

13. *Horse Girls* by Jenny Rachel Weiner

14. *Little One* by Hannah Moscovitch

15. *Scratch* by Charlotte Corbeil-Coleman

16. *I Am For You* by Mieko Ouchi

17. *Scorch* by Stacey Gregg

18. *Joan* by Lucy Skilbeck

19. *SHE* by Renée Darline Roden

*Note: This is a crowdsourced list and certainly not comprehensive.

HELEN SCHULTZ

Helen Schultz (she/her) is a creative producer, currently producing programming and public art for Times Square Arts, the largest public arts organization in the United States. Her criticism has appeared on broadway.com, TheaterMania, *and* Stage & Candor. *Helen is a proud former member of the HowlRound staff, having served as the staff assistant in 2015 and 2016. Helen lives in New York City and received her BA from Emerson College.*

ON "MINORITY" ARTIST DEVELOPMENT PROGRAMS

04 DECEMBER 2017

ASIF MAJID

I've recently come through a number of "minority" artist development programs at a variety of major (read: primarily white and able-bodied) theatre venues and cultural institutions, and have found them to be consistently wanting in a few ways. As a theatremaker and performer engaged in transnational "minority" theatre work in both the United States and the United Kingdom, it's frustrating to see well-intentioned programs that can serve to helpfully challenge white supremacy fail on basic programmatic aspects.

I find it hard to believe that such failures would be accepted as adequate were these programs not alternately blessed and cursed with being exclusively for minorities, people of color, or other disenfranchised groups.

What is needed is an institutional reassessment of why such cultural organizations engage in such work in the first place. Is it as a diversity box-checking exercise? Are they trying to change audience demographics? Are they fattening their bottom line, ever aware of the increasing cuts in arts funding on both sides of the Atlantic? Or are these types of programs reflective of a true activist commitment to unlearn and dismantle structural inequalities? Unfortunately for that last one, exceptions like actor, playwright, and director Kwame Kwei-Armah prove to me that these institutions aren't in the business of loosening their stranglehold on resources, preferring instead short-term "development" projects that result in minorities fighting with one another for leftover table scraps.

So, I've put together a few pointers that may be useful for staff at such institutions when they are tasked with executing a "minority" artist development program, one that may or may not be conceived or designed by those who implement it. Specifically, I'm speaking to middle management: to those who are simultaneously facing pressure from supervisors in offices upstairs to implement a "minority" development program and from "minority" artists on the ground who are frustrated at the program's failures. (There is, of course, a broader discussion to be had about whether or not these programs ought to be conceived as they are from the top down and how that creates the space between a rock and a hard place that middle management inhabits. I recognize the importance of that topic, but it is beyond the scope of what I'm covering here.) Suffice it to say, for the moment, that such initiatives are sometimes as unwanted by the so-called "community" that they target as they are by those who are responsible for implementing them. When that's the case, here are some tips on how to make the best of a bad situation.

I. AVOID LUMPING.

A recent program for ethnic "minority" and disabled artists offered a standard bursary to attend programming at a major arts festival so participants like me could learn about taking work there in the future. The program connected me and my colleagues to festival programmers and artists who had presented work at the aforementioned festival in the past. Yet the program seemed blissfully unaware that additional financial and logistical needs might be relevant for colleagues of mine who had disabilities, until those colleagues advocated for themselves. This was based on a serious flaw in logic: that ethnic "minority" and disabled artists can be lumped together and treated in an undifferentiated way, as if the needs of ethnic "minority" artists and disabled artists are one and the same. To engage with difference is to both recognize that it exists and accommodate it on its own terms, rather than on the terms of the majority.

2. RECOGNIZE INTERSECTIONALITY.

Just because a program identifies a particular identity marker that it seeks to target or focus on doesn't mean that the person who applies for and participates in said program is a monolithic robot. Rather, it is important to recognize that the needs and objectives that participants have for participating in such programs may differ widely from other program participants, even if they share some surface-level characteristic that the program has ascribed to them. A prime example of this came when an opportunity recently arose for me to apply for one of multiple part-time civic engagement positions that was oriented towards members of "minority" groups. I turned it down for a host of reasons, not least of which is that the creation of only a few slots for "minority" individuals continues institutional strangleholds on resources at the same time as it allows institutions to be perceived as improving opportunities for minorities despite increasing competition among them. Intersectionality is useful here because it showcases the ways in which multiple aspects of identity must be catered to. For those unfamiliar with the term, it is worth investigating further, as it is part and parcel of the discourse used by "minority" artists on both sides of the Atlantic.

3. INDIVIDUALIZE SUPPORT.

This builds on the two points above. It's no use offering a group of ("minority" or majority) artists a series of workshops as a form of compensation for not paying them enough, and then being astonished when attendance dwindles over time. What is needed for true artist development is the personalization of attention and resources, meeting artists where they are rather than where a program believes them to be. If an institution's approach is to commission a piece in an effort to work with artists who haven't engaged with that institution before, it is essential to invest in what that artist wants out of the relationship so that they feel part of a collaborative process and willing to engage with that institution in the future. Where too many institutions fail in their development programming that is oriented towards "minorities" is in their preference for product over process, rather than the other way around (the renowned and respected Sundance Theatre Lab is a notable and positive exception). It's only through good processes that we end up with good artistic products.

4. SILENCE INSTITUTIONAL ASSUMPTIONS AND RESPECT WORK THAT IS PRODUCED.

Often in the rush to create showable content like a script, sharing, or something of the sort, crucial decisions are taken out of the artist's hands. As part of a recent monologue-writing project, the results of which were to be showcased in nearby community venues, I developed a piece that included foul language. The institution that ran the project never asked me to remove the cursing, despite asking for other useful edits to the script that made it a better piece. Yet later they claimed that it was because of the foul language that they chose to not take the piece to some community venues where young people would be present, a decision I wasn't consulted on or made aware of until shortly before performances were to take place. (To be clear, my objection is not to their choice, but rather to how it was made.) If an artist is participating in a "development" program, how does it strengthen their craft to leave them out of dialogue on important decisions about their own work? I have no issue when an institution objects to content and form in an effort to improve a work's quality. But it should always do so in a manner that treats both the artist and the work with respect.

5. UNDERSTAND WHY THIS PROJECT IS BEING UNDERTAKEN, ON BOTH A PERSONAL AND A PROFESSIONAL LEVEL.

Theatre director Anne Bogart, in *And Then, You Act*, talks about the importance of "stay[ing] close to the why" when making theatre,[1] but it's management consultant Simon Sinek who makes the relationship between why, how, and what a bit more explicit.[2] Starting with *why* we are engaging in a project allows us to ensure that *how* we do *what* we're doing connects to our initial purpose. Too often, the ends are seen to justify the means: that if a program checks a bunch of diversity boxes and brings audiences into the theatre who

1   Anne Bogart, *And Then, You Act: Making Art in an Unpredictable World* (New York: Routledge, 2007).
2   Simon Sinek, "How Great Leaders Inspire Action," TEDxPuget Sound, September 2009, video, 17:48, https://www.ted.com/talks/simon_sinek_how_great_leaders_inspire_action.

might not otherwise attend, then all will be forgiven. Actually, it won't. Word will spread among "minority" artists about the failure of such programming. This can often result in such artists choosing not to work with these institutions, despite their heavyweight status. To be sure, it is primarily white and able-bodied institutions that need "minority" artists, rather than the other way around.

6. ADMIT MISTAKES AND LEARN FROM THEM.

After I (and other artists) completed the aforementioned monologue-writing project, the institution sponsoring it asked for quotes and sound bites about the effectiveness of the project. In this way, they assumed that the project had been a resounding success and sought to use project participants (myself among them) as a way to check off boxes about diversity and show that they were engaged in complex, innovative, and brave programming. An alternative, and better, approach would have been to conduct a thorough and in-depth evaluation of the program that was honest and rigorous in admitting its mistakes. Instead, I felt used by the institution, as it sought to further its own funding and public-relations objectives. The institution's lack of commitment to its own growth came across as a failure to care for the artists it sought to "develop," adding a troubling layer to an already problematic project.

These pointers can allow primarily white and able-bodied theatre institutions to put "minority" artists and their development at the heart of what they do, rather than on its fringes. It's good that such organizations are interested in diversifying their artistic input and output, and it's important that this work continues even if institutions don't understand white supremacy or intersectionality or think that these concepts matter. But for the sake of both the project and the headache that the institution and the artists in question go through when serious miscalculations occur, it is imperative that process is privileged over product. At every moment when the end results seem to be taking primacy, I would encourage arts administrators who work at the middle-management level to return to the why of the project, and to remember that the artists they are working with are talented individuals in their own right, worthy of far more respect than they are often afforded.

ASIF MAJID

Asif Majid (he/him) is a scholar-artist-educator working at the intersection of racialized sociopolitical identities, multimedia, marginality, and new performance, particularly through devising community-based participatory theatre. Currently, he is assistant professor of theatre and human rights at the University of Connecticut. He completed his PhD (anthropology, media, and performance) at the University of Manchester and has been a Mellon/ACLS Public Fellow with the San Francisco Arts Commission. Asif has published in multiple books, peer-reviewed academic journals, and popular media. His performance credits include work with the Kennedy Center and Royal Exchange Theatre, among others. asifmajid.com.

CONSCIOUS CASTING AND LETTING PLAYWRIGHTS LEAD

14 FEBRUARY 2018
DAVID VALDES

Can a Japanese family be Mexican? That question was at the heart of an email exchange with a theatre doing one of my plays. It wasn't really a debate; the roles had already been cast. But the director wasn't trying to pull a fast one—in writing my play's character notes, I had sent mixed messages about what I valued and expected. And I know I'm not alone in still learning how to navigate this terrain.

The debates over so-called "color-blind" and "color-conscious" casting have been heated in recent years, especially when a theatre's decisions do not align with a playwright's wishes. Sometimes, a theatre contravenes the express indications of the author without permission (as happened to Lloyd Suh's *Jesus in India*); sometimes (as in the infamous 2017 *Who's Afraid of Virginia Woolf*), a theatre makes a choice without permission because it feels that ethnicity is not specified, only to discover otherwise mid-stream.

More often, however, the shoe is on the author's foot, so to speak. What should you, as a playwright, do when a theatre *does* ask if they can depart from your character descriptions, leaving you to determine how color- and gender-conscious the play must be? If you're a playwright whose writing is intentionally diverse, how do you decide when to draw firm lines in the sand and when to be open to interpretation?

A few years ago, I stopped writing race-neutral plays. Instead of waiting to see more diverse faces onstage, I wanted to help bring them into the spotlight. But this applied to more than race. As a mixed-ethnicity Cuban American gay man, I was hungry for characters whose lives, like mine, were intersectional. Every play since has featured what I refer to as non-majority characters, often with specific ethnicities, races, orientations, and gender identities noted. (In some scripts, I have stipulated that the play may not be staged by an all-white cast without express permission.) I advocate for holistically conscious casting, not just of race and ethnicity, but of gender identity and expression.

The Japanese family I mentioned above shares a play with characters who are Latinx, mixed ethnicity, straight, gay, trans, and non-binary. Every theatre that has worked on the play has found its creative team wrestling with casting questions. Does trans mean trans only, or non-binary or genderqueer as well? What equals authenticity for the Cuban American characters: being of Cuban descent specifically, or of any Latinx heritage, or (as Latinx people are racially diverse) simply being plausible? And when a character's intersectionality involves both race and gender identity, does it do harm to honor one more than the other?

Questions like those can make a director's head spin. Too many playwrights have encountered people in casting who simply decide not to do the hard work of examining their choices in situations like these. The oldest dodge is to spout some variant of the argument that we don't require authenticity of experience for actors playing other parts, the default example being murderers. That claim is true, but only to the extent that all theatre is a form of illusion: we go to a play knowing it is fictive. But that's too easy by half. Character *functions* do not come attended by the same weight of history represented by character *identities*. When a murderer is played by a (presumably) non-homicidal actor, that portrayal does not inherently come bundled with a society-deep backstory of stereotype, exclusion, legal injustice, and erasure. To acknowledge that theatre trades in pretense does not let us off the hook in confronting what our choices mean and how they further or limit our shared conversation. If a theatre has a request to make around the identities of your characters, you deserve a more active intellectual exercise than a claim of "it's all pretend."

Perhaps the second most common defense of casting adjustments has to do with a theatre's audition pool. Many an inclusive playwright has heard this line: "We want to do your show, but we do not have the population for it." Some artists argue that the question answers itself. Michelle Tyrene Johnson asks, "If a theatre can't cast my play adequately, why are they doing it?" She adds, "I think that as a playwright of color, it's critical I stand firm on my casting."

For some pieces, it may well be that any debate around casting truly ended the moment the play was written. Playwright Zahra A. Belyea explains, "I guess what I feel is that once the playwright gets the text to a point where it is able to be produced, the heavy lifting of character choice has been made." This is especially true when non-majority life experience is at the heart of the play.

A writer can't always predict what might challenge this choice. Patrick Gabridge found himself in a unique situation when a South Korean theatre proposed doing his play *Distant Neighbors*, which included a Black character. "There's just no way that they're going to be able to find a Black actor—they're all going to be Koreans." This led him to consider adapting the text, but not simply for ease; he looked at how to "maintain the integrity of the script and the themes," which include trust and mistrust between neighbors, and the potency of human connection. Staging an American play on this topic in Korea at this moment is itself a powerful act, so the change merited consideration.

There are times when such latitude in casting is more organic. In an interview for the *Root,* Katori Hall noted that a production of her play *Children of Killers* featured ethnically and racially diverse actors playing Rwandans to "drive home the major theme: that lines of identity were arbitrarily drawn by colonial powers, rendering signifiers of 'racial' identity unreliable."[1] In her case, that was less a departure than a game plan. In seemingly dissimilar fashion, Johnson, Belyea, Gabridge, and Hall are all making the case that, from page to stage, it should be the playwrights who get to choose what casting means.

To make conscious choices sometimes involves confronting opposing values—and perhaps determining just what the high value is. Melinda Lopez, whose work often features Cuban Americans and Cubans, notes that, "When you write a specific culture rather than 'Latinx generic,' people always freak out—and I get it, there just aren't a lot of Cuban American actors in Wyoming, for example. Even though *I* know the difference between a Puerto Rican actor and an actor of Mexican heritage—or an actor who has Argentinian heritage—I don't know that it's going to make or break my play." As she points out, "I would rather have the play being done" in a community rarely or never exposed to the viewpoints of artists and characters of color. In this case, inclusion of Latinx life becomes the high value over fidelity to a specific culture.

That distinction comes up a lot for plays with people of color. My Japanese family has now been played by Japanese, Chinese, and Vietnamese actors. If the play was being performed in Tokyo, this might seem more glaring, but for majority-American audiences, the top note that registers is the presence of an Asian family at all. This in turn raises

---

1   Katori Hall, "Playwright Reacts to the White Casting of MLK in The Mountaintop," *Root*, 9 November 2015, https://www.theroot.com/playwright-reacts-to-the-white-casting-of-mlk-in-the-mo-1790861704.

competing issues: Is it differently racist to cast non-Japanese Asian actors in the roles? Will not staging the play because Japanese actors could not be found add to Asian erasure? Every possible answer starts a new conversation.

Conscious casting is simply not a one-size-fits-all proposition. Eleanor Burgess says of her process:

> I think the right approach varies enormously from script to script. I have written plays where a character's heritage is central to the conversations they have and the actions they take—for those plays, alternative casting would make a mishmash of the dialogue and put an undue burden on actors to represent points of view that no longer make sense. For other plays, I've specified heritage partly to nudge/force theatres to cast in a way that reflects the modern world, but the character's background isn't a plot point. It often represents something a little more abstract—a recent history of immigration, a position of relative comfort or discomfort, a unique source of insight or expectations.

A theatre may not be able to discern what a playwright deems absolutely core to the character as distinct from that which can be handled otherwise and still be thematically true. This means that playwright ownership of character descriptions is a powerful thing. When I define character identities more clearly in my cast lists, my goal is to yield more specific (and in turn more truthful) characters, while steering theatres away from the tendency to default to white, cisgender, and ability-typical actors for almost every role.

But I'm still learning how to communicate these values. In the same script, while I was explicit about who could be cast in trans and non-binary roles, I was less concrete otherwise, simply noting that the stated character races and ethnicities were what I envisioned but were not firmly proscribed. The message I *intended* to send was, "Let's talk about diverse choices for these roles." But the message I *actually* sent was, "Make diverse choices as you see fit." When I expressed surprise about casting choices to one director, he rightly suggested that I needed to reframe my instructions to say what I really (and fully) meant: "Ask first; cast later."

So how did my Japanese family become Mexican? Beyond showing the diversity of America, the primary role of ethnicity for the family was in their struggle with the conservative opinions of elders back in the parent's country of origin when it came to the gayness of an American-born grandchild. This is a scenario that would resonate with many first- and second-generation immigrant families, including the Mexicans, who comprise a large part of that theatre's local population. As the director explained, the traditional bias against homosexuality remains common among older generations of Mexicans, influenced as they were by the Catholic tradition. This casting wasn't a meaningless choice but a decision that still reflected the diversity of the world, while drawing a specific audience into the ideas of the play.

Learning as I go, and benefiting from the wisdom of my fellow scribes, I've landed on a quartet of useful mantras for playwrights as they champion diversity in their work:

- *Conscious casting starts with conscious writing.* I can't expect a theatre to commit to diversity if I don't, and my choices on the page must show both intent and an awareness of meaning.

- *Commit to choices, not reactions.* Should a theatre ask for casting adjustments, my answer should never be a mere reaction to the request, but a real choice about what the new representation says and does, and whether the play's integrity is preserved in the choosing.

- *Consider the high value.* In the end, it's up to me to determine what is the high value and what is non-negotiable. Does a particular play hang on authenticity of identity, faithfulness to theme, audience exposure to new ideas or new worlds, or something else?

- *Set the terms of the debate.* If I really want theatres to cast consciously and make meaningful choices that reflect the high value of each play, I can and should be blunt about what I do or don't expect. It shows respect for my own work and gives them the right tools for doing their best.

Truly conscious casting requires that theatres and playwrights make the effort to be on the same page. As Burgess puts it, "The point is always to be thoughtful. Thoughtful about how to offer great roles to underrepresented actors, thoughtful about offering the audience a powerful experience, and thoughtful about casting actors in roles where they can *enliven*, rather than *fight*, the text."

DAVID VALDES

David Valdes (he/him) is the author of more than two dozen plays that have been staged across the United States and abroad, most notably Mermaid Hour *and* Brave Navigator. *His essays have been published in the* New York Times, Boston Globe, American Theatre, HowlRound, *and elsewhere. He is the author of nonfiction books, including* Homo Domesticus: Notes from a Same-Sex Marriage, *and several novels, including* Spin Me Right Round.

THE UGLY TRUTH ABOUT ARTS INSTITUTIONS LED BY WOMEN OF COLOR

09 MAY 2018

TERESA COLEMAN WASH

As the founder and executive artistic director for the Bishop Arts Theatre Center (BATC) in Dallas, Texas, I experience racism, sexism, and classism almost daily. It's no secret that racial and gender disparity is a chronic problem for women in leadership at arts institutions in the United States, but for women of color there is a severe, unconscious level of prejudice.

I'm so grateful for the 2016 study on women artistic and managing directors in the League of Resident Theatres (LORT), commissioned by American Conservatory Theater.[1] It not only gave me the lexicon to talk intelligently about the issues I was experiencing, but, more importantly, it made me feel less like a martyr.

The study found zero women of color as executive directors in LORT, the largest professional theatre association in the United States, and only one woman of color as an artistic director. This is a dismal reality for women like me who are founders of their own theatre company, hoping to transition to jobs at LORT theatres in the future. The ugly truth, which was revealed in the study, is that, "hidden behind a gender- and race-neutral job description, is an expectation grounded in a stereotype" of what a theatre leader needs to look like: white and male.

White men are the long-standing majority of those in top positions, which translates to who funders trust to provide financial resources, who the media decides to give a platform to, and who board members select to lead their organizations. Many female leaders experience deeply entrenched inequalities and are pushed away from economically viable opportunities; by and large, women of color are not looked upon as masterminds or artistic leaders in the field.

Last year I attended Theatre Communications Group's (TCG) Fall Forum on Governance in New York City. While I knew white men were the dominant culture for artistic directors

1   Sumru Erkut and Ineke Ceder, "Women's Leadership in Resident Theaters," Wellesley Centers for Women, Wellesley College, December 2016, https://www.wcwonline.org/pdf/proj/theater/womens_leadership_theaters_FinalReport.pdf.

in the industry, the affinity group breakout sessions made it crystal clear—in the one made up of tenured founding artistic directors of twenty-plus years, I was the only woman of color. Throughout the forum, it was refreshing to learn that TCG was creating much-needed dialogue about issues never discussed before and asking bold questions about what leadership should look like in our field. But it was discouraging to hear many attendees lament that the same conversation has been happening for years. It's apparent very little progress has been made.

In November 2016, just days after Donald Trump was elected, I attended the Facing Race conference in Atlanta. We had all arrived depleted, in a state of disbelief. Roxane Gay, best-selling author and recent Guggenheim Fellowship award recipient, outed white women who had voted for Trump. It was there many of us learned that, despite Trump having been caught on tape boasting about sexual assault, more than 53 percent of white women voted for him.[2] Most attendees wondered how a sexual predator could have been elected as our commander-in-chief. It was an honest question that we all wanted answered.

At the end of the conference, we collectively agreed to forge ahead and tackle whatever problems would inevitably arise in the months to come. Our marching orders were to get comfortable having uncomfortable conversations—whether political, professional, or personal. For me, it meant to show up more authentically in my relationships and call out discrimination in any form, whether it's a staff member who is not accustomed to being led by a woman of color or a colleague who throws rocks and hides their hands.

2   Katie Rogers, "White Women Helped Elect Donald Trump," *New York Times*, 9 November 2016, https://www.nytimes.com/2016/12/01/us/politics/white-women-helped-elect-donald-trump.html.

The BATC has grown from a small community theatre to a multicultural, multidisciplinary resource center for the neighborhood. We offer a full season of theatre performances, jazz concerts, speaker series events, and year-round arts education programs. Property ownership has afforded us the autonomy to diversify our income and sustain our organization independent of government grants, but I was taken aback when a national funder declined a grant application citing disapproval of our multidisciplinary programming. Places like the Public Theater and the Denver Center for the Performing Arts are lauded for the innovative use of their spaces. How is the BATC different? I couldn't help but recall Janelle Monáe's line in the movie *Hidden Figures*: "Every time we have a chance to get ahead, they move the finish line."

Nonprofits led by women of color are judged by unrealistic standards set by funders who fashion themselves as allies. On occasions, I've had the good fortune of recruiting and securing former trustees from regional theatres to join our board. Their expectation is always to raise the same level of funding as they had in other positions, but the reality is that small to midsize theatre companies, like mine, and particularly theatres led by women of color, have very few million-dollar donors in their Rolodex compared to regional theatres. In addition, the allocation of funds from corporate and wealthy private-sector donors is hugely skewed. I have found that while a funder might grant the BATC a $5,000 gift, he will fund a larger institution at a disproportionately higher level. It is a deeply entrenched racial and (in my case) gender imbalance strategically designed to keep women of color away from economically viable resources and under the radar.

In 2015, our theatre was invited along with five other organizations by the Embrey Family Foundation (EFF) to participate in an RSF Social Finance Shared Gifting Circle. EFF is a small family foundation in Dallas that supports groundbreaking socially conscious projects centered around racial and gender inequalities. The gifting circle was a revolutionary grant-making process where six selected nonprofits distributed $60,000 in funds among each other. Each organization was guaranteed a minimum of $2,000.

Although this was a new approach to grant making for our organization, I learned the concept has been around for over a decade. RSF's model of shared gifting gives full decision-making authority to a group of grantees who evaluate each other's proposals and make funding decisions together with transparency. Here's how it works: The funder decides how much the participating organizations will share and distribute. A meeting date is established and each group is asked to submit a proposal for operating support or an upcoming project, which is reviewed by the participants prior to the meeting. On the meeting date, participants share personal stories and organizational biographies. There is an open discussion about each proposal and each representative determines how much to grant the other nonprofits. The process is designed to be simple and logical from an economic perspective and socially constructive from a community-building perspective. In an innovative and unusual twist on traditional grant making, participants are both grant recipients and grantors to each other.

Our organization walked away with a $10,000 grant that year—not a bad day's work, right? But what was even more empowering was that I was able to gift thousands of dollars to a different arts group led by another woman of color—and she did the same for my organization in return. We had been in the trenches together, doing great work under the radar for a long time, and it gave us both a personal sense of satisfaction to reward the other's organization. In 2016, I had the pleasure of co-facilitating a shared gifting circle for EFF that was made up of all women. And this month, I'm the lead facilitator for the 2018 cohort, which will mostly include women of color artistic leaders.

The shared gifting circles are cathartic in many ways for minority female artistic leaders. We learn that until we talk to each other and affirm that our experiences are the same, we can't fully support each other. Oftentimes we are pitted against each other, but with shared gifting, competition becomes collaboration.

Hillary Clinton's book *What Happened* should be required reading for any young woman interested in a leadership position in any field. The chapter on sisterhood had me bearing witness, out loud, like a congregant at a tent revival down a country road in rural Georgia. In it, Clinton recounts a conversation with Sheryl Sandberg, the chief operating officer of Facebook: "The more successful a man is, the more people like him. With women, it's the exact opposite. The more professionally successful we are, the less people like us." Women leaders, particularly women of color, suffer implacable hostility.

I am a member of a professional women's group in Dallas called It's Lonely at the Top, which is made up of executive directors in the Dallas/Ft. Worth area. I'm the only woman in theatre and only one of two women of color in the group, and I've found that while I share many similar concerns as the other women, my experiences as a leader are unique. Women of color struggle with disparities in funding, media attention, and recognition compared to our white male and female counterparts. Implicit bias is layered and complex, and, while it might be subtle to others, women of color know when we are being discriminated against. I've experienced firsthand being pushed to the margins in ways that should have been crippling.

There is a cadre of impressive young theatre practitioners, many of whom are women of color, being trained to be leaders in the field. At TCG's Fall Forum last year, I was impressed with panelist members from artEquity, a dynamic organization that seeks to build practical and analytical skills necessary to address diversity and inclusion issues at an interpersonal, group, and organizational level. One of the most salient points made was that there must be a major paradigm shift in the industry if these young innovators would even consider leading arts institutions—currently, they are reticent because they feel there is not enough meaningful effort being made to dismantle systemic racism. Moreover, these young people want to see more than lip service. No one wants to be set up for failure. The industry has been talking about dismantling racism and systems of oppression for fifty years, but the reality is that change is slow. Female artistic leaders must be given leeway to experiment and fail and explore again without public shame. There must be the same financial investment in women of color as there have been in our white male counterparts.

Unconscious bias is layered, and when left unchecked it rears its ugly head in subtle ways that is oblivious to most people. White supremacy maintains its power in liberal advocates who are touted as progressives but who unconsciously discriminate against minorities and women of color on a daily basis. But I have always been an incorrigible optimist; it is a mindset that has helped me overcome seemingly insurmountable odds and left detractors befuddled. Indeed, a new day is on the horizon, and I am joining the legions of women and men to help usher it in.

TERESA COLEMAN WASH

Teresa Coleman Wash (she/her) is a producer, writer, and founding artistic director for the Bishop Arts Theatre Center in Dallas, Texas. Teresa is a graduate of the National Arts Strategies Chief Executive Program at Harvard Business School and holds an MA in arts management from Goucher College. She is a recipient of Theatre Communications Group's Peter Zeisler Memorial Award and the National Guild for Community Arts Education's Milestone Award. Teresa has also earned several Irma P. Hall awards including the 2020 Theatrical Excellence Medal. She was elected to the Dramatists Guild of America council in 2017 representing the Southern region, where she also served on the steering committee.

DECOLONIZING CREATION PROCESSES BY RECLAIMING NARRATIVES

28 MAY 2018
ROBERT GOODWIN AND MARY KATHRYN NAGLE

Robert Goodwin: When you talk about decolonizing Western theatre, how do you explain it?

Mary Kathryn Nagle: I think it means different things to different people.

"Decolonization" is used a lot nowadays, and I think that's a good thing. People are becoming more aware of the ways in which our lives are predetermined by colonization, and they don't have to be—we have a choice. We live within a system, of course, but certain things we accept, or we frame things in certain ways in our minds because that's what we've been taught... Realizing you don't have to see them that way can be really liberating.

There's a lot of discussion happening about decolonization but not a lot of true education. That's not on anyone in particular. I think we need to go deeper into particular aspects of decolonizing the theatre.

Robert: The deeper, tougher questions—and the conversations that broaden the definition of what theatre can be—are the ones that tend to scare theatre practitioners who come from what could be perceived as a traditional colonial construct.

People get nervous when you start talking about systems and tradition. And it makes sense, because storytelling within cultures is an offshoot of different peoples' traditions. And sometimes when you start expanding those traditions, people get scared and want to maintain what they know.

But I think there's a beautiful opportunity when you have folks coming from different ethnic and cultural traditions, all showing ways of broadening storytelling. I've always constructed theatre as a means of telling stories, and I think there's such an interesting possibility when you get to expand how stories are told and what kind of stories are told. I think they're also connected to who will then be hearing and participating in those stories.

That then extends all the way to the audience: from who's producing to what kind of entities are being formed, and if folks can get those stories within established entities without nervousness and anxiety. It gets people nervous for some reason. I guess I understand; I don't necessarily agree with it, but I understand.

Mary Kathryn: I think those people don't understand storytelling's role in colonization and colonialism. They're just really not aware of why they live in the world they live in. American colonialism utilized—and continues to utilize—a very specific form of storytelling that dehumanized different groups of people and characterized the land we live on and with as a commodity, and that's the narrative and the story that got told. And it's still told today. We're still living and breathing and consuming a Manifest Destiny, "go west young man," "this land is yours" narrative in the United States.

For me, the biggest thing you can do to decolonize the theatre is to put all voices on stage, especially those who have been historically underrepresented or silenced in this country.

The historic silencing of underrepresented voices in this country is no accident. The silence is for a reason, right? Because when you do get to tell your story, you reclaim your power. And that's very threatening to colonialism and colonization. You can't exercise power over people if they are defining their own identities and sharing their own stories.

Robert: Yeah, you change the narrative. The narrative is taken back.

Mary Kathryn: Exactly. So, when I hear people talk about decolonizing the theatre, that's what I immediately go to. Who has been historically silenced, who are we now going to invite to the table and allow to define and share their own stories?

Robert: Right. And I think that's the interesting part of the conversation, which, like you said, gets deeper into all systems and begins to look at all of our history, especially in America.

We have to look at Manifest Destiny politics. We have to look at slavery and how world colonization allowed America to come into being what we know it to be, and how it allowed a lot of folks to be unaware because a whole system was created based in privilege and lack of awareness. You didn't have to worry about what was going on in the world. Somebody else was doing the heavy lifting, and people were benefiting from that. Especially when you and I, Native folk and folk who were brought over, are a real direct reintegration and reclamation of the narrative of the founding of our country, and consequently our stories.

I have a picture that I'm looking at right now of my maternal grandmother's sisters. There are twelve or thirteen of them, and they're sitting with my great-grandmother and great-grandfather. My great-grandmother is African American and my great-grandfather is Cherokee. Meanwhile, you and I are having this conversation exploring colonial narrative when those stories are represented in this picture. I wonder what that play would be, what that story would be, and how it would turn narratives that either aren't told or are maybe mistold on their heads.

Mary Kathryn: It's interesting to think about some of the criticism my plays, such as *Sovereignty* and *Manahatta*, have received so far. There are people who have said they're too educational. You really have to unpack that. Because the way in which my plays are educational is that they expose and reveal a narrative that has been purposely silenced by a colonial government. Our authentic stories have been silenced, removed, erased, and replaced with performances like redface and blackface and yellowface, and other forms of erasing or dehumanizing performances.

There is a reason that redface became a nationally adopted performance in the 1830s, around the same time Andrew Jackson was campaigning for president on a platform that advocated for Indian Removal. We, Natives, have stories—true authentic stories. People of color have authentic stories and narratives that are not the redface or blackface that colonialism created.

But when you put authentic narratives of Natives into a play, there are a lot of people who say, "Oh my gosh, I've never heard this before. I've learned so much." And they're excited, and they recognize it as a true story and they want to learn more. Just like you would any time you hear a good story.

Then there are the people who really challenge it, and I'm still figuring that out: How are they challenging it, why are they challenging it, what does it mean, and where does it come from? I think a lot of us hold onto colonial narratives without even fully consciously recognizing it. Just because it's the narrative we've grown up with, the one we've been taught.

Letting that go and opening ourselves up to other narratives is very tricky and requires a lot of thought and actual purpose. And so, right now, throwing writers of color who are challenging the colonial narrative straight into American theatre, without thinking about how they interface with critics—critics who derive their practice from a narrative that erases the writers' communities— leaves our writers of color disproportionally vulnerable in their artistic practice. We're literally changing the white colonial model of storytelling and infiltrating it with stories that have been purposefully silenced and erased, so there is going to be pushback. But how do we navigate that? And how does an artist honestly take in criticism they receive from an institution designed to erase them?

It's a challenge. Because I do need criticism for my plays. But when the critique is that my play was too educational... No one says that about a play about a white founding father. And we have tons of those, and those plays aren't educational because they're telling us something we already know. And why do we know it? Because it's the colonial narrative.

So therefore it's been deemed, in colonial fashion, to be good art because it's telling us what we already know. And plays by historically silenced people tell us what we don't know. Their authentic stories do educate us. Personally, I think the question of good art is simply: Is it a good story? And when it's a good story that also educates an audience about a narrative that has been hidden from them, that is the kind of art most humans attribute authentic value to.

Robert: I think it becomes systemic analysis. Then the challenge becomes grounded in the fact that when we look at other narratives and stories we don't know, we have to pull the thread on all parts of the form: how things are produced, who's in the room when stories are being critiqued. It forces a complete analysis.

And then we go to the next level, which is how human beings interact with each other in our country, in systems, and in the world, and then you start uncovering rocks. What's under the rocks that haven't moved for a long time?

I was doing some reading about how decolonizing work is happening in South Africa. One of the age-old playwrights, Welcome Msomi, paired Zulu history and stories with Shakespeare, layering the story of Shaka Zulu with Macbeth, for *uMabatha*. The narrative points to work not only of the Apartheid past, but present-moment issues that deal with social and political power, with accessibility and narrative offering, who controls the narrative... And it just makes folks have to be far more open to merging constructs.

You talk about the breadth of criticism, or who's in the room. I had to learn how to broaden my artistic palate. I grew up in a culturally specific theatre as an actor. I was told by old, experienced journeymen actors that if I was going to get really good at my form, I needed to go train classically. That gave me another set of tools in my box, and when you continue to expand your tool set, your way of working expands.

But if you choose to only have one frame of reference in terms of the tools that you use to build, to fix, to renovate, and to analyze, then you're making a choice. To view things in a particular way, to only fix things in a particular way, is a choice.

That says a lot of the desire of many people to maintain story structure. I know that we have both had experiences with others not understanding anything but linear temporal storytelling.

Mary Kathryn: Yeah. Linear, linear, linear, linear, linear.

Robert: Everyone across the world, other than the West, tells stories in all kinds of circles.

Mary Kathryn: Oh yes. I love a good circle.

Robert: In my experience working in regional theatre, it's a hard sell for some audiences who are used to the linear temporal form, but the expansion of exploring story structure in a different way is just like the circle. It becomes far more inclusive, far more whole.

But you have to say yes to it to be able to really get immersed and get an idea of what it could be. Not only to the institution—the audience, box office, the whole thing.

Mary Kathryn: One really exciting thing about a circle—and if you consider that a form of decolonization in the theatre— is that, automatically, everyone standing together is in relation to one another.

So much of colonization, and theatre that supports colonization, is about isolation and actually separating us from one another. That's the power of what you can do in a performance, in theatre, that you can't do in another political arena.

Robert: Right, the value and power and strength is when we do stand together holistically in that circle and engage with one another. It's an experience that asks us to engage in a way that makes us have to really see each other. And educate, and learn, and be entertained.

I think it's so interesting that you had a criticism about your piece being too educational. Isn't that what the form is supposed to do? Isn't it supposed to educate as much as it is to entertain? That's in my definition. You're supposed to take something away from it. I hope that I'll always take something away from every theatrical experience I have. That's what storytelling is about.

Mary Kathryn: For sure. Well, it has to be interesting to think about decolonization when you're at a company that focuses on producing Shakespeare. Do you think Shakespearean theatre contributes to colonization? Or do you want to plead the fifth.

Robert: I think about this often. I wonder if he would think that he was participating in a colonial act. Would he say, "Not only am I trying to do the exact opposite by taking antecedents and explore and pull threads"? Or, "My original ideas are pulling threads from at least different nationalities"? I think he would have a problem with how he's constructed as a cultural icon, if you will, because it seems like he was trying to be pluralistic. I think he was trying to be pluralistic.

That being said, I think, quite honestly, he's being used as a colonial reinforcement. And that's unfortunate because you see in some of the lines that are written the desire for folks to be true to who they know themselves to be intrinsically. And if you're asking people to be personally authentic, it's hard to say that the cat was trying to make a culturally isolating or even hegemonic statement.

I think, unfortunately, he's been used that way. And I think that's why it's even more incumbent on institutions that present Shakespeare to do their best to be progressive, and innovative, and pluralistic, in order for us to have spaces for all people versus resorting to a generic rationale that Shakespeare is universal. That's pushing people away because often the "universality" point does nothing but reinforce the status quo.

Especially if you know that during Shakespeare's time Britain was one of the major colonial forces in the world.

Mary Kathryn: The narrative of colonialism was one that supported colonial regimes but that has continued to reinvent itself over time. And it evolves. So we have in America today this post-racial colonial narrative: "We're all the same, we're all equal, there are no differences." But that lack of specificity, that "we're all just the same"... We're not all the same. How a Native person is affected by something is different than how a person from another community is affected by the same thing because of a very specific history: colonization.

Sometimes, as a progressive thing, we try to erase history, and I think that's really problematic. A Shakespeare play can get done in a way that seems "progressive," but actually, sometimes, the more you take it away from its original context, the more it contributes to this idea that our communities' relationships to colonization don't matter when they really, truly do.

I think it's easy to not really investigate what Shakespeare was exploring and what he was ignoring. And what colonial narratives he was promoting, and maybe what he was challenging. But that requires a lot of specificity. You have to really understand his context and investigate that. I think a lot of times the new colonial narrative that supports maintaining our status quo in contemporary Unites States prevents us from asking the hard questions about our history and where we come from—questions we desperately need to ask.

Robert: Exactly. I think that's the challenge. But let's pull the thread some more. What are we really saying about theatre? And are we up for the challenge for this next period of time in terms of theatre practice as well as theatre consumption? Because the more we try to stay in this neutral, undefined, non-specific history—and the more we ask people to come and consume, in a time when it's clear that specificity in storytelling is exactly what people are consuming—the more we risk losing the very people we want to invite to participate.

A colleague of mine said that people don't have to come to the theatre: there's great content across all technological platforms that we have now, and it's specific. It's more than Baskin-Robbins, it's more than your thirty-one flavors. It's very, very vast. So I can find the story. Like, I just found a platform for African American storytelling called kweliTV that's got a ton of specific content to my particular culture and ethnicity.

Then why do I go to the theatre? The live storytelling argument is, to me, coming into question more and more because those same forms—film, TV—are stealing the best from the theatrical traditions in terms of storytelling. And so the lines are being blurred in terms of aesthetics, how we as practitioners ideate and build stories, and how the public then consumes them. So, what are we telling people who go to the theatre?

Are we setting up the same kind of traditional theatre spaces that have been problematic for decades? Are we saying only certain people can go to the theatre, people with money or from a particular class? Are we saying that the (Western) "classics" are the only classics? We are again setting the stage for people who want to maintain a particular kind of story tradition. That's who comes. And it's a maintenance of a particular narrative, a particular idea, a particular mode. If we don't want to keep that as the narrative, then some of the decolonizing work has to happen to open the doors. I wonder if we want that.

Mary Kathryn: It goes back to the fact that if we really do want to decolonize the theatre, it's more than just saying, "Who are we inviting to make theatre and who are we inviting to watch it?" There's a lot more that has to be prepared responsibly if we don't want to harm anyone. And I actually think there is potential to harm. I've learned that by doing plays that challenge the colonial narrative. You are automatically engaging in narratives that have supported things like genocide, so people are going to get triggered. And there's a lot of trauma there.

I think theatre has the power to heal. But you have to know what you're working with and go about everything intentionally. You can't just stick it up there and say, "Let's see what happens." I think that's something I hadn't fully realized until I was completely engaged in it.

Healing the colonial narrative is going to be painful. Because there's a lot of pain, and that pain didn't go away because we didn't talk about it.

Robert: Right. Generation to generation to generation to generation. And when you crack the ground, water hits everyone. Not only the generation that was hurt by the colonial action.

As someone who does contextualizing and engagement work for a major theatre, I know I'm constantly trying to make sure that we pull threads in order to cover not only dramatic action, but to apply what we're focusing on in the theatre to everyday life and political action.

That's what you have to do in order to leave folks with some sort of construct that gives them a chance to close the loop on what they've seen. Give them opportunities to get more information in order to encounter, explore, and even reframe the narrative so they can go and interact in the world.

It points to the reason we have to have critics from across cultures, ethnicities, and orientations. Producers, executive directors, the whole nine, all through. I think that's when you start getting into interesting territory in this conversation because it does pull a lot of threads.

Mary Kathryn: Yeah, and that kind of systemic change can scare people for sure.

Robert: To say the least.

ROBERT GOODWIN AND MARY KATHRYN NAGLE

Robert C. Goodwin (he/him) has worked as performer, content creator, and independent producer. His work spans performances in regional theatre, television, and film as well as journalism and documentary filmmaking. He is a 2021 Sundance Institute Interdisciplinary Program grant awardee and has worked as a learning and creative-engagement practitioner for the majority of his thirty-year career, starting as a teaching artist and moving through the ranks to organizational department head. Robert currently serves as the vice president of Lyric Unlimited-Learning and Creative Engagement for the Lyric Opera of Chicago.

Mary Kathryn Nagle (she/her) was born in Oklahoma City, Oklahoma, and is a citizen of the Cherokee Nation of Oklahoma and an honorary member of the Ponca Tribe of Nebraska. She studied theatre at Georgetown University and went on to study law at Tulane Law School, where she graduated summa cum laude. Her play Sliver of a Full Moon *was presented at Joe's Pub in September 2014 and Yale Law School on 31 March 2015. Her other plays include* Miss Lead *(produced by Amerinda at 59E59 in January 2014),* Fairly Traceable *(developed in the Civilians 2014 R&D Group), and* Waaxe's Law *(presented at the Smithsonian's National Museum of the American Indian in October 2011). She currently lives in New York where she writes briefs and plays.*

FLIRTING WITH THE TABOO AT THE CAIRO FESTIVAL FOR CONTEMPORARY AND EXPERIMENTAL THEATRE

31 OCTOBER 2018

ADAM ASHRAF ELSAYIGH

" That was something, wasn't it?" my dad mutters with a forced nonchalance.

We are driving out of the parking lot of El Gomhoureya Theatre in downtown Cairo. It's 9:55 p.m. on the 18 of September, day nine of the Cairo International Festival for Contemporary and Experimental Theatre (CIFCET). My dad had decided to join me at the last performance of the evening, a Moroccan adaptation of Jean Genet's 1947 one-act play, *The Maids*, by Iraqi director Jawad Al-Assadi. In this production of the Genet classic, the tension is high as the two maids (Jalila Al-Talmasi and Rajaa Khirmaz) take turns pretending to be their mistress. Their relationship oscillates frantically from beat to beat: one minute, one of them sadistically attempts to choke the other to death; the next, they straddle each other, discussing the mistress's last sexual encounter. It's undeniably homoerotic.

My father is, of course, right. Al-Assadi's adaptation wouldn't be flagged as obscene or graphic on a Berlin or New York stage; yet here in Cairo, as a part of the Silver Jubilee programming of a state-sponsored festival, it's something.

"I've never seen subjects like that discussed on stage before."

I keep my amusement at his referring to queerness and female sexuality as "subjects like that" to myself and tell him, instead, that sexuality is not exactly a unique subject in theatre, even though it might be in this city.

I've explicated the elephant in the room on this ninety-five-degree night. Two blocks later, still awkwardly quiet, we pass by a traffic light. A decaying billboard close by, which has probably been there for over a year, announces that *Arabs Got Talent* will be accepting new auditions this summer. On one side of it, a huge sticker quoting Islamic Hadith reminds women to cover up. On the other, graffiti of President Sisi's face adorns the wall. I ruminate over the conversation with my dad. It's not that this is the first time censorship has come up since the beginning of the festivities. Yet the conversation with my father is the one that hits me most because I find his thinly veiled internal conflict so emblematic of the paradoxes of the Arab middle class: wanting to engage with cosmopolitanism and all it offers in culture, yet being flustered at the first threat to a conservative worldview. That paradox is in the very billboards before us. The signal turns green.

I ponder over the thing I have enjoyed most about the festival so far, which is the apparent absence of censorship. A lot of the performances (which are often graphic, explicit, or political) wouldn't have passed the censors here if they were being presented by an Egyptian company as an Egyptian production, or if they were being presented outside the festival.

Despite being a vibrant community of politically engaged artists and scholars, Egypt's theatre scene, for political and structural reasons, is reminiscent of Peter Brook's "deadly theatre." The majority of widely produced theatre is state sponsored, and the subjects artists are encouraged to present are often depoliticized historical fiction or farce. This policing is executed by the Censorship Bureau, an ever-growing major department of the Ministry of Culture with branches in every governorate in Egypt. Every book, film, television, or theatrical production to be circulated in Egyptian arts establishments must pass by the censors before release, and the censors cater to the aforementioned anxieties of the middle class. Just this summer, a dozen young actors were acquitted after having spent six months in a military jail for producing an anti-military play in a community club, which offended audiences despite receiving prior approval from the censors.

CIFCET is unique in its positionality because it challenges the constraints and stagnancy of this scene in ways that go well beyond censorship. The festival has three key components: the workshops, the conference, and the performances. All free of charge and open to the public, these initiatives allow local theatre students, artists, scholars, and everyday theatregoers (a tragically diminishing demographic in Egypt) to learn more about emerging styles, themes, and scholarship in experimental theatre communities from all around the world. While the festival does not categorize performances by theme, aesthetic, or country of origin, the selection committee this year seems to have been invested in showcasing works that explore migration, displacement, and the diasporic experience. This emphasis gave way to multiple joint productions between Arab and Western companies.

A particularly well-received production was the Syrian-German joint production *Hadra Horra (Free Presence)*. The highly stylized, contemporary dance piece subverted modern pop costuming and iconography to create visceral images that pertained to the experience of Syrian displacement and diaspora. The dancers—some German, some Syrian—employed a contemporary German dance aesthetic reminiscent of Pina Bausch. A particularly salient moment happened towards the middle of the performance when the stage lit up in sharp red and the dancers disappeared. A suitcase was left standing center stage—the only prop left—and it began to shake violently for almost a full minute as tunes from Syrian folklore were interspersed with moments of silence. When the suitcase finally broke apart and a dancer escaped from within, a choreography that evoked a sense of entrapment began.

Another particularly striking performance I saw early on was *Shaqf (The Raft)*, a Tunisian-Canadian co-production directed by Cyrine Gannoun and Majdi Bou-Matar, which first premiered in the Carthage International Theatre Festival in Tunisia. *Shaqf* tells the story of eight people from different regions of the Middle East as they attempt to cross the border from Tunis to Italy, seeking refugee or asylum status. Through the story, the undocumented Arab immigrant archetype is deconstructed from a monolith to a variety of three-dimensional characters—from the Sudanese child soldier attempting to escape servitude to the rural young Lebanese woman who wants to go to dance school in Europe. In some scenes, an actor tells his story in a five-minute monologue. In others, the Lebanese young woman pretending to be Syrian to gain refugee status expresses her trauma through contemporary dance.

Over the course of the eighty-minute one-act, *Shaqf* intersperses the Western dramaturgy of the well-made play with a variety of non-realist traditions such as contemporary dance, monodramatic storytelling, and musical interludes. The performance was a compelling example of experimentation that embraced both North American realist theatre aesthetics and Arabic aesthetics, such as the oral storytelling tradition of the *hakawati*. One of the play's main characters is explicitly queer and is treated very empathetically; another is blasphemous and blames God for displacement from rural Lebanon due to being a religious minority; a couple talk about how they would like to have sex on a raft.

Censorship comes up in conversation with an Iranian Canadian scholar as we exit the theatre. I tell her the performance would never pass the censors if a local writer had written it and that, for no apparent reason, it seems that international productions are given a pass. She responds with:

Well, that's the point of these festivals, right? The average theatregoer may not want or be able to see stories like this, but here they're confronted with it. Shows that are generally banned sometimes get performed in festivals and when they're good, the censors change their mind and they get approved outside of the festival.

As a diasporic Egyptian who has spent the past four years studying theatre between Abu Dhabi, New York, and European metropolises, I find myself in conversations about censorship with visiting scholars and artists throughout the festival. I don't always feel like I have the authority to speak as a local; I only relocated to Cairo this May. I struggle with how to talk about censorship. How do I contextualize the limitations on free speech here without confirming stereotypes about freedom of speech and human rights in the Middle East?

CIFCET incites discourse and provides opportunities for young artists here in Cairo in ways beyond seeing the visiting performances. The conference, for instance, called for submissions on philosophies of the body in contemporary theatre. There were lectures from Switzerland, Morocco, the United States, India, Canada, and beyond, which addressed the politicization of the female body, domination in theatre, racializing dramaturgies, and theatre of the absent body. Two major questions asked were:

- What is the positionality and politics of performing Arab identity—and specifically Egyptian identity—in Western settings?

- How can artists, scholars, and stakeholders in different theatre communities facilitate the exchange of art, writing, and performance within the larger international theatre ecosystem through commissions, festivals, and translations?

Discussions that arose from the talks sparked debates between young artists on the politics of performance within censored theatre communities.

Beyond the productions and conference, censorship remained a predominant subject of discussion. This was the topic of conversation at the playwriting workshop, where I acted as Arabic-English translator between the facilitator, Swiss director Erik Altorfer, and twelve aspiring theatre artists from Cairo. The participants felt that the subjects they'd like to explore in their writing—sexual harassment and state corruption, to name a few—would never be approved by the censors here. Erik had a different stance: that removing censorship was going to have to be a gradual process rather than an immediate one. He argued that countries that suddenly stopped censoring art, post-revolutions, ended up producing work that took advantage of the freedom of speech in ways that came off as shallow or lacked nuance.

I found myself of two minds. On one hand, I do not see the degree of censorship in local theatre here as productive. On the other, some of the best dramatic writing produced throughout history came under authoritarian rule with heavy censorship. I left the workshop that day thinking, *How can artists leverage the constraints of censorship to create innovative dramaturgies rather than approach the constraints as hurdles? How can we maintain what's compelling about these dramaturgies beyond censored theatrical environments?*

The Cairo theatre community needs a space where discussions on the philosophies of the body can happen uncensored. It needs a space where actors can talk about the diaspora from experiences seldom heard here. The international community needs better access to Arab narratives, which every day become harder to export due to strained economies. The more time I spend in Cairo and the further I develop my understanding of the nuances of Egyptian society, the more I value the space for free discourse and cultural exchange the festival creates.

ADAM ASHRAF ELSAYIGH

Adam Ashraf Elsayigh (he/him) is an Egyptian writer, theatremaker, dramaturg, and producer living in New York. Through his writing, Adam interrogates how intersections of queerness, religion, immigration, and colonialism inform our daily lives. Some of Adam's plays include Memorial, The Marginalia, Jamestown/Williamsburg, *and* Drowning in Cairo. *Adam's producing practice aims to develop, present, and produce transnational theatre that does not fit in a box, with a particular focus on Arab plays. Adam is the co-founder and former co-producer of the Criminal Queerness Festival in partnership with National Queer Theater. He is a fellow at Georgetown University's Laboratory for Global Performance and Politics. Adam's work has been seen at Golden Thread Productions, NYU's Tisch School of the Arts, the LaGuardia Performing Arts Center, Dixon Place, and the NYU Abu Dhabi Arts Center. Adam holds a BA in theatre with an emphasis in playwriting and dramaturgy from NYU Abu Dhabi and is an MFA candidate in playwriting at Brooklyn College.*

HOW REFUGEES ARE USING THEATRE TO WELCOME PARISIANS INTO THEIR LIVES

13 DECEMBER 2018
VERITY HEALEY

It's supposed to run for just over forty minutes, but it's been going for an hour. Jack Ellis, a volunteer artist at Good Chance Theatre in Paris, peeps hastily through the curtains and motions cut.

Alexandre Moisescot, curator at Good Chance and director of and actor in this Hope Show—a weekly presentation of work made during the week by refugees in theatre workshops—immediately falls into an improvised gag with Bashir, an Afghani refugee playing a security guard in a take on Samuel Beckett's *Waiting for Godot*. It ends with the audience clapping enthusiastically. Most are on their feet; some, like me, hide a tear.

When does theatre ever match this sense of closeness and sharing? Not too often—and probably rarely in geodesic domes, which were used by Good Chance when the theatre first formed in the Calais Jungle as a place where refugees could express themselves away from the problems they were facing. Now, as the company's production arm prepares to transfer its show *The Jungle* from London to New York City, the moveable domes sit like beating hearts outside Paris's Cité nationale de l'histoire de l'immigration (Museum of Immigration), where Good Chance has been in residence for the museum's season, aptly titled "Welcome."

"Who is allowed to welcome? Normally the people who have been in a place for the longest time," write co-founders and co-artistic directors of Good Chance, Joe Murphy and Joe Robertson, in an email. "Who is not allowed to welcome? The people who don't know the place very well." They have decided to invert the notion, with recently arrived refugees welcoming born-and-raised Parisians. The point of this is to demonstrate that the people who are arriving and building new lives in the city have just as much to offer, with their unique perspectives and experiences, as those who know their environment well. "It is not a case of 'refugees welcome,'" Murphy and Robertson say, "it's a case of 'refugees welcoming.'"

Good Chance's residency is about refugee empowerment. It is the first time they have worked so openly in the public eye. Since the destruction of the Calais Jungle, the company has built its domes outside French refugee centers far from society's gaze. Now, refugees have to travel from centers in Paris via public transport to Good Chance, intermingle with the public at the museum, and "welcome" them to their dome. As audience members arrive, they get patted down at the doors by actors dressed as security guards; while it's done as a joke, it's probably the refugees who are more used to this kind of intrusion than everyday Parisians. Deliberately flouting the conventional theatre etiquette, actors then "welcome" the audience members, show them to their seats, and talk to them like friends.

Of course, this is nothing new. Belarus Free Theatre has sometimes operated in the same way, and actors interacting with audience members is commonly used, especially in children's theatre. Here, though, it seems to give the refugees a sense of ownership and to promote an egalitarian atmosphere. "In the theatre everyone is equal," says Bashir, who is a member of La Troupe, a group of regular Good Chance workshop attendees borne out of the Paris domes.

Indeed, gone are the usual stiff silences before lights down or motionless ushers standing to attention; instead, it feels like everyone has come along for a gig, where anything can happen. Modern-day theatre protocol and all its trappings—brightly lit box offices and swanky bars—has been stripped away. "This is Shakespeare," says Claire Béjanin, Good Chance's international executive producer of *The Jungle*. "Theatre is too bourgeois today; it is for the educated, it is not vital anymore, it has lost an essence," she says.

But perhaps the refugees along with Good Chance are helping to put this vitality back into theatre. When the clapping finishes at the end of this Hope Show, the audience mingles with the actors, keen to talk to them—something that is less common in conventional theatre. According to Bashir, this is what theatre is for: to have conversations where different groups of people can begin to talk to each other.

Naomi Webb, executive director of Good Chance, explains that the company "came to Paris because there are thousands of refugees on the streets and there is no dialogue between them and the Parisians." For her, the work seems more urgent in the wake of President Macron's hostile new immigration bill. "In central Paris, refugees are ignored or not known about," concurs Dina Mousawi, Good Chance's creative producer.

When I visited Jardins d'Éole as an embedded critic—with volunteers and Malang, who is from Afghanistan, and another member of La Troupe—to encourage newly arrived refugees to come back to the theatre for a day of workshops, I got to see just how isolated this population is. This isolation partly comes through indifference. The park, rather than welcome centers, is home to a host of men from Eritrea, Chad, and Sudan—these individuals live out in the open, exposed to the elements and within full view of nearby apartments. Two Parisians are even exercising amongst them without batting an eyelid. But the isolation also partly comes from the opposite: from not blending in. As we walk back to Stalingrad Metro with the men who've decided to join us, I notice people looking, wondering who we are.

At the theatre, though, things change. We all eat together—a chance for people to hang out socially, even if, due to the many languages spoken (around twenty sometimes), people can't always understand each other very well. Later, a vigorous workshop, where the men are encouraged to play fight, allows them to let off steam and high five and fist bump people like Bashir, Malang, and Alpha, another Good Chance regular. It's Thursday and we don't know if anyone will return the next day or for Saturday, the day of the Hope Show, but they seem to be enjoying themselves.

Refugees do come back, though. "With this residency refugees can come into the museum and be seen," says Mousawi. "There is a pride in that." If it seems crazy that refugees living out in the open or with other huge worries on their shoulders would decide to partake in theatre workshops, even if they've never had an interest before, it's put into perspective by Bashir. He tells me that upon his arrival to Porte de la Chapelle, a welcome center for refugees, Good Chance volunteers—Mousawi in particular— were the only people who spoke to him and wanted to include him in something. It's "theatre of necessity," says Moisescot. Later, Webb tells me Good Chance believes that being able to express oneself is as important as the human right to food, warmth, and shelter.

But there's no room for any self-pity in the Hope Shows, although the Parisian audience must surely see the *Waiting for Godot* skit—where Bashir sits around waiting for the arrival of Godot, who never comes—as a metaphor for the situation many refugees face. That same night, Yousef, who has political refugee status and is a Syrian poet and history teacher, recites a tender but angry poem about the state of the world—but not about himself; private traumas remain private, although refugees can contribute story ideas at the workshops. "The war has broken all things, has broken human beings on the inside," Yousef says. But Yousef's sadness and attention is not directed at himself, it's directed at the "sick ideology, at Assad, Putin, Hezbollah." As he recites his poem, the silence is so great you can hear someone shouting down the street, far from the theatre.

Time away from their problems gives the refugees mental space, but in Yousef's words it also encourages him to think about what more he can do to help: "When I'm eating I think, how can I eat, how can I sleep? Maybe my writing can do something. Everyone can do something."

Back onstage in the Hope Show, the refugees enjoy each other's company. Marzin, a Sudanese refugee who has been in France a few months, says for the first time he feels he is in a group he likes and that he is a lot happier. But there is something more raw and visceral at work too. Malang, who is interested in how he can use his body onstage, says, "I want people to come and see [the Hope Show] because I have something to say, not necessarily in words." Malang, who wants to "go further in acting and dancing," says that Good Chance Theatre gives people what they need to exist: "It's about being seen, being heard, being recognized."

What does this do to an audience? Charlotte, a volunteer from Paris, believes that French theatre is "missing the human connection" and that Good Chance, working with refugees, is helping add that back in. But this means there is a need to "get rid of the condescension," says Moisescot, referring to audiences who would enthusiastically applaud the early Hope Shows, even if they weren't very good. By continuing to work with people like Malang and Bashir through La Troupe, to build up their skills, the Hope Shows can now "have some irreverence, cruelty, violence, and fun," says Moisescot, and "people who see the show have the feeling to be part of it, not just a spectator."

The audience's relationship to the performers has changed—it is less conciliatory and more respectful and equal. And, in a way, because the refugees have actively invited the audience into their space, without money changing hands (the Hope Show is free), it is a gift. It might not be totally perfect, but it is participatory.

"If we had to summarize what we expect of the audience, it's to get them to leave the Hope Show with more questions than certainties," writes a representative from the Museum. And it can happen—one female audience member tells me it has changed what she thinks art is for.

Some people might query if there is a chance that audiences will see a Hope Show and then forget it, or if the people who need to see it just won't go, but these might be the wrong questions to ask. "We can't force people to change their opinions [of refugees], we can only do it slowly," says Webb. However, she reveals that one Parisian was so moved after seeing a Hope Show they donated a large amount of money to help with future projects. But the co-founders make me realize that I have not quite understood theatre's latent powers. "Good Chance believes in the power of theatre to stay with people, to continually affect and challenge," Murphy and Robertson write. "Live, unrepeatable experiences have a particular energy that allows them to change in an individual's memory, allowing them to feel consistently relevant and difficult to simplify." This fits. We can't actually measure the impact art has; its effects are more hidden.

From my brief stay in Paris, it is apparent that everyone is affected by Good Chance's presence: from the bored security guards at the museum who shout "Good Chance!" as a salutation to refugees as they enter the domes, to the café-bar across the road, where we decamp every night, whose attitude towards its very international guests has become warm and welcoming.

The refugees are suddenly walking tall. "When he arrived, Malang was so down," says Chris, a volunteer who met him when he first came to a refugee center in Paris. But now, "he is like this: head up, shoulders back." The empowerment is apparent in how Malang, Bashir, Marzin, and the others treat the domes: as if they are their second homes.

"When I come here every Saturday I make shower; I make elegant because I am coming to meet my family," says Yousef. Good Chance has become a way for people to live, to meet, to socialize. It's more than a job for its staff, and there seems to be no cutoff point for the refugees who regularly attend the workshops. The work they do and the art they create seeps into their private lives; both Bashir and Malang are often the first to arrive early and amongst the last to leave at night. Good Chance is not just theatre but a living, breathing way of life.

Refugees need Good Chance; this is obvious. But, the co-founders are clear to point out, "their stories are needed by us" too.

This is something that even liberal audiences need to learn: "Even if people are open-minded, there's still work to do in levels of understanding," says Webb. Good Chance and its refugee performers are filling the gap that exists between audience and performer in traditional theatre in order to increase understanding and break down boundaries. They are also inverting need, taking away its propensity to encourage power imbalances and making it more equal.

As Marzin says, Good Chance is "a beautiful idea," and the fact that he travels five hours every day from his center outside Paris, just to come to the theatre, says it all.

VERITY HEALEY

verity healey (she/her) is a London-based writer, photographer, and filmmaker who writes for HowlRound, WhatsOnStage, *and* The Stage, *amongst others. She recently completed editorial commissions for Belarus Free Theatre in Minsk.*

PRODUCING WITH A DISABLED LENS

28 MAY 2019

CLAUDIA ALICK

To be successful, cultural productions, including theatre, require the artistic, technical, and administrative staff to have expertise in the areas they desire excellence. If the people who create or experience the work cannot access the production process or space, there's an immediate barrier to creating or experiencing excellence. Work that does not center justice is centering injustice, which makes for negative artistic outcomes. Practically speaking, it is important for the production teams to have expertise in the areas they want to be successful in. And when it comes to accessibility, disabled artists have the lived experience necessary that will lead to more successful outcomes.

I acquired my disability in 2009 but was lucky to experience disabled culture from a young age as an abled youth. In high school, I was a counselor at Camp Challenge for adults with developmental disabilities. Later, I engineered audiobooks at the American Foundation for the Blind. I studied disability culture in graduate school, where I learned the importance of the social model of disability: while the medical model centers "the problem" inside the individual's body, the social model recognizes that "the problem" is in the systems and physical spaces that create inaccessibility.

When I became community producer for Oregon Shakespeare Festival (OSF), I felt confident in my cultural competency and allyship. I knew that if I wanted to curate an artistic series that reflected our full culture, I would need to be intentional in my choices. I booked artists with visible and invisible disabilities, artists whose work centered on their disabled identity, as well as artists where disability was not an explicit part of their content. I curated diversely because the disabled community is not homogenous. This required reaching out to D/deaf, blind, mobility-impaired, and neurodiverse artists. It required seeing a broad spectrum of work and building relationships. Finally, it required increased resources to dismantle barriers to access.

At OSF, we built our dressing-room spaces with wheelchair clearance in mind from the beginning, which saved us some bother later on. We booked sign interpreters for the D/deaf artists. With grant support from New England Foundation for the Arts, we built a ramp to modify our stage for AXIS Dance, who perform with wheelchairs. I felt we were meeting most of the needs of our audience and the artists. Then my perspective radically shifted, and I saw where we were institutionally failing ourselves.

In my second season at OSF, I had a sudden-onset illness and found myself in chronic pain, with spasmodic muscles and decreased mobility. Areas of inaccessibility in our institution suddenly became hypervisible to me. The complications of requesting modifications (let alone knowing which ones I could ask for) were a barrier. Our rehearsal and meeting communication practices, locations, and expectations were all designed for abled participants. The numbers of stairs I needed to climb to access the executive director's office was a barrier. These were all barriers I'd failed to dismantle because they had not been visible to me before.

I began using a power scooter, and I met audience members in wheelchairs and scooters. One couple shared with me issues regarding the theatre's bathroom access. They hadn't felt comfortable sharing the feedback with anyone in person until they met a producer who was literally on their level; this was feedback I was uniquely able to empathize with and understand. I expressed that these were issues I'd also experienced and we were working on them. They were longtime supporters of the theatre; they felt heard and in turn would contribute more in the future.

It's incredibly useful to have people with disabled expertise involved in production processes from the beginning. Familiarity with concepts like "inspiration porn" (stories that reduce subjects into objects for ableist inspiration) or "disability drag" (abled actors playing disabled characters) can be the difference between creating work that helps or harms people and the institution's bottom line. When the disabled perspective is prioritized, the work centers on outcomes of excellence for everyone.

For instance, having a neurodivergent theatremaker on my producing team allowed us to identify and dismantle barriers in communication practices. This was in addition to him being an effective administrator and performer. Working with a physically disabled director created circumstances where we were always planning the most physically accessible paths on and off stage for everyone, including the creative team. When someone turned an ankle and became temporarily disabled, we were already prepared.

A few seasons before I left OSF, we cast actress Regan Linton in the rep company. I had booked dancer Alice Sheppard for an outdoor performance on dates where Michael Maag, our resident lighting designer, and Regan Linton were both available. All three artists use wheelchairs. I recognized I was uniquely able to produce and facilitate a cross-disciplinary conversation about access that would have no ableism embedded in it. The result was a powerful hour of educational programming, and relationships were created that have resulted in original work and international collaboration outside of OSF.

With my company, Calling Up Justice, I produce transmedia performances of justice online, onstage, and in real life. I've helped museums and conferences design for accessibility, worked with executive staff to develop and rehearse ways to respond to microaggressions, helped curate projects for funders to invest equitably, built and facilitated online spaces, and produced art with structures and stories of justice. We also devise and share resources, tools, and concepts online.

In addition, I participate in several national and international cohorts such as Unsettling Dramaturgy: Crip and Indigenous

Process Design in the Studio, on the Stage, and in the Street. This cohort is an online research colloquium that brings together crip and Indigenous dramaturgs and theatremakers from across the Americas. Crip theory centers on "the disabled" as an identity to be recognized and celebrated while also acknowledging the historical exclusion of Black, Indigenous, people of color and LGBTQ+ within the community. "Crip," as used here, is considered to be an inclusive term, representing all disabled peoples.

For the past year I've been working with the concept of "crip time" as a tool to create universally designed accessible rehearsals and meetings. Alison Kafer, author of *Feminist, Queer, Crip*, says that "rather than bend disabled bodies and minds to meet the clock, crip time bends the clock to meet disabled bodies and minds."[1] Theatre is chronically under-resourced, and we fill that monetary gap with sweat equity. There is an ethos in the theatre community of doing whatever it takes to make sure the show happens—"the show must go on"—and there's a reason why so many people in our industry hide their disabilities. Our field has a track record of punishing perceived weakness. When I became disabled I was afraid I would no longer be able to work at the level that was expected of me. I was sometimes treated that way. However, in the last decade, I've surpassed my old goals and produced prolifically with high success and reach, creating even more ambitious intentions that I am now beginning to fulfill.

My lived experience has forced me to reckon with legacy colonialist and capitalist structures in order to create more

---

1   Ellen Samuels, "Six Ways of Looking at Crip Time," *Disability Studies Quarterly* 37, no. 3 (summer 2017), https://doi.org/10.18061/dsq.v37i3.5824.

humane ways to work together. The results are a healthier process and better art. There are many thought leaders who have been working on these concepts for many years. A piece of wisdom that informs my practice comes from Sins Invalid, a performance project that incubates and celebrates artists with disabilities, centralizing artists of color and queer and gender-variant artists as communities that have been historically marginalized. One of the ten principles of disability justice, shared by Patty Berne and the Sins Invalid family in their book *Skin, Tooth, and Bone— The Basis of Movement is Our People: A Disability Justice Primer* is sustainability: "We pace ourselves, individually and collectively, to be sustained long-term. We value the teachings of our lives and bodies. We understand that our embodied experience is a critical guide and reference pointing us towards justice and liberation."[2]

I often publicly tell the story of creating access for others and then needing that access for myself. It's a little funny. I built a ramp for disabled artists and would have been prevented from using my own stage without it. Accessibility is literally for everybody! I used to share the story in order to encourage non-disabled and abled producers to present and cast disabled artists. Today, I share this story to encourage everyone to include disabled collaborators as producers who have the power to make choices in design, representation, and access to resources. Practically speaking, it's the smartest way to achieve success.

2   Sins Invalid, *Skin, Tooth, and Bone: The Basis of Movement is Our People* (San Francisco: 2016).

CLAUDIA ALICK

 Claudia Alick (she/her) is a performer, producer, designer, writer, and inclusion expert. She serves as co-president of the board of NET and on the HowlRound advisory council, and she co-produces Unsettling Dramaturgy (crip and Indigenous international digital colloquium). She is founding producer of the transmedia social justice company Calling Up Justice, whose projects include Producing in Pandemic, the Every 28 Hours Plays, We Charge Genocide TV, Justice Producers, co-artistic direction of the BUILD Convening, directing Electra with Access Classics, digital design of the Festival of Masks, partnering with Trek Table in addition to building and facilitating the Mosaic Network (an alternative to Facebook for BIPOC theatres and funders), as well as consulting and advising funders and companies around the country. Public speaking highlights include the conversation "Disability + Pleasure Activism," an interview with AI for the People Black in 2042, and being on the panel for Claiming Space: A Symposium on Black Futures, part of the Smithsonian Afrofuturism Series. She produces performances of justice onstage, online, and in real life.

#METOO AND THE METHOD

13 JUNE 2019
HOLLY L. DERR

H*e would send one actor to listen to a piece of jazz, another to read a certain novel, another to see a psychiatrist, and another he would simply kiss."*

—Arthur Miller on Elia Kazan,
in Kazan on Directing

#MeToo has raised many questions about what kinds of intimacy are created in rehearsal rooms and classrooms, and to what end. As I've listened to the stories of survivors, I've been struck by the fact that the abusers in these cases, mostly men, weren't doing anything that their predecessors in the American theatre didn't do openly and without repercussions. At least three of the fathers of the American Method—Lee Strasberg, Sanford Meisner, and Elia Kazan—had reputations for treating men and women differently, as well as for treating both women actors and women characters as sex objects. It made me wonder: Is there a connection between use of the Method and the behavior called out by #MeToo?

Since the 1930s, American theatre has been operating under the spell of the oh-so-seductive Method, a psychological acting technique that asks actors to draw on their own memories and to act "truthfully" on "instinct." The Method is derived from Konstantin Stanislavsky's Method of Physical Actions, usually called the System, which is a psychophysical technique that posits that engaging in physical action in pursuit of solving a problem—otherwise known as "playing an action"—will lead an actor to have a real emotional experience.

Significant scholarship—shout out to Sharon Carnicke's *Stanislavsky in Focus*—has shown that the American progenitors of the Method, namely Harold Clurman, Elia Kazan, Lee Strasberg, Stella Adler, and Sanford Meisner, misunderstood the Stanislavsky acolytes and interpreters through whom they learned the System, and wrongly placed their focus on generating emotion for its own sake. Clurman and Adler later caught their mistake when Adler traveled abroad to work with Stanislavsky himself, and they redirected their evolving processes towards physical action. But though they shared their experience with their comrades, Strasberg chose to continue to neglect the physical aspects of the System in favor of a process that centered on delving not just into the characters' psyches, but also the actors'. Meisner, on the other hand, came to prioritize instinct. Kazan did use physical action but shared Strasberg's interest in generating emotion using the actors' real lives.

Due to the popularity of some of the movie stars trained at Strasberg's Actors Studio (anyone heard of Marilyn Monroe?), Americans today, even non-actors, still use the parlance of the Method to talk about acting, and most people still conflate the Method with Stanislavsky's System. Having a shared vocabulary can be valuable, but the parlance and practices that accompany the Method are rooted in a history of sexism and exploitation. Though many of Stanislavsky's techniques work, the powerful men who left us our particularly American legacy didn't just create an American version of his System, they created a technique for both acting and learning to act that has the ongoing potential to reinforce patriarchal norms.

> *"Today, purely in looks, you were more attractive. You looked sexier. In [Cat on a Hot Tin Roof], the girl, no matter what she is, has to be attractive, otherwise the play becomes unpalatable.... Frankly this quality is essential for your progress, acting-wise and career-wise."*
>
> —*Lee Strasberg giving feedback to an actor, in Strasberg at the Actors Studio*

Stanislavsky was without doubt a patriarchal figure, and from his own writing we learn that his classrooms were not free of gender stereotypes. The women, for example, did an awful lot of fainting. But he was horrified when he accidentally had a student do an improvisation that mirrored her personal experience of losing a child and she was, understandably, devastated. This is because the System asks actors to create emotional experiences by focusing on the problem the character is trying to solve (the task or objective) and the tactics they use to solve it (the actions), not reliving past emotional experiences—usually traumatic ones—as the Method asks. Because Method directors and teachers believe that creating emotional moments on stage requires delving into the actor's subconscious mind, they tend to take on the role of guru, opening the door for far more manipulative behavior than Stanislavsky ever advocated.

In her 2012 book *An Actress Prepares: Women and "the Method,"* Rosemary Malague zeroes in on Strasberg and Meisner as the primary culprits of using the Method to affirm and reinscribe harmful gender stereotypes. Topping her list of feminist critiques is the idea that the goal of the Method is to produce "truthful" performances, and yet what is considered "truthful" is, in itself, a gendered concept. According to Malague's extensive research, Strasberg's responses to women's acting in class often took the form of remarks upon their sexuality and desirability, as he encouraged them to play sex kittens and weeping women. In his classes, he gave different acting exercises to men and women. And when he rewarded actors for performances that he deemed truthful, he tended to reward women for being seductive and men for being fighters.

Is there a connection between use of the Method and the behavior called out by #MeToo?

Strasberg's goal was to "break actors down," which often meant manipulating, confusing, and shaming them, particularly the women, then encouraging them to re-suffer that shame every time they performed. In his own accounts of his practice, quoted below from *An Actress Prepares*, Strasberg admitted this could be unhealthy:

> *In fact I once had a Private Moment which was terrifying. An actress came in who I realized was very bound to convention and didn't move from within.... She had an emotional disturbance, and she should not have done Private Moments because they only lead to a re-affirmation of whatever bothers you.... She did a Private Moment which was one of the greatest I've ever seen. I sat in amazement. I wouldn't have believed that this girl had it in her. But she couldn't recover from it, it was so strong.[1]*

As Malague put it, "The most intriguing statement in Strasberg's account...is his declaration that this woman's private moment was 'the greatest' he had ever seen. Watching a woman in total breakdown fulfills Strasberg's (aesthetic?) goals."

Meisner's particular subgenre of the Method, called the Meisner technique, trains actors to act on instinct. The psychology underpinning it comes from Freudian theory, which, as we know, is already an extremely binary,[2]

1   Rosemary Malague, *An Actress Prepares: Women and "the Method"* (London: Routledge, 2012).
2   Sigmund Freud, *New Introductory Lectures on Psychoanalysis* (New York: Norton, 1933).

gendered[3] approach to the human mind, making even the simplest Meisner exercise a minefield of gendered assumptions. Malague points out that the repetition exercise, which encourages actors to make uncensored observations about one another's physical appearance— "You are wearing a blue shirt. I am wearing a blue shirt"— could go very badly for actors whose gender identities are non-binary, or for those with nonconforming bodies or who are a minority presence in the room.

Meisner's exercises, like Strasberg's, tended to be different for women than for men. In his book, *Sanford Meisner on Acting*, he recounts a class in which he demonstrated a version of the repetition exercise twice, once with a man and once with a woman. In the first instance, he begins with "Can you lend me twenty dollars?" and, when the student eventually says no, he calls him a "big shit." When working with the woman student, Meisner begins with "Will you come to my house tonight?" and, when she says no, he ends by calling her "a professional virgin."[4]

Meisner was not alone in this tendency towards encouraging aggression from men and victimization, usually sexual, from women. Apparently, Kazan used to stand next to actors as they rehearsed and poke them with a rapier; he deemed most of the women in Tennessee Williams' plays to be motivated by a desire for sex or protection, in contrast to those of the men, who were encouraged by conflict. In fact, for Kazan, the tendency towards violence is an inherently biologically male

3   Nancy Chodorow, *Individualizing Gender and Sexuality: Theory and Practice* (New York: Routledge, 2012).
4   Sanford Meisner and Dennis Longwell, *Sanford Meisner on Acting* (New York: Random House, 1987).

phenomenon. In his notes on *A Streetcar Named Desire*, published posthumously in *Kazan on Directing*, he says Stanley is "desperately trying to squeeze out happiness by living *ball and jowl*, and it really doesn't work because it simply stores up violence until *every bar in the nation is full of Stanleys ready to explode*." Under the heading "Mitch," he wrote, "Violence—he's full of sperm, energy, strength." And he characterized Blanche as a kind of succubus: "Blanche's spine: to find protection, to find something to hold onto, some strength in whose protection she can live, like a sucker shark or a parasite. The tradition of woman (or all women) can only live through the strength of someone else."[5]

> *"I'd known her when she was a plump young girl, and I had a theory...that when a girl is fat in her early and middle teens and slims down later, she is left with an uncertainty about her appeal to boys, and what often results is a strong sexual appetite, intensified by the continuing anxiety of believing herself undesirable."*

> —*Elia Kazan on casting Maggie in* Cat on a Hot Tin Roof, *in* Kazan on Directing

Malague, as she herself documents, was not the first feminist scholar to point out these issues as they apply both to the rehearsal room and the classroom. Feminists have been warning about the consequences of the continued popularity of the Method since at least 1985, when Linda Walsh Jenkins and Susan Ogden-Malouf wrote the article "The (Female) Actor Prepares."[6] Stanislavsky emphasized

5   Elia Kazan, *Kazan on Directing* (New York: Random House, 2009).
6   Linda Walsh Jenkins and Susan Ogden-Malouf, *The (Female) Actor Prepares, Theater* 17, no. 1 (February 1985), 66–69. https://doi.org/10.1215/01610775-17-1-66

what he called "faith and a sense of truth,"[7] vaguely defining truthful acting as acting in which the actor believes in what is happening. Though Stanislavsky's idea of "truth" was broad and could even be expressed in nonrealistic ways, Method practitioners reduced the "truth" to patriarchal, gender-normative behavior. This, Jenkins and Ogden-Malouf argue, is problematic because with the Method the actor must rely on an all-knowing guru to get to the "truth," and the "truth" they must believe in is actually a stereotype.

"The (Female) Actor Prepares" was followed by Sue-Ellen Case's book *Feminism and Theatre* in 1988, in which she singles out anything based in Freudian psychology, as the Method was, as likely to replicate the Freudian hierarchy that places men in the subject position while treating women as derivative and subordinate. She goes on to explicitly reject the Method for asking women actors to believe in, identify with, and see the world from a patriarchal point of view, particularly regarding their sexuality.[8]

In 1989, Deanna Jent published her dissertation "Sex Roles in the Acting Class: Exploring the Effects of Actor Training on Nonverbal Gender Display"[9] about her qualitative study, over the course of six months, of gendered behavior in a group of college actors training in the Method. She found that their nonverbal behaviors changed during that time "toward more stereotypic behavior, indicating an inflexibility of traditional masculine and feminine movement patterns." Most striking is her example of an emotional recall exercise in which "three women were

7   Constantin Stanislavsky, *Faith and a Sense of Truth in a Performer* (UK: Read Books, 2012).

8   Sue-Ellen Case, *Feminism and Theatre* (London: Routledge, 1988).

9   Deanna Bantz Jent, "Sex Roles in the Acting Class: Exploring the Effects of Actor Training on Nonverbal Gender Display" (PhD diss., Northwestern University, 1989).

asked to perform scenes involving 'terror'–all three relived moments of victimization and helplessness." By retelling these kinds of stories and not looking at the gender issues they raise, Jent found that this exercise reinforced the notion of "woman as victim" or "woman as helpless."

The idea that successful acting requires psychologically unhealthy behavior has a strong grip on American actors to this day.

For more than a decade, feminist theatre theory, by Elin Diamond, Jill Dolan, Peggy Phelan, Elaine Aston, Ellen Donkin, Susan Clement, and more and more and more, continued to reject the Method, often eschewing the tradition of psychological realism altogether. Yet, in the world of traditional professional theatre practice, no one listened. Adler, who died in 1992, probably would have found that depressingly familiar.

> "Suppose that when the actress playing this part was five years old, a gang of four or five local ruffians dragged her into a deserted lot and ripped off her clothes. The horror, the disgrace of this experience is still so alive in her that whenever she recalls it, she breaks down. So that might be a useful preparation for the opening of this scene."
>
> —Sanford Meisner, in Sanford Meisner on Acting

Use of the Method crossed over from rehearsal rooms to classrooms and from theatre to film, and it remains standard practice in both private studios and academic institutions. The Actors Studio still offers classes in the Method, as do the Lee Strasberg Theatre and Film Institute and the Sanford Meisner Center. NYU's Tisch Drama offers two-year-long intensives in Strasberg and Meisner, and colleges and universities all over the country, from state schools like Ohio University to private schools like Rutgers University, offer classes in the Method. Meisner's technique is particularly popular in LA, and movie stars like Angelina Jolie, Scarlett Johansson, and Steve Buscemi all say they use Method acting. Supposedly, Jared Leto once used the Method as an excuse to send a dead pig and a sticky *Playboy* magazine to his costars.[10] The idea that successful acting requires psychologically unhealthy behavior has a strong grip on American actors to this day.

The stories told by #MeToo survivors (and Jared Leto's castmates) attest to the fact that Method-based practices are still doing gender-based harm, whether in the form of guru gatekeepers who use their power inappropriately, gender-differentiated training that affirms stereotypes, directors and teachers who treat women actors and characters as objects instead of subjects of their own action, or actors who act irresponsibly while "in character."

To the leaders of the American theatre just now grappling with these sexist practices in response to #MeToo, on behalf of the scholars and practitioners who identified these problems last century, I'd like to take a moment to say: Told ya.

And now, some antidotes.

After Carnicke's *Stanislavsky in Focus* was published in 1998, feminist scholars began to reconsider their wholesale rejection of the System. Scholar and director Rhonda

10   Marc Malkin, "Jared Leto Sent Used Condoms and Anal Beads to His *Suicide Squad* Co-Stars (Yup, You Read That Right!)," *E! News*, 12 April 2016. https://www.eonline.com/news/756288/jared-leto-sent-used-condoms-and-anal-beads-to-his-suicide-squad-co-stars-yup-you-read-that-right.

Blair's 2002 article "Reconsidering Stanislavsky: Feeling, Feminism, and the Actor" argues that recent developments in cognitive neuroscience and neurophysiology validate Stanislavsky's systemization of acting.[11] For example, in real life, we create what Stanislavsky called "throughlines" by "proto-narrativizing"; we turn events in our lives into meaningful stories driven by cause and effect, just as Stanislavsky asks actors to do on stage. In fact, humans have been doing this for so long that the process is embedded in our brain structures.

Blair shared that in her practice as a director, she finds Stanislavsky's idea of a mental film of highly personal images useful for actors to emotionally connect to their roles. She also uses objects of attention, action, imagery, and physicality to engage actors, and she changes Meisner's mantra "get out of your head"—which she calls anti-intellectual, narcissistic, and mystifying—to "get out of your neocortex," where we over-rationalize and control things, "and into your subcortex," where we respond to circumstances spontaneously.

J. Ellen Gainor's article "Rethinking Feminism, Stanislavsky, and Performance," published at the same time, points feminist actors towards a Stanislavsky/Brecht hybrid technique, in which the actor combines Stanislavsky's ideas about physical action with Brecht's alienation effect, enabling the actor to both empathize with a character and comment on the ways in which the character's gendered behavior might be a performance or a product of historical circumstance instead of "instinct."

11   Rhonda Blair, "Reconsidering Stanislavsky: Feeling, Feminism, and the Actor," *Theatre Topics* 12, no. 2 (September 2002): 177–90. https://doi.org/10.1353/tt.2002.0008.

In Jent's dissertation, she posits that plays with traditional gender roles might be more healthily rehearsed if the characters' gendered behaviors are treated as given circumstances instead of physiologically motivated characteristics inherent to the characters. For example, Blanche might not be biologically motivated to seek protection through seduction—she might simply be living in a world in which women have to play that role. (Having grown up in the South, I can tell you belles are not born, they are made.) Likewise, Stanley and Mitch may not be violent because they have balls and sperm—a dramaturgical choice that excuses violence against women as "instinctive"—they may *choose* violence as a way of controlling women.

Certainly there is plenty to explore in *Cat on a Hot Tin Roof* if Maggie is not inherently oversexed but is rather responding to her circumstances in the only way she can, by playing the role of Southern seductress. According to Malague's research, Strasberg felt that the audience had to want to sleep with Maggie for the play to work, but what if the audience, instead of seeing her as an object of desire, sees her as the subject of her own actions, a woman trying to use the only means she's been given by a sexist society to secure her economic future? It isn't, after all, seduction that gets her what she wants from Brick in the end.

Today, feminist theatre theory embraces the possibilities in Stanislavsky's System, particularly as taught by Adler. In my own practice, I recognize that often an actor can find an emotional anchor in a scene just by focusing on the right given circumstance, a fact about the imaginary reality of the play-world that is meaningful to them. An actor can also experience real emotion in performance by focusing their attention on the other actor(s) instead of on themselves, reacting in the moment to what's actually happening on stage instead of to a memory. Sometimes, it's simply a matter of finding the right subtext.

Directors can also avoid directing actors into gender stereotypes by taking a closer and more gender-conscious look at the actions they're asking them to play. Must men always fight? Must women always seduce? Seemingly harmless verbs, like "protect" for a man, can create a binary, gender-normative character and play-world, in which women need men's protection, even where that is not necessarily written into the text. What if women are encouraged to play actions like "to fight"? What if men are encouraged to play actions like "to heal" and "to comfort"? There exists no one right action for any moment, and many different actions can be played with the same text to great effect.

> *"It is not essential that you should want to fuck the leading lady, but it is essential that you should feel emotions well past those of ordinary friendship or respect."*
>
> —*Elia Kazan, in* Kazan on Directing

Because of #MeToo, people are finally listening to women who say the behavior typically associated with Method practices creates a toxic work environment. Under the motto "whatever the truth requires," Profiles Theatre in Chicago put actual violence—not stage combat—on stage along with sexual behavior that was not consensually choreographed.[12] Not surprisingly, the guru in charge there

---

12   Aimee Levitt and Christopher Piatt, "At Profiles Theatre the Drama—and Abuse—Is Real," *Chicago Reader*, 8 June 2016. http://chicagoreader.com/arts-culture/at-profiles-theatre-the-drama-and-abuse-is-real.

used his gatekeeper status to sexually harass the women who worked for him, and the theatre programmed play after play in which women are sexually victimized and men are violent. After important reporting gave voice to abused employees, Profiles closed. At long last, widespread agreement is slowly emerging that treating women actors and characters as sexual objects is no longer acceptable.

Furthermore, the new field of intimacy choreography now encourages directors and teachers to work with consent when sex and violence are involved, rather than having actors act on "instinct." And new acting techniques, which are more physical and less emotional, like the Viewpoints, proliferate. In *The Viewpoints Book: A Practical Guide to Viewpoints*, Anne Bogart and Tina Landau explicitly frame the Viewpoints as a solution to one of the problems caused by the Method:

> *The Herculean effort to pin down a particular emotion removes the actor from the simple task of performing an action, and thereby distances actors from one another and from the audience. Instead of forcing and fixing an emotion, Viewpoints training allows untamed feeling to arise from the actual physical, verbal and imaginative situation in which actors find themselves together.*[13]

Though thoroughly post-modern in spirit, the Viewpoints are actually more true to Stanislavsky than the Method is.

Though theatre does not need the Method anymore, I do not mean to argue that no one should ever use it again—

---

13   Anne Bogart and Tina Landau, *The Viewpoints Book: A Practical Guide to Viewpoints and Composition* (New York: Theatre Communications Group, 2004).

we can't let Jared Leto ruin everything. But even well-meaning directors and teachers need to be aware of the ways it can normalize toxic behavior. The aspects of the Method that rely on instinct and emotional truth fail to account for subconscious bias, meaning that a director or teacher who uses it could easily end up validating feminine (e.g. seductive) behavior from women and masculine (e.g. aggressive) behavior from men as "truthful," even where other possibilities exist and even when they don't consciously intend to do that. Because the Method removes critical thinking from the equation, artists who use it are not likely to see and check their own problematic "instincts" to create gender-binary characters. Likewise, unchecked subconscious biases can lead directors and teachers to reinforce racial, ethnic, and every other kind of harmful stereotype as "truthful" simply because they are easily recognizable and passionately performed.

So, if you're a director or teacher, use the Method if you must but educate yourself about its toxic possibilities (Malague's book is a great start), learn how to help actors have genuine emotional experiences without breaking them down (go back to Stanislavsky), and be wary of your own tendencies to define "truthful" as gender normative (check yourself). Don't just teach alternative techniques (do try the Viewpoints), but actively expose the harmful aspects of the Method, dispelling the long-standing myth that suffering is the secret to good acting (it's not).

Finally, I hope survivors will keep speaking up about the harmful potential of these techniques, calling to account the people who continue to practice harassment, discrimination, and abuse under the name of the all-powerful Method. (Thank you.)

HOLLY L. DERR

Holly L. Derr (she/her) is the artistic director and head of graduate directing at the University of Memphis. She holds an MFA from Columbia University and a BA from UNC Chapel Hill and was the founding producer of SKT, Inc. She has directed for the Know Theatre, Ashland New Plays Festival, Oregon Shakespeare Festival School Visit Program, Saratoga Shakespeare Company, and the Stonington Opera House. Holly has taught at Smith College, the ART Institute at Harvard University, the Brown University/Trinity Repertory Company Consortium, CalArts, UC Riverside, and Chapman University. She has been published by the Atlantic, HowlRound, Ms. Magazine, Slate, and Bitch.

A MANIFESTO FOR STAGING GENDERED VIOLENCE

11 JULY 2019

SHARANYA

The performance and staging of gendered violence is a political issue, and not a recent one. Gendered violence can be understood as a spectrum of acts, ranging from physical, sexual, and emotional abuses against marginalized women, to acts that nullify and demean women's resistance to patriarchy.

Women's resistance takes on a variety of forms, such as anger, joy, care, self-preservation, and protest. Historically, all of these forms of gendered resistance have been tamed in their representations in theatre and performance: rather than being viewed as radical ways to claim agency over women's narratives, they have been seen in patriarchal terms as enacting violence *in turn*; as protesting too much. In Anne Carson's "The Glass Essay," she writes:

> *You remember too much,*
> *my mother said to me recently.*
>
> *Why hold onto all that? And I said,*
> *Where can I put it down?*[1]

The work of dominant dramaturgy has been to align the narratives of suffering women with a cis-hetero-patriarchal gaze. Performances that resist this gaze are those that actively make place for women's narratives—a space to *put it down*, à la Carson. Violence against women isn't exceptional and extraordinary; it is routine and banal. We need to challenge traditional dramaturgies that frame it as the former rather than the latter. But undertaking such a challenge involves a tremendous overhaul of the institutional practices that support, sustain, and monetize these traditional dramaturgies.

As a researcher and practitioner who spends a fair bit of time thinking about violence against women and the ways in which it enters this world, I have six thoughts on restaging gendered violence.

---

1   Anne Carson, "The Glass Essay," *Glass, Irony, and God* (New York: New Directions Publishing Corporation, 1995).

I. VIOLENCE AS SCRIPTING.

In her deeply significant book *Rape on the Contemporary Stage*, Lisa Fitzpatrick examines professor Sharon Marcus's idea that the representation of sexual violence, such as rape, has the power to be scripted and, also, the power to script—meaning that through the writing and staging of such acts, social and cultural notions of sexual violence are created. In other words, gendered violence isn't a single, unified idea or set of practices that are replicated constantly and in the same way across different productions. It is, in fact, a form of ideology that is lined in the choices we make. It is very much constructed, especially when it feels or looks accidental. Thinking about gendered violence as something we as performance-makers can actively script helps us identify how to change existing problems with traditional representations and stagings, issues such as the fetishization of women's bodies, sexualizing violence against women, "miming" acts of violence, and relying on old tropes to convey them—and thereby reinforce them!—instead of imagining new narratives.

Gendered violence isn't always specific acts of harm either: the tropes do as much ideological violence because they perpetrate misogynist stereotypes. Think about the sexualized adulteress, the promiscuous schoolgirl, the "mad" Black or Brown woman, the (white) manic pixie dream girl, the blonde who isn't as sharp. Think about the scream of horror, or the "ruined" woman, or the absence of consent in sexual acts. These representations exist across film and theatre, and they are actively scripted each time. If we change how pleasure and consent are represented, we change pleasure and consent cultures in the world around us.

2. DE-SPECTACLING VIOLENCE.

I am constantly dazed by the fact that enactments of gendered violence, especially in performance, are so spectacular. Not in a, "Wow did you see that?" way, but more in an, "Ugh was that really necessary?" kind of way. Violence against women may consist of explicit acts that feel like they're out of the ordinary, but that's not all it is, and it only appears to be so because we continue to lack a vocabulary and method to make such acts commonplace in dramaturgy. What if domestic violence wasn't the premise for a character development arc? What if casual sexism (that phrase—what on earth is "non-casual" sexism, and how does it matter if it's casual or not?!) wasn't the main joke? And so on. Gendered violence as it plays out in performance needs to take a step back: its potency in representation arrives from its integration with the everyday lives of women. It happens to us every day. The banality of gendered violence is rarely a spectacle. Such violence is tedious, institutional, and hoary—our lives are not contained by it.

Last year, I tried to think about what it means to "de-spectaclize" grief and loss in women's lives. I was the dramaturg for a fifteen-minute devised dance theatre piece by actor-dancer Namaha Mazoomdar titled "What is Fully Mature is Very Close to Rotting (after Clarice Lispector)." This was part of a longer performance titled *Kaal: Dancing with Time*, by Drutam Dance Ideas Lab in Mumbai, which explored time. Namaha wanted to showcase the rise and fall of a woman who grieves after she discovers the loss of a source of great joy.

We played with temporality and tried to devise different ways to mark the passage of time using speed, space, and repetition of movements. What proved to be a bigger challenge was showcasing the violence of loss without resorting to conventional signifiers like hysterics. What we did, instead, was make the loss part of her dramaturgical journey, after which she continues to grapple with grief. The costume consisted of nondescript colors and everyday clothing. Namaha played with the repetition of certain actions traditionally associated with despair, such as spinning by herself on stage, but by changing the tempo of these twirls and using the entirety of the space to execute them, she made the process of loss and the time taken to adjust to this loss more visible, rendering it less of an exceptional event. Grief is a turning point, a marker of a change, but it is not a spectacle.

3. REPRESENTATION IS MORE THAN LEGIBILITY.

"I have a voice! Sometimes that voice is high-pitched – a grotesque scream. It is illegible," writes Kate Zambreno in her chapbook *Apoplexia, Toxic Shock, and Toilet Bowl: Some Notes On Why I Write*.[2]

2   Kate Zambreno, *Apoplexia, Toxic Shock, and Toilet Bowl: Some Notes On Why I Write* (New York: Sarah McCarry, 2013).

"Mimicking" acts of violence against women in a performance context takes us back to the old conundrum of repeating conventional representations of violence. The first problem with relying on such conventions is that they have frequently evolved from appeasing patriarchal norms—acts of violence become sexy, titillating, metaphoric, and a source of voyeuristic pleasure. Secondly, realism or psychorealism as a style fudges the fact that violence against women is scripted (see point 1!) and therefore sets up irresponsible expectations for what such violence "looks like" outside the performance. Cue cries of "but that doesn't look like a violation!" Maybe violation doesn't look like that.

Representation of gendered violence is about more than just making it "legible" or "visible." It is also a matter of changing what this legibility looks like. In 2016, I watched Sarah Kane's *Cleansed*, directed by Katie Mitchell at the National Theatre—the first time any of Kane's plays had been staged there. Kane, known for her ability to write into the heart of gendered violence (where men and women are both victims of patriarchy), also wrote stage directions involving rats carrying away bodies and sunflowers bursting through the stage. In Mitchell's production, sunflowers did burst through the stage floor, but the rats were shot. The shooting of the rats is a small but overwhelming gesture towards the mindless violence that patriarchal practices entail.

4. REFUSAL IS NOT A BINARY CODE.

"History is full of people who just didn't," writes Anne Boyer in her essay "No," which was published in *A Handbook of Disappointed Fate*. "They said *no thank you*, turned away, ran away to the desert...lived in barrels, burned down their own houses...killed their rapists, pushed away dinner, meditated into the light."[3] The power of the feminist refusal is immense; it can shatter dynasties and turn a second act into a first.

Refusal isn't just saying no, though. Refusal can take a variety of forms: it can look like a back-and-forth, it can be a monologue, it can present itself as silence, and it can be enacted through an emphasis on ambiguity. Non-realism, again, can be very powerful here, allowing for the use of choruses, choreography, ensemble work, and intermedia.

The "confessions" and chorus work in Suzan Lori-Parks's *In the Blood* are powerful instances of feminist refusal. The play revolves around Hester, a Black American woman living in poverty with her five children, and her relationships with the key figures in her life: a reverend, a doctor, a social worker. These individuals all have monologues or confessions that indict them in their exploitation of Hester. The ultimate confession, though, comes from Hester, who has the last word on the life she's pushed back against, and on the society—the chorus—that has inflicted this life of violence on her.

---

3   Anne Boyer, "No," *A Handbook of Disappointed Fate* (New York: Ugly Duckling Presse, 2018).

5. WHO IS THE MONSTER?

Women have always been represented in cultural texts as monsters. We are terrifying in our demand to be treated with dignity, fairness, and care. Sometimes, we get real loud about this. Sometimes, even speaking softly is speaking too loud. Feminist theorist and teacher Sara Ahmed writes poignantly about how an Indigenous student made a complaint about white supremacy in the classroom, and in the student's refusal to let the problem of her complaint disappear became "an indigenous feminist monster," a brute force merely for calling out the brute force to which she was subjected.[4] Monstrosity comes in all forms and shapes: it can look like anger, refusal, resignation, silence, a chin up, a step back, a spotlight. It can look ambiguous, like uncertainty, a space for holding doubt against power.

Part of the work of reclaiming the mode of monstrosity, or defamiliarizing the monstrous, involves legitimizing the right kind of ambiguity—hesitations that resist patriarchal violence; that punch up, not down, and hold powerful individuals accountable, rather than those they marginalize. I call this "ambiguity" partly because resistance does not look like a yes/no question, and partly to highlight the fact that characters who grapple with power do not exist outside of it. The most interesting and potent performance work excavates these relationships, where the origins of violence are less meaningful than the ways in which they manifest.

4   feministkilljoys, "Refusal, Resignation and Complaint," *feministkilljoys* (blog), 28 June 2018, https://feministkilljoys.com/2018/06/28/refusal-resignation-and-complaint.

Adrienne Kennedy's remarkable one-act play *A Lesson in Dead Language*—described succinctly by Hilton Als as occurring "in a classroom, where the students' menstrual blood stains the backs of their white dresses and the Latin teacher is a white dog"[5]—deals with, in Kennedy's own words, "the fear of growing up,"[6] and is a complicated unpacking of how young women's bodies, Blackness, gender, and white supremacy manifest in nightmarish and surreal ways in everyday spaces such as the classroom. What is effectively highlighted by Kennedy is the patriarchal view of menstruation as possessing monstrous proportions, especially in the context of young Black women.

6. YOU ARE NOT FRAGILE, THE INSTITUTION IS.

I mean, you *are* fragile. So am I. It's important to hang on to that, especially in the face of a daily existence that hinges entirely on making it through another day of patriarchal violence of varying proportions and degrees. Without using fragility as an excuse for another's oppression, we should be allowed to crumble and fall.

And so should institutions. This is perhaps the most difficult and yet the most insidious aspect of performance-making to examine and discuss. Cultural and educational institutions that support performance-making—such as

5   Hilton Als, "Adrienne Kennedy's Startling Body of Work," *New Yorker*, 5 February 2018, https://www.newyorker.com/magazine/2018/02/12/adrienne-kennedys-startling-body-of-work.

6   Jennifer Dunning, "Adrienne Kennedy Decides That the Classroom's the Thing," *New York Times*, 28 December 1977, https://www.nytimes.com/1977/12/29/archives/adrienne-kennedy-decides-that-the-classrooms-the-thing.html.

theatres, performance groups, funding bodies, university structures, awards organizations—are complicit in the conversation and cultural production of gendered violence. Not only do they support work that frames and scripts narratives about gendered violence, they are also involved in propping up such structures themselves, such as through hiring practices, how women are represented in marketing and advertising, in the designing of the architecture of the space, as well as in safety and inclusion practices for marginalized people.

These actions take forms that frequently suit the institutions' own ends; events about diversity and sexual violence frequently become one more way to rake in the cash with no real systemic or structural change in sight— you know, the kind that would actually halt the profit-making machines of these institutions. When we put our work in the hands of institutions, we are giving them our trust. When they break it to support and sustain a capitalist enterprise that is only concerned with anti-racism and anti-patriarchy in the shallowest of terms, surely there must be consequences?

THERE ARE NO STRAIGHTFORWARD ANSWERS

Even though there are no easy answers about how to stage gendered violence without falling into racist patriarchal traps of representation, it is important to be aware of the challenges of such staging and writing. I wrote these thoughts partly as a manifesto, and as a call to action, but also as a tool kit for challenging patriarchal narratives in performance—whether they take form in a rehearsal space, in a brainstorming session, or at a writing table. The next time you feel the waves of patriarchy swelling up in a cultural conversation about gendered violence and performance, I hope you find these of some aid in stemming the tides.

SHARANYA

Sharanya (she/her) is lecturer in theatre at Brunel University London. Her work has previously appeared in Theatre Research International, Performance Research, *and elsewhere. She is part of the editorial team of* Contemporary Theatre Review's *online platform* Interventions. *In 2021, she was a fellow at the Mellon School of Theater and Performance Research at Harvard University.*

WE HAVE SUFFERED ENOUGH: THE COST OF PERFORMING TRAUMA FOR WOMEN OF COLOR

12 SEPTEMBER 2019
MELISA PEREYRA

Since the beginning of my career in the American regional theatre, I have been embodying roles from what the West considers "classical" plays. Beloved female characters have, through my body, been verbally, mentally, and sexually abused; mutilated, murdered, and exiled. I can count on one hand the times my characters weren't harmed.

I have suffered enough.

I'm an Argentinian immigrant from Villa Caraza, Buenos Aires. I watched my father look for work in a town where there was none to be found until the day he died. I watched my mother clean houses for a living while she battled cancer. By the time I was eleven, I was an orphan. Eventually, not knowing how to speak English, my older brother brought me to the United States, where I lived with a foster family in Idaho.

The same body that lived through all that later began a career in the American regional theatre. Today, when asked why I am a storyteller, I often say it is because it gives my sorrows and my joys a greater purpose. But throughout the years I have noticed that, more often than not, I am sharing my sorrows and not enough of my joys.

TRAUMA IN PERFORMANCE

Men are quick to be praised for their work in theatre, called geniuses when they stage a scene I could have done with my eyes closed, told they were so moving when all they had to do was stand there and wield their power over everyone else. We, women of color, are praised when we suffer. White spectators from all over the country told me they loved me as Lavinia, and Claire in *The Maids*, and Lady Macbeth— particularly in the "mad scene," they were quick to say. What is that about? Why do women of color gain space in someone's consciousness only when we show them the depth of our suffering?

When I worked on *The Maids* a few years ago, a play by the French writer Jean Genet, the goal of the production was to show what life might be like for immigrants in the United States. To that aim, the maids were cast as Latinx and a white person was cast as Madame. Performing in that play was one of the hardest things I have ever done.

My scene partner and I hurled our hearts all over the stage every night for anyone who would listen. We beat each other and yelled at each other and hated each other for the sake of the story. After a while, I began to ask, "What's in it for me? What do I gain by exposing my heart on the stage, drawing from a well of trauma audiences might never understand?" As an artist, I should love getting to play big roles like this and show off my acting chops. But when you're an immigrant in this country and you are playing a maid in a play called *The Maids* to a majority white audience... the cost is personal. And hard to shake off.

HOLDING OUR TRAUMA UP TO NATURE

I want to protest the state of American theatre. Not in general, but for women. And not just for women, but for women of color. I am doubly traumatized by both embodying and seeing violence—physical and mental—inflicted on the bodies of women of color for the sake of storytelling. We carry the weight of grief on our shoulders so often that it is difficult to navigate when and where it is okay to allow ourselves to feel something else, to tell a different story—one in which we use our bodies to express the joy that makes us warriors and survivors.

The bodies of women of color are used to convey violent stories. On stage, we are expected to be invincible but not aggressive, vulnerable but not passive, Brown but not too Brown. To complicate things further, if we are stepping into a role that was written for a white woman, the challenge to accomplish those tasks becomes even more difficult. My proximity to whiteness does not make me part of that world.

For example, embodying a maid intended to be played by a white woman in a play written by a dead white man will not help me shed light on any part of my story nor my community's. It is a dangerous practice on my body and one that should be the exception, not the rule. We cannot keep stepping into problematic stories that do not properly address issues of race, ethnicity, or gender without someone on the other side of the table who's aware of the possible effects these stories will have on our bodies.

If the work we do on stage holds the mirror up to nature, then when the lights go down and we leave the theatre, we walk back into a reality that is just as painful as our make-believe world. A reality that has only gotten more difficult since the election of Forty-Five. Taking into account the current divisiveness of this country, as people of color are being brought into predominantly white institutions with majority white audiences, who is to say that the stage is a safe space to even practice our art, let alone embody trauma that might refuse to leave our bodies long after the performances have passed?

I know I am not alone in experiencing the way our current political divisiveness shapes the work we do on stage. It affects our bodies in a different way than it used to. Last year, the prolific powerhouse playwright Quiara Alegría

Hudes gave a speech at the Association for Theatre in Higher Education conference in Boston, later published in *American Theatre* magazine, that gave me the courage to speak on the issue. Under the title, "High Tide of Heartbreak: Has theatre wounded me as much as or more than it's healed me?" she weighs in on whether the stress the job has had on her body is still worth the ride and discusses her desire to keep her characters, who are also women of color, from fetishizing their pain.

In attempting to highlight a different side of women of color she was met with resistance. More suffering, is that what audiences want? How do we help them and ourselves seek something more? Until we undo this attachment to pain, we will keep telling stories—both old and new—in the same way we've always told them. This process has manifested in my psyche as anxiety and in my body as constant tremors, joint and chest pains—things that have led me to seek the help of chiropractors and physical therapists.

SUFFERING IN THE EYE OF THE BEHOLDER

I just heard Kholoud Sawaf, a Syrian professional director and theatre artist who studied in Arkansas, describe the feedback she had received on one of the early drafts of her play *10,000 Balconies*, loosely based on Shakespeare's *Romeo and Juliet*. She was told she was misrepresenting Syria because she wanted to focus the play on a love story, leaving out stereotypes about Muslims and Arab culture. One critic accused her of "misrepresenting Syria by leaving out honor killings." Women of color attempting to broaden the scope of our narratives are being met with resistance. The plays that do get written are seldom produced, with only a few exceptions.

Recently I acted in *The Book of Will*, which was written by white female playwright Lauren Gunderson and centers around the making of Shakespeare's First Folio. For a play about two men, there was significant attention given to the often-unseen women behind the story. My character didn't experience trauma the way I was used to feeling it in my body; she wasn't supposed to be looking out for danger, she wasn't going to be hit at any point in the story. I didn't have to worry about protecting my body in any fear-driven way. My heart didn't sink into my chest. My shoulders felt relaxed. My jaw wasn't afraid to drop. There was nothing physically demanding about my role—it was really fun and free for me.

Reviews across the country said the play was not as great as it *could* have been. Some criticized the structure, others the language, but I began to wonder if what they were trying to identify, in a veiled way, was the lack of suffering inflicted on the women. In Gunderson's play, the lens is different. Women are living their lives until life leaves them, rather than struggling to survive.

Have we seen so many stories that inflict pain on the bodies of women that, without it, the narrative feels incomplete? Since *The Book of Will* is about putting a book together—a book of plays that have aided in both indulging our imaginations with beautiful poetry and also solidifying ideas of racism, classism, anti-Semitism, and misogyny—shouldn't it include some of that history in there too? This made me wonder: If it did, would I be okay with suffering in another Shakespeare story, and a new one at that? I had to check my frame of reference. After embodying the pain of so many other characters, was I now feeling incomplete, like some of these critics were, playing a woman who doesn't get traumatized?

BEYOND THE SUFFERING

As actors, our minds may know violence on stage is part of play, but our bodies don't. The reality of what we do is such that, if a scene requires my scene partner to put shackles on my wrists, forcefully kiss me, or sexually assault me, there is no way to communicate to my muscles that I am not in danger. And for women of color there is no way to communicate that to the transgenerational trauma that may be present in the body.

Telling traumatic stories over and over is the reason I am afraid to take a space in rehearsals. It is the reason I don't breathe deeply enough and my jaw clenches. It is the reason I am afraid to speak loud enough. My mind and body need space to create this trauma for the stage but I am still trying to identify what that looks like and how I can do it safely. It's more complicated and more dangerous, because this country is more complicated and more dangerous. Is there a place we can actually go to suffer a little less?

I want stories about women of color that highlight resilience in a non-violent way. I want more stories of triumph and fewer stories about the trauma of triumph. The American theatre has pitched their tent next to the school of thought that tells us women are only as talented as the traumas we are willing to bring to life on the stage.

I am more than my trauma, more than the tension in my hands, more than my broken heart, more than my oppression, more than my survivalist nature, more than my shortness of breath, more than my pain, more than my screams, more than my tears. But it is hard to convince my body otherwise if that's all I'm being asked to bring to the table.

MELISA PEREYRA

Melisa Pereyra (she/her) is an Argentinian actress, writer, theatre director, and educator. She has spent time at Boston University's College of Fine Arts as assistant professor of acting and is a core company actor at American Players Theatre in Spring Green, Wisconsin. She believes that the future of theatre will be changed by community building and organizations like HowlRound building bridges across cultures. In Melisa's own words, "Keep building and writing until the voices on the outskirts of our theatrical platforms are centered. And then, beyond. Let us overcome the tradition of silence and make the future in our dreams, our reality. ¡Juntos lo logramos! ¡Ponete las pilas!"

THE AMERICAN THEATRE WAS KILLING ME: HEALING FROM RACIALIZED TRAUMA IN AN ART WORKSPACE

18 NOVEMBER 2019

AMELIA PARENTEAU AND LAUREN E. TURNER

For those unfamiliar with the term "racialized trauma," counselor Ayanna Molina of True Love Movement explains: "Trauma is hurtful, emotionally damaging situations that you cannot control. [With my clients], the racialized component is that [they] happen specifically because you are Black." Racialized trauma happens because of the system of white supremacy we live in, which is detrimental, out of control, and disturbing socially, emotionally, behaviorally, and/or mentally.

White supremacy culture, says Molina, makes it is very difficult to isolate this kind of trauma, since racism exists in every part of the system.

Resmaa Menakem, another trauma-specialized counselor and author of My Grandmother's Hands, *concurs. "When I think about institutions and organizations, white-body supremacy is allowed to sustain itself through standard operating procedure," he says. "Institutional things are decontextualized over time." According to him, superficial equity, diversity, and inclusion work is insufficient and is not getting at the fact that every institution in the United States that exists has been built through the efforts of enslaved people, on ground gotten through genocide.*

As a microcosm of our nation, American theatre cannot evolve to truly embody the values of equity, diversity, and inclusion that artists and arts administrators are rushing to embrace without doing the long, hard work of confronting the ingrained systems of oppression embedded in the field. In the following conversation, theatremaker Lauren E. Turner recounts her courageous healing journey from the depths of sustained racialized trauma working in a New Orleans theatre to the launching of her own theatre company, No Dream Deferred, *into its first season this fall. Given the persistence of racialized trauma in white theatre institutions, we interrogate how—and if—people of color feel they have a place within them.*

Amelia Parenteau: Can you describe the role theatre has played in your life?

Lauren E. Turner: I am from Raleigh, North Carolina, and I was raised through the arts. I went to a performing arts high school, and I had very real role models in the arts. When I was a kid, my mother created a nonprofit organization for Black children to have access to Black professional artists, where I learned African dance from Chuck Davis, who ran African American Dance Ensemble, and was taught voice by Black opera singers who were my mom's friends. Beverly Botsford would teach African drumming.

I was taught creating space was my duty. The idea of what was out there and available for performers of color was accessible, and I knew there was power in being able to tell a different story in different ways.

Had I not had that experience, I would have just assumed theatre was strictly for white people. I was able to take what I knew to be true from a predominantly white high school, where I was the only person of color in advanced theatre courses, to a historically Black university theatre program, where what I knew to be true was met with affirmation, all the way to my graduate program, where I was the only African American woman and one of two students of color.

I was able to share the information I had with the Black undergraduate students who were hoping for it, and I've carried that with me. What guides me even now in my work is knowing there's another possibility than a white-dominated theatre field, and I'm really grateful for that, because I don't know how I'd be able to stay in this field if I didn't know that for sure.

Amelia: We've spoken a little bit about the mentality of being a trailblazer and holding the door open for others, and the generational differences in what it means to be a person of color working in the American theatre. Can you talk to me about how you perceive that?

Lauren: Although I was born in 1983, I don't consider myself a millennial, I consider myself a "xennial"—someone who's caught between two shifts in generational thinking, both that have merit. My mother is of the generation where people were literally kicking down doors for future generations, having been raised by people who kicked down doors, people who were putting their bodies on the line. I consider my mother's generation the "make good" generation. So you have my grandmother, who was on the line, and then you have her children, who had to make good on the work she started.

Then you have our generation, who were taught by the make-gooders to do the same thing, that our job is to get into these spaces we were denied entry to, and our job is to hold the door open. And then you have the generation I consider right below me, which has been reexamining the cost of that, because a lot of times what happens is that while you're holding that door open, you're being verbally abused, harmed, and traumatized in those spaces.

While the previous generation's motto was "Stay there, stay strong, and hold this door open," the millennial generation is asking, "Do I even want to be in this building? Do I even want access to this space that isn't for me?" It's revolutionized the way I think about myself moving forward. I've been letting go of the idea that it's my job to hold the door open, which has been really hard. But it's also opened up a lot of possibilities.

If my job isn't to hold the door open, and my job isn't to endure abuse from the institution so that someone else can come in and endure the same abuse, then what is my role? How do I lead from the outside? How do I create a space that is the opposite of that, where people can feel equally or even better than what is being presented to them in these other predominantly white institutions and organizations?

It's changed the way I think about so many things, but especially when it comes to caring for myself. When I was having a particularly hard time, my mother said, "You have to decide if you're willing to be a martyr." That never left me, because that is the decision that has to be made by so many people of color who are the first and the only: "Am I going to martyr myself?" I decided I didn't want to be that.

Amelia: How did you come to realize that?

Lauren: Three years ago, I was awarded a grant to join the staff of a theatre in New Orleans, working in community engagement. It happened at a time when the theatre—a predominantly white arts institution—was moving to a historically Black neighborhood. My arrival was a huge benefit to them. For the first year I was there, due to my salary being covered by the grant, I felt they were able to associate the work I was doing with being beneficial, but not having any worth. Because of that, the power dynamic was already way off—I'm still struggling with how that works, but since we live under capitalism, I believe if you don't allocate resources to something yourself then you don't feel like it has value.

I was so used to being the only person of color in theatre spaces that I didn't understand what being the "only" in New Orleans theatre implied. I had just accepted that this is a field where I may end up in rooms and be the only person of color, and that's just the way it is. Being in a city that's 60 percent Black, and that, before Hurricane Katrina, was 70 percent Black, a blind spot I was not examining was how and why this art space has remained monocultural, all white. How is that even possible? Had I stopped to ask myself what people have to do to maintain the whiteness of a space in a city like New Orleans, I would have been able to foresee a lot of problems in the future. I also would have been able to understand the value of who I am and how that impacts the work I'm doing, and what that would bring to the organization I was working for.

Another blind spot I had was around being tokenized. I didn't understand I was going to become the face of this community-engagement programming, and that I was the only one, as far as the Black community was concerned, who had something to lose. I was wagering my own personal relationships with folks in a way that no one else in the organization had to. If programming was a success or failure, it was being attributed to me personally. That added to some of my anxiety. This was my community, and if I screwed it up, I was basically ostracizing myself from it.

Throughout my two-plus years at the theatre, going from being a grant-funded person to an employee, I faced a tremendous amount of microaggressions. I realized some folks at the theatre didn't care about any of the things we'd been discussing at all. They were looking at Black people as props who could be manipulated and looking at my role as bringing Black people to the theatre. They were not expanding the vision around equity, diversity, and inclusion.

Here are a few examples of the microaggressions I experienced. Every time I would write something for new programming, there was this huge delay around putting it out because there were questions about the quality of my writing. I would be told that basically everyone at the company had to review and edit the piece before it could go out, because I did not have a firm understanding of the brand. It made me question my own ability.

The office was very small, so if I received an email and I didn't respond within ten minutes, someone would come ask me why. If I wasn't smiling, someone would ask me what was wrong. I had to respond to the microaggressions that were happening on a daily basis in real time. I didn't have any processing space, and I was on display every day, 24/7. One of the employees used to come up and rub my head and say I reminded them of a little kid. That would have to be processed in that moment. There were tons of times where I felt like people were looking to me to bring up the obvious, but I was also reprimanded for doing so.

The biggest thing that happened there, which kind of shook me to the core, was at a staff meeting after the Black community had some very public actors say they were not happy with the way things were going, because equity, diversity, and inclusion promises had been made when the theatre moved into the new space, but none of those promises were made good. We had a meeting where everyone asked me what we should do, and I said, "Well, we still have three full-time positions available, and we should really prioritize hiring a person from the neighborhood or a person of color, preferably both, but at least one." One person responded that what they heard me saying was that we had to fire all the white people, and another expressed that they felt like some people wouldn't be happy until a Black woman replaced them, and that that was never going to happen.

I remember thinking, *This is something they feel is okay to say in front of me at this point.* But the silence at that table from others spoke way louder than the horrible things that were actually said. That meeting shone a light on this pervasive, unjustified fear that something is going to be taken away from white institutional leadership if they let in "other" people and treat them humanely; look at what's happening on the border right now, it's the same fear.

After the meeting, people came up to me and were literally patting me on my back. I remember thinking, *You just sat there and watched this violence happen to me, and you said nothing.* I felt violated in that conversation.

Over time, these experiences created a work environment that cut at my worth and caused me shame. I had allowed myself to stay in a position where I was not only being treated harmfully, but where some of the actions the theatre was taking were harmful for my own community. I had to do a lot of work coming out of that to heal.

Amelia: That risk goes much further than your work at that institution, since New Orleans is your home. I recently read an interview with playwright Jeremy O. Harris, and the interviewer asked him about his experience of regional differences of racism, because he grew up in Virginia, went to school in Chicago, and was working in New York. Is that something that resonates with your own life experience?

Lauren: Racism is racism is racism. There's no "worse." It's bad any way it shows up. But every place has a different story. Even within the Deep South there are variations. There is something different about the way white folk and Black folk interact in New Orleans from the way white folk and Black folk interact in North Carolina. What you have going on in New Orleans is a long history of disenfranchisement of Black artists. You have a city that is basically built upon the creative and artistic genius of Black people. And very few of those Black people are as financially successful as the city itself—and white people—for owning that genius, for owning that art.

It bleeds into the way art institutions treat or interact with Black artists and Black folk. There is a sense of paternalism and propriety that reigns. The theatre I was working at was worried about what I was doing with other theatres, because they felt proprietary over me.

A lot of local Black artists did not understand how I got selected to work with this company, because they had been denied access there for so long. They didn't know I had chosen to work there. They thought the company chose to work with me. I had a lot of people tell me that art institutions here tend to not want to work with local Black folk, and it was because I was from somewhere else. I think that's very specific to this place and the history of enslavement here.

For many decades, New Orleans was a place where there were more enslaved Black folk and free people of color than white people, and the fear held by white people throughout history has been that Black people could rise up and revolt and take over, so laws and policies were put in place to keep that from happening. Even to this day there are things that happen with that fear at its core, because there are still more Black people in New Orleans than white people.

Amelia: As we all get better at seeing the structures and patterns of racism and white supremacy, it's useful to be able to get specific and recognize local history and context. How do you think the theatre where you worked got to be so stuck in these ways?

Lauren: This particular organization is no different than any other regional theatre in the country, since I believe regional theatres were created in part as a result of white flight. White folk were fleeing cities and urban areas for suburban areas, and they wanted to maintain the cultural practices they had enjoyed in the cities, so they created regional theatres. These spaces were never built with inclusion, equity, or diversity in mind. This is reductive, but they were places where white people could be with other white folk and enjoy art.

With that as the foundation, if you don't actively work towards dismantling all of it, you're just going deeper and deeper and deeper—you've built an audience, you've built a board, you're just continuing the legacy. The more time passes, the harder and harder it gets to undo it. But I think it comes from being too scared to do something drastically different. If you don't have enough creativity to envision what a theatre could be, then this is what happens. In a city like New Orleans, I don't see how any theatre can afford not to be thinking about changing completely.

It also becomes a system of cheating, because right now funders are interested in community impact. So it's like, "How can we pretend what we're doing is community work so we can continue to get the funding that we so desperately need because we don't have ticket sales at all, because our audience is getting smaller by the minute, so we're dependent on this grant?" There's so much energy being put towards trying to pretend and saying the right words. "What Black person can we hire to put in a position to write a narrative for this so we can get this money?" All that energy could be put into actually doing the work.

Amelia: Can you talk to me about not having a generous leadership model as part of the systemic problem?

Lauren: This connects to scarcity, holding onto the old ways of doing things, where a single artistic vision leads us forward. No leader will survive this way. It's impossible because each success but also each failure is attributed to that person. It's harmful to the person in charge.

Shared leadership is something I'm currently exploring, and also sharing leadership with the community you're in. The idea that community members might be able to assist with programming—that statement alone is enough to send some artistic directors into cardiac arrest, because they feel like they're losing something. But if you are not programming with community in mind, what are you doing?

One of the characteristics of white supremacy is that there's only one right way to do things. The idea that one person is right and holds all the artistic vision for the entire company is also how you get to the point where you're creating an oppressive work environment and a work culture that can be traumatic.

Amelia: Let's talk about healing. After you decided to leave the theatre, what were your first steps coming out of that experience in identifying it as trauma, seeking safety, and seeking healing? How did that look, or how does it continue to look?

Lauren: I spent a lot of time confused as to what had happened to me. Throughout my time there I had multiple breakdowns, where I would just be depressed, sobbing, and not really understanding why. At the end, I had a final massive sob, and I had this enormous sense of grief. I didn't know what had happened to me. I knew that racist incidents had taken place, I knew I was dealing with microaggressions, but I didn't recognize what I had been through as a trauma event.

I thought that was something completely different. I didn't know there was something called racialized trauma that has an effect on your body, something you have to heal from. I spent a lot of time in the beginning very angry and sad, and also trying to figure out what to do about it. I wanted to immediately take action. It wasn't until a great friend of mine told me that what I had experienced was equivalent to being in an abusive relationship—emotionally, psychologically—that I gained perspective on what had happened to me. Then I was able to put a plan together to move forward.

The first thing I had to do was name racialized trauma as the thing I had endured and accept the fact that it would be a healing process to get whole again. In order to do that, I had to let go of all the shame attached to it, the thinking that I could have done anything differently. Then I had to seek counseling. There aren't that many people who specialize in racialized trauma in the workplace, though it is a growing field.

One of the most important things was that I had a tremendous network. Not only locally did I have friends who cared and who were there to support me, but also nationally. I had just been part of the New Orleans cohort for artEquity, one of the most powerful, supportive networks I could possibly be a part of. For a person who's been in an abusive relationship, there's nothing more comforting than being able to talk about what you went through without also having to prove you went through it at the same time.

Speaking to people without having to explain or prove or convince is a tremendous blessing. It's re-traumatizing when what you're saying is questioned.

Amelia: Tell me about No Dream Deferred. How is that helping your healing process?

Lauren: No Dream Deferred is something I have been working on since 2016, but it is just now launching its first season. No Dream Deferred is anchored in creating theatre for this space—we're not going to New York and seeing a bunch of shows and saying, "Let's bring all these plays and same experiences back to New Orleans." We're saying, "What stories exist? What stories have yet to be written that are relevant to this place?" And we're creating theatre experiences that make sense for the people who live here.

We are equitable in our envisioning and implementation of all of our programming, and I can honestly say I consider myself as having a doctorate in what not to do. I have insight, having experienced it myself, to build something that needs to be different. India Mack, who's my producing partner, and I are creating the space New Orleans deserves: a place of healing for people who have had traumatic experiences in other spaces.

I'm reminded of a quote a friend of mine shared about trees: "This tree is deep and has many roots, and the best you can do is enjoy the shade in the summertime, and admire the leaves as they change, but you better have your own tree planted somewhere." No Dream Deferred was my own tree. I look at predominantly white institutions as those trees with deep roots. It's going to be hard—damn near impossible—to change them from within. To me, the shade is the funding, and I'm not going to harbor animosity for people who choose to enjoy the shade. Predominantly white institutions are still able to maintain the majority of the funding for the arts that exists in this country. There's shade there, there's funding there, people can get paid and create lives for themselves. The leaves may change, leadership may look different. There may be times where we have more leaders of color in the positions that matter. But that doesn't change the roots, the foundation. Having my own tree planted somewhere has been a saving grace because I've been able to divert all of the anxious, depressed energy from what I went through into building something better.

If I didn't have anything to look forward to, I would be like so many people of color who endure racialized trauma in art organizations where they just leave the field. And if we don't get to the root of this and fix it, we're going to lose people, those who are our best resources. We don't have a lot of money, we don't have a big audience, but we do have some really gifted and talented people, and if they're deciding they can't be in this field because our workspaces are toxic and harmful, we might as well go ahead and close up shop.

It's easy to see how racialized trauma and microaggressions affect a company's bottom line: people call out more, people are physically getting sick. Black women are dying from high blood pressure and heart disease based on the racialized trauma they're enduring at work. Even corporate America has been able to say, "We've got to invest in workspaces that do not have these elements." When is it going to be our turn to take a good hard look at this within our institutions and organizations?

Amelia: In a forward-looking sense, what feels like justice? What's the happiest resolution to this trauma in your life, and also in the bigger context of this institution existing in New Orleans?

Lauren: As far as for the trauma in my life, justice feels like complete healing, and the completion of building something that's on its way to being the opposite of what I experienced.

It's important that people know that institutions like the one I was at exist—they're the majority of arts institutions in the country. The answer that's in my heart is that they have to be dismantled. I know it sounds very revolutionary, very impossible, but that's really what has to happen in the end. The foundations on which these institutions are built do not suit us anymore. These organizations do not serve us anymore. America is a place where we know how to redefine and reinvent ourselves probably better than any other place. Why are we holding onto a model that's no longer serving the people who live here?

I'm going to the National Performance Network Conference soon, where I will be giving a talk about art institutions as monuments. Monuments are special because they are physical representations of what we value, what we hold dear. These institutions, similar to the Confederate monuments, need to come down because they are no longer reflective of what we value. There are tons of people talking about dismantling and what it looks like. The next conversation is, "What do we put in its place?" That's the more interesting conversation to me. Once we dismantle something, we have to take it apart to diagnose it and then we can build something better.

Amelia: Is there anything we haven't talked about today that you want to make sure gets into this conversation?

Lauren: I want to make sure people understand that pay inequity goes hand in hand with racialized trauma in the workplace. There's a lot of pressure on me to talk about them as separate things, but they're interconnected. People also need to understand that racialized trauma in the workplace doesn't just affect people of color, it affects the entire health of that workplace. It's not good for anyone to be experiencing racialized trauma.

And people are leaving. This isn't a future prediction—I can name ten people right now who have left theatre for good. Specialized people, people who have their master's degrees from top-notch institutions, who have left, citing racialized trauma in the workplace. It is very real.

Amelia: Can you talk about what your career looks like and what your relationship to institutions is, as well as the self-reflection you've accomplished and how scary it might be for other people, but how worthwhile as well?

Lauren: Coming out of all of this, I had to ask myself if I'm suited to work within these institutions, and the answer was no. It's harmful to me. I can't imagine, in thirty years, what shred of myself would be left. I don't think I would recognize myself if I stayed in a predominantly white institution for my whole career. So I had to say, "How am I building my career if it's not going to be measured by the same success metrics that currently exist?"

That's really hard for folks. There aren't other models to look at. People need to be honest with themselves about their capacity to do this work outside of what's been established as generally successful and reexamine what success might look like. I'm trying to figure out how to lead from the outside. Some people are suited to work within these organizations, but people have to ask themselves if that's for them.

Amelia: Absolutely. I love that terminology, "leading from the outside," because it's exactly what you're doing, while recognizing there are different positions. We all have a role to serve, and people have to listen to themselves and figure out what theirs is going to be. Thank you, Lauren.

AMELIA PARENTEAU AND LAUREN E. TURNER

Amelia Parenteau (she/her) is a writer, French-English translator, and theatremaker with a passion for social justice, based in New Orleans. An alumna of Sarah Lawrence College, she has worked with 600 HIGHWAYMEN, Ping Chong and Company, the Civilians, the French Institute Alliance Française (FIAF), the Lark, the New York International Fringe Festival, the Park Avenue Armory, and Theatre Communications Group in New York City, as well as Trinity Repertory Company in Providence, Rhode Island; People's Light in Malvern, Pennsylvania; the Eugene O'Neill Theater Center in Waterford, Connecticut, the Théâtre du Soleil in Paris, France, and Intramural Theater and No Dream Deferred in New Orleans, Louisiana. Her writing and translations have been published in numerous outlets including American Theatre *magazine,* Asymptote, Contemporary Theatre Review, *and HowlRound. amelia-parenteau.com.*

Lauren E. Turner (she/her) is a director/performer/producer and community facilitator. Lauren is the founding producing artistic director of No Dream Deferred NOLA, a community-anchored multimedia theatre production company that is dedicated to the development of new works originating in the South. She is driven by her interest in equitable, place-based, culturally relevant theatre especially as it pertains to the Global South, and her work lives where storytelling, community building, and politics intersect. Lauren received her MFA in performance from the University of Southern Mississippi and her BA from North Carolina Central University. Lauren lives joyfully in New Orleans with her partner Jason and their three children, Austyn, Elijah, and Nia.

PARENTS OF COLOR AND THE NEED FOR ANTI-RACIST THEATRE PRACTICES

03 DECEMBER 2019

NICOLE BREWER

I'm at a theatre conference, and I hear the children before I see them. Bubbly giggles erupt from their bodies as they take flight, running for the pure joy of the experience. For a moment I'm lost in thought as I measure the emotional cost of me being here—which is time away from my own children—and what it would mean for them to accompany me into these highly problematic, racist spaces. Confident I made the right decision to leave them at home, I return to the reality of the conference.

In another instance, I'm part of a convening planning committee for an organization that lives the justice it teaches others to fight for. During the planning process, we learn there will be two infants present. My reaction was: "We're child friendly, the more the merrier!" But that thought was the extent of my support around their presence. Though my intention was to be inclusive, I mistook the term "child friendly" as sufficient, which resulted in an exclusive gathering with no tangible plan for parental support and childcare, including having things like mats in the space and plush toys for the kids. Only when a parent spoke out during the gathering about the lack of support did any of us organizers realize our misstep. As a parent myself, I was dismayed I had upheld the narrative "parenthood is an independent issue for parents to overcome," especially because my lived experience has been shaped by systemic inequities.

PARENTHOOD AND RACE

Dr. Robin DiAngelo, author of *White Fragility*, says, "You cannot talk about any other issue without talking about how race informs that issue."[1] When we don't view systematic inequity through the lens of race and racism, our anti-oppression practice remains rooted in oppressive values and inactive language.

The term "child friendly," as I understand it, is an abstract noun, which is something that exists in thought without

1   "Debunking The Most Common Myths White People Tell About Race | Think | NBC News," NBC News, 25 September 2018, video, 3:47, https://www.youtube.com/watch?v=wjHg65JORi8.

being concrete and, in many instances, operates to protect white supremacy culture through generality and vague, unofficial policy. Due to the indeterminate nature of the conference's family-friendly policy, I had intuited the space as inhospitable for my children to attend, which was further fortified by seeing only white children present.

For the convening I helped plan, "child friendly" functioned as a demonstrative expression lacking application, which resulted in my failure to advocate for parent support. My personal lack of interrogation of the term is in part due to how normalized my experience of not being supported is, paired with the toxic "exceptional Black womxn" myth that reinforces that I should be able to carry the weight of everyone's needs before attending to my own.

Certainly if the issue of parent support was reconstructed as an issue of race and racism, my response would have been activated to right the imbalance of superficial resources enacted to support parents of color in the arts.

GOING BIG TO GO SMALL

Looking first at issues that parents of color face can provide a more holistic and deeper understanding of the obstacles in front of them, which informs what resources they may need in order to feel supported. For example, my gender and race make me susceptible to lower pay; people like me earn roughly $0.74 for every dollar a white man earns. Womxn are more likely to be penalized for taking time off work to care for children or aging family members than men. Black womxn stagnate in their careers and are less likely than white women to make it to executive level positions; when they do, they are often put in charge of organizations that are in disrepair. Black womxn are also more likely to be watched over by their white counterparts, which leads to lower performance reviews.

Knowing that the roots of the theatre industrial complex are overwhelmingly capitalist, racist, patriarchal, and ableist—a sentinel of white feminism and staunch advocate of meritocracy—provides a wider framework for organizations to begin to effect the necessary long-lasting change that will have considerable impact for parent-artists. Enacting anti-racist policies and practices, which function to create equitable workplaces and events, changes the way we perceive the world and generates a ripple effect on the decisions we make. The task of uprooting oppression is for all of us to do and is more effective when we prioritize anti-racist and anti-oppressive ideology in our decision-making.

STEPS TO SUPPORTING PARENT-ARTISTS WITH AN ANTI-RACIST LENS

There is such a long history of mistrust between white people and Black, Indigenous, and people of color communities, which cannot be remedied by a generic "family friendly" invitation to a conference. It's difficult to repair trust when communication is not clear around whose experience and comfort is being prioritized.

In terms of parent-artist support, there needs to be an active acknowledgement and commitment through written policy about harm reduction, harm prevention, and relationship repair. These tenets provide the foundation of transparency, accountability, and admission, acknowledging both how American society utilizes policies to destabilize families of color and what is being done to counter those policies.

Here are some ways organizers and organizations can work to recognize, address, and counter bias and racism to standardize equitable support systems for parent-artists of color:

- Make sure the historically invisible communities have a say and a stake in the resources provided for parents and caregivers.

- Implement institutional-wide policy. The problem with case-by-case parent support is that it allows bias to influence language used to describe working parents, which in turn determines an institution's willingness or reluctance to grant parent support. For instance, bias in language ascribes negative or positive words to different parents for doing the same action, e.g. a white mother who brings her infant to work is "hardworking" and a mother of color who brings her school-age child to work is "unprofessional"; a father who brings his children to work is "a good dad" but a mother who does the same is "a mess." Rachel Spencer Hewitt, founder of the Parent Artist Advocacy League (PAAL), shares, "Without intentional parent support and protocol, implicit bias will always dictate the words we choose to describe contributors who are caregivers."

- Develop a written public anti-racist ethos outlining your commitment to anti-racist and anti-oppression parent-support work. Be honest about your institution's past and present bias, prejudice, and racist behavior toward parents, and create pathways of accountability that ensure those oppressive values don't resurface.

- Sustain child-positive practices rather than child- or family-friendly practices. "Child positive" is a term I use to refer to the purposeful inclusion of children in any space by accounting for their needs, abilities, and limitations. All of these factors impact how children, parents, and non-parental people function in a space and determine whether or not the needs of all participants are being met, valued, and centered. "Child friendly," on the other hand, is akin to tolerating the presence of children with minimal attention given to how they impact others and the space.

- Invest in anti-bias training that provides people with resources to address and mitigate microaggressions to children from adults and from children to children.

- Apply principles of restorative justice to how you integrate parent-support policies.

Recently, both my children and I were invited to the national PAAL Summit—me to present on anti-racist principles and my children to engage with other children of parent-artists via provided childcare. The invitation to do my heart's works without leaving behind my heartbeats was a rare moment and one worth fighting to have again. It is now on us to decide where we are going from here, letting go of all that is unnecessary to cultivate embodied liberation for everyone. It is my hope us artists will be guided by, as theatre artist Douglas Turner Ward puts it, the desire to construct anew "not out of negative need, but positive potential,"[2] leaving for the next generation a more transformed and just society for all.

NICOLE BREWER

Nicole Brewer (she/her) is an actor, director, and educator who was compelled to speak out against the harmful and unnecessary practice of cultural erasure in the theatre industrial complex. She has shared her approach on anti-racist theatre at various panels and has presented at Theatre Communications Group conferences; National Black Theatre Festival; and Goldsmiths, University of London in the United Kingdom. Nicole is currently faculty at the David Geffen School of Drama at Yale and is a 2021 recipient of a Kennedy Center American College Theater Festival medallion. Nicole's a proud member of the 2018 artEquity National Facilitator Training cohort. She resides with her two children on land stewarded by the Piscataway and Conoy colonially known as Washington, DC.

2   "Quote," *Douglas Turner Ward Quarterly* (blog), 14 March 2011, https://douglasturnerward.wordpress.com/2011/03/14/quote.

PANDEMIC THEATRE AESTHETIC

07 APRIL 2020
JONATHAN MANDELL

It was sunny and eerie after I left my apartment building for the first time in more than a week and walked gingerly through the empty streets of my neighborhood, Greenwich Village, to the corner that brings forth vivid memories of two past crises—the AIDS epidemic and the terrorist attack of 9/11—and the aesthetics that each generated.

The corner was where St. Vincent's once stood, a hospital that had served the neighborhood for 161 years until it went bankrupt and shut down in 2010. It was razed and replaced with condominiums. That local officials didn't save the only hospital in the Village was a shortsighted inaction that's coming home to roost right now.

The hospital was at the epicenter of the AIDS crisis, the place that young men went to be treated, and to die, in the 1980s and 1990s. It is surely why the City of New York decided to construct the New York City AIDS Memorial Park in St. Vincent's Triangle right across Seventh Avenue from what used to be the hospital.

I walked to the memorial, where the only other people around were a group of men, each with Grubhub bags, waiting for the next delivery orders. Lining the sidewalk were the posters created in the heat of that epidemic: one with the slogan "Silence=Death" on a black background underneath a pink triangle and one of two dancers as a pair of green scissors cutting a red serpent that twists around them, beneath the words "Stop AIDS," designed by Keith Haring.

St. Vincent's was also one of the closest hospitals to the World Trade Center site. This is why on 9/11 its walls were taped with square pieces of paper, each a photocopied photograph of a missing loved one and a phone number in case they were found. When it became clear there would be no survivors to treat at St. Vincent's, the sheets of paper were turned into little memorials, from paper to cardboard to glazed tiles. A decade after the death of the hospital, some of those tiles still hang from that fence: a heart-shaped one with "Port Authority of NY & NJ" surrounded by the names of the employees who died; a square one with a drawing of an apple and the words "9/11. We Will Always Remember"; many with childlike renditions of the American flag.

Last year, a play about St. Vincent's, *Novenas for a Lost Hospital*, was presented at Rattlestick Playwrights Theater, which is about a block from the old hospital site—so close that at the end of the play cast member Kathleen Chalfant led the audience on a procession to the AIDS memorial, where we stood in a circle to show our respect.

Like every other theatre in New York, Rattlestick was ordered shut down in mid-March, to help curb the spread of COVID-19. On the Rattlestick stage at the time were previews for Ren Dara Santiago's professional playwriting debut, *The Siblings Play*, about an isolated and vulnerable family in Harlem. Rather than allow it to close before it opened, Rattlestick's artistic director Daniella Topol decided to do something she'd never done before: stream the show. They had been planning to record the 14 March performance anyway, so on 23 March, thanks to a new agreement by Actors Equity, they streamed that recording online for patrons who had purchased tickets to canceled performances, as well as to new viewers for $15 a ticket.

By the time Rattlestick began streaming, other theatre companies had rushed to do the same: New York City's HERE Arts Center's production of *Anywhere*, Chicago's Theater Wit's production of *Teenage Dick* (having recorded its one live performance in front of an audience), San Francisco's American Conservatory Theater's productions of *Gloria* and *Toni Stone* (both with "pay the price that works for you" models), New York City's En Garde Arts's production of *Fandango for Butterfly (and Coyote)*. These joined the long-established theatre-focused online streaming services such as BroadwayHD and OnTheBoards.TV.

But in that same week after the shutdown, something else was happening in theatre. Instead of just streaming prerecorded stage performances, theatre companies and theatre artists were livestreaming original shows created hastily and unfolding virtually. This was theatre created for the internet, without ever having been performed on stage.

It may be too grand—or at least premature—to proclaim a new theatre aesthetic for the 2020 pandemic. But just like the AIDS and 9/11 crises were accompanied by clear visual aesthetics, which came out of the need and urgency of those posters and missing notices, so too I sense a theatrical aesthetic emerging from the need and urgency that confronts us because of the pandemic.

On 13 March, the day after the Broadway theatres were all shuttered, playwrights Lily Houghton and Matt Minnicino and actress Ali Stoner created a new Instagram account, Theatre Without Theater, inviting theatre artists to perform excerpts of shows that had been canceled.

On 16 March, the day after all remaining New York City theatres were ordered closed, the well-known Broadway musician, writer, and radio host Seth Rudetsky and his husband, James Wesley, launched "Stars in the House" on the YouTube channel of the Actors Fund with guest Kelli O'Hara singing and answering questions from the hosts in her own home. The twice-daily livestream episodes (which remain available on YouTube) are a hybrid of variety show, talk show, Actors Fund fundraiser, and coronavirus public service announcement, with a doctor or two on call. At the beginning of April, they added a twice-weekly "Plays in the House," livestreaming readings of popular plays; the first one was Wendy Wasserstein's *The Heidi Chronicles*, performed by the original cast, albeit each in isolation.

On 17 March, the 24 Hour Plays—which, faithful to its name, has a twenty-five-year history of writing, rehearsing, and performing an original production from scratch in twenty-four hours—presented Viral Monologues on its Instagram account. The twenty monologues, each about four minutes long, were written by twenty noted playwrights and performed by twenty well-known actors; they were released one by one every fifteen minutes online, where they are still available. Exactly a week later, Viral Monologues Round 2 streamed another twenty-four original plays pairing a new set of playwrights and actors. And then, a week after that, Round 3. Whether or not the Viral Monologues continue, Methuen Drama reportedly plans to publish the scripts as a book.

I put together a post, "Where To Get Your Theater Fix Online, Old Favorites and New Experiments," initially on 19 March and found I had to update it almost immediately. The task of updating has turned from challenging to impossible, as has watching it all. New online theatre is announced every day, from the one-time resuscitated the Rosie O'Donnell Show to La Mama's weekly Downtown Variety livestreaming on HowlRound TV, from R&H Goes Live to National Theatre at Home, which offers its National Live recordings of its stage performances online for free.

Among new online theatrical platforms are Play-Perview, co-founded by theatre producers Jeremy Wein and Mirirai Sithole, which promises "unique, one-time-only, live-streamed theatrical events and original series," and TrickleUp, the brainchild of Taylor Mac, which is charging a subscription fee of $10 a month in hopes of raising money for artists in need. TrickleUp launched on 23 March with a group of downtown artistic directors and artists, as well as a raft of promotional partners. It promises "videos of solo performances, conversation, and other behind-the-scenes goodies." Its catalog so far features such fare as Mac reading scenes from *Gary*, Sarah Ruhl reading some of her poems, Mia Katigbak singing "La Vie en Rose," Dominique Morisseau doing a monologue from *Skeleton Crew*, Suzan-Lori Parks singing "Colored All My Life," and Lucas Hnath reading material cut from his play *A Doll's House, Part 2.*

There are even some experiences in immersive theatre for an age of self-distancing: Sinking Ship Creations has created three LARP (live-action role play) plays via telephone, *Adventures on Phone*. And This Is Not A Theatre Company has created *Life on Earth*, an adaptation for chatroom of Charles Mee's *Heaven on Earth*.

It would be tough to group all this activity as belonging to a single theatrical genre, but, for all the variety, I do detect an emerging aesthetic. It's low-tech, low-key, one-on-one, close-up. And, in keeping with the much-used hashtag #AloneTogether, there's copious use of split screens, notably in the many concerts of "virtual orchestras" and the Plays in the House performances—presenting individual people in isolation together on the screen artfully or (more often) inartfully. There is a sense of informality, like even the most accomplished professional is a do-it-yourself amateur, which is underscored by the comparatively low technical quality of the transmissions. Playwright David Lindsay-Abaire agreed. "It's advanced technology that's making all of this online theatre possible, and yet by and large what's being shared is mostly low-tech and homespun in a way that harkens back to the most primitive around-the-campfire storytelling," he told me. "You strip away fancy sets and costumes and giant chorus numbers and you're left with one person in their home telling you a story."[1]

Even the new scripted plays in Viral Monologues project a sense of casual intimacy. Many of those monologues are specifically about life during the pandemic. In "A Story of Survival" by David Lindsay-Abaire, Rachel Dratch portrays a character who discovers "a bottle of Purell on the bottom shelf, sad and lonely, just like I am right now," but notices that an older woman in the store has her eye on it too. So, to win the bottle, she engages in direct combat... by coughing. She tells this story so close to the camera that her face looks distorted, as if to emphasize how inexperienced her character is in talking to an audience.

Eric Bogosian's "Injustice," performed by Clark Gregg, creates a character in the entertainment industry, spot-on for its depiction of the narcissism and self-importance even during a worldwide crisis: "Now we have this craziness. We're lucky here. We have food, we're taken care of. I'm not complaining. But I'm complaining because this baby.... Look I know that others, those poor folks in wherever are suffering and obviously...that's terrible but this is my job.... We have to be ready to jump back in the saddle.... Yes, the world is going to hell in a handbasket but, my friend, without us, without what we do to convey the message of empathy, of what it's all about, then what's the point?"

What's most instructive, though, are the plays that have nothing to do with the pandemic. In "Grandma Taught Me

---

1   Jonathan Mandell, "Playwright David Lindsay-Abaire's Viral Monologues: 'Charting My Journey Through the Pandemic' and the Emerging Online Theaters," *DC Theatre Scene*, 2 April 2020, https://dctheatrescene.com/2020/04/02/playwright-david-lindsay-abaires-viral-mono-logues-charting-my-journey-through-the-pandemic-and-emerging-online-theaters.

How to Kiss," by Bekah Brunstetter, Ashley Fink portrays a character talking on a hands-free telephone to her grandmother in her car outside the home of her brand new boyfriend. "It's been a year since I kissed anybody," she tells her unseen grandmother. I briefly wondered whether she hadn't kissed anybody because she had self-quarantined, and if the play was taking place in the future. But there is no indication that this is the case. What this suggests is Instagram, and other online platforms, offer congenial showcases for original theatrical dramas and comedies.

One more aspect common to many of these shows, even the prerecorded plays, is that almost all have a live, in-real-time component to involve the audience. Instagram permits comments, of which the Viral Monologues audience took generous advantage. When BroadwayHD offered the 1988 *Oklahoma* with Hugh Jackman for free over the weekend, it was in partnership with the Rodgers & Hammerstein Organization, which offered (and solicited) in-real-time commentary on Twitter. The tickets to *Teenage Dick* and *The Siblings Play* included a live aftershow conversation, via GoToMeeting and Zoom respectively.

It's these conversations, oddly enough, that made me feel most as if I were attending live theatre: when an audience member at *Teenage Dick* observed that the video "brought back a little moment of normal" and that it had "that live feel like I could have been sitting there"; when an audience member at *The Siblings Play* observed: "There's such a sense of isolation in the play that I think can resonate differently right now," that we all more identify with "a household of people so stuck and spiraling." And then there was Theater Wit's artistic director Jeremy Wechsler sharing a prediction with us: "Playwrights will start writing Zoom/ GoToMeeting/Skype plays that can be acted remotely."

This is happening already, although perhaps not yet on those specific platforms. Will this emerging approach in an emergency have a lasting effect? Right before the shutdown, United Kingdom critic Lyn Gardner reminded readers of the plague in Shakespeare's times. "The closure of theatres in 1606 eventually ushered in a new era with the creation of the indoor playhouse. It is possible the Covid-19 virus may play a similar role in shaping the theatre of the future."[2]

Or, as the Segal Theatre Center's Frank Hentschker likes to quote Bertolt Brecht: "New times need new forms of theatre."

JONATHAN MANDELL

Jonathan Mandell (he/him) has written about the theatre as a critic and journalist for a range of publications, including Playbill, American Theatre *magazine, the* New York Times, Newsday, Backstage, *npr.com, and cnn.com. He currently blogs at New York Theater and tweets as @newyorktheater.*

2   Lyn Gardner, "Whatever Havoc Coronavirus Wreaks, History Tells Us Theatre Will Survive," *Stage UK*, 6 March 2020, https://www.thestage.co.uk/opinion/whatever-havoc-coronavi- rus-wreaks-history-tells-us-theatre-will-survive.

I AM THE DAMAGE WE HAVE DONE TO THE EARTH: INTERSECTIONS OF THE CLIMATE CRISIS AND DISABILITY

28 APRIL 2020

HANNA CORMICK

For some of us, the crisis isn't coming, it's here: air we can't breathe, water we can't drink, food and resource scarcity, sun that blisters our skin, pollution so thick that everything becomes a poison. I have been living inside a sealed room for five years, disabled by the environment that we have created through our actions.

I have a rare immune disease, but the systems of my
body are not wildly different from a regular person, just
accelerated, amplified. My cells, ravaged by the effects
of humanity's addiction to fossil fuels, have mutated,
and through the damage done to my body by the toxic
environment we have created around us, I feel the damage
we do to the planet. I may be in the vanguard for humans,
but I'm alongside a host of other early climate casualties
that don't usually have a voice: animal and insect species
going extinct, glaciers melting, coastlines disappearing, and
bushland aflame.

> *"I wasn't listening to the tremors that were running*
> *through my cells*
> *that were the same tremors running through the*
> *coral, the sea-bed, the roots*
> *that we are not on the Earth, but of it"*
>
> —The Mermaid

I'm especially susceptible to air pollution, though what
classifies as a pollutant is perhaps more broad than you
realize: if someone walks past me with a coffee, I'll have
a seizure because of the way the dairy particles pollute
the air; I can't open the window of the single room I live
in because if a neighbor has hung their laundry out, the
petrochemicals in the fragrance of their laundry powder
will trigger my mutated white blood cells to mount an
allergic response, causing respiratory distress. To need
an EpiPen because of the fossil fuels in someone else's
perfume or the odor of their takeaway meal is an observably
direct example of how our little—and what we assume to
be personal—actions affect those beyond us; your lunch
invades my cells, the planet is inside my veins.

My performance artwork uses my body as a metaphor for the damage we do to the earth. But it isn't really a metaphor. We are indivisible from the planet; the damage we do to it we are also doing to ourselves. Our environment shapes us, our function and identity, as surely as the organs inside our body and the thoughts in our head. The social model of disability interprets disability as the barriers that are created by the environmental and social structures we find ourselves within. This is in specific contrast to the outdated medical model of disability, which interprets disability as stemming from something being "wrong" with one's body.

RADICAL VISIBILITY

The Mermaid, my first performance artwork after a three-year art hiatus, debuted in 2018 at Art, Not Apart, a festival in Canberra, Australia, with later remounts at Ainslie + Gorman Arts Centres, for I-Day 2018, and Sydney Festival 2020. This work was my "coming out" as disabled; for years, I had been hiding my illnesses from my colleagues and friends with a subterfuge of vague excuses and radio silence, but with this work I claimed my new identity in a public act. I put my body at risk to speak out and be seen—a radical action against the shame born of internalized ableism and the cultural invisibility that facilitates us hurting each other and our planet.

The character of the mermaid is a symbol of the social model: in the water the mermaid moves freely, but on land she presents as disabled; it is the environment, not her body, that creates the barrier. *The Mermaid* asks us to consider what our shared resources are and how our pollution of those resources disables the people, creatures, and systems around us.

Placing my real mobility and medical aids—a wheelchair, oxygen tank, full-face respirator, saline IV drip, and body orthoses—against the image of a mermaid, I spoke of my experience of disability, illness, and climate in the same space as the public. This sharing of space, however, meant sharing the air, and it ran the risk of triggering serious allergic events, including anaphylaxis, seizures, dystonic storms, and episodes of paralysis, which could "interrupt" the work at any moment, any number of times. The audience found their places inside the ruins of the abandoned coal tunnels of the Coal Loader—an old coal processing station, now turned sustainability center, on Sydney Harbour's edge—but, if they were wearing fragrance or cosmetics, they were asked to move to an upstairs area or the rear of the space. Segregation, something routinely experienced by the disabled, affected their access and framed their experience.

This risk variable was built into the structure of the piece with a kind of dark and irreverent humor. For example, a mast cell seizure, which left my body thrashing about on the floor in a state of complete vulnerability and lack of agency, would result in very loud surf rock music playing as assistants held up cue cards and reiterated through a megaphone that I was having an allergic reaction, what it was potentially triggered by, and the audience's complicity in that event. These medical events happened ten times over the two years in which the work was performed; sometimes not at all, sometimes multiple times in one showing.

Why expose myself to this danger and put moments of such fragility and trauma on display?

Invisibility is the mechanism that allows us to continue to operate in a mode of "business as usual," safe from the threat of retribution or the crush of guilt; if someone, or something, isn't acknowledged, you don't need to acknowledge its rights or the suffering that your actions cause it. We also create a system that perpetuates that invisibility through the mechanism of stigma and shame. These are true for many forms of oppression and exploitation, not just victims of the climate crisis. And I knew that giving in to those internalized feelings of shame would only facilitate further oppression.

Invisibility doesn't make the problem go away; I am at the mercy of these systems whether I am in public or not. Shining a light on my own situation is also a means of shining a light on other people, species, and ecosystems, especially those that do not have the capacity to speak out or the privilege of a platform, as I do.

SICK PLANET

"On the ride back from the hospital, I saw the rocks peeking from the mountainside
and I felt like I looked at the ancient face of the country
And I said: 'help me, I'm sick'.
And it replied: 'me too'"

—The Mermaid

The Sydney Festival season of *The Mermaid* in 2020 coincided with the catastrophic bushfire emergency in Australia. Enormous swathes of land had been destroyed by mega blazes, fire tornados, and pyrocumulonimbus storms. The air was thick with a bright orange haze and the taste of ash. Suddenly, people were wearing respirators to go outside, like me. They had to seal the cracks where the air seeped into their houses, and they could smell smoke particles from an event miles away that blew into their bedroom. They started to realize how the air could hurt them. Their experience was catching up to mine, the earth was starting to wear her sickness visibly.

As I write this, COVID-19 is sweeping the globe, and other people's lives are again starting to mirror my own: a hyperawareness of the vectors of transmission between us, our safety at the mercy of how others use our shared spaces, and the loneliness of being excluded because of a hostile, contaminated environment. We are starting to understand that we are all participants in this global event, and we need to work collectively to prevent the contamination of the air in our lungs, the fluids on our skin, and the people around us.

CANARY IN THE COAL MINE

In contrast to the embodied practice of *The Mermaid*, my work *Canary*, a short-form piece commissioned by the Arctic Cycle for Climate Change Theatre Action 2019, highlights the absence of my body. I was interested in the way privilege can be leveraged in activism—particularly the sort of activism that puts one's body on the line. I drew inspiration from the way allies encircle and protect marginalized protestors at Black Lives Matter marches so that they would be arrested instead of their peers, or the way the often-denigrated white, middle classness of Extinction Rebellion protestors (or of outspoken protestor celebrities) affords a kind of safety. Protestors with privilege can go out there and champion their message, and if they are arrested it ends up as a slap on the wrists, whereas for other marginalized people, that same arrest for that same action could result in incarceration, unemployment, deportation, violence, or murder. It is the responsibility of those with privilege to use it to protect the planet.

As someone who is vulnerable to harm in situations that implicate my body—though predominantly through immunologic rather than carceral channels—I became intrigued by the use of a surrogate to participate in civil disobedience. Not as a replacement of one voice for another (always something to be wary of), but as a conduit for the marginalized voice to be present without risk. I wanted to see how this could be extended to my protest-art; if, as a performer, my body could be manifested through someone else.

Canary asks another body to stand in for my body, an activism by proxy in which my absence becomes the illustration, and, like *The Mermaid*, asks the audience to be aware of their complicity and their responsibility in making the space inaccessible for me and those like me. The text weaves my own medical story with that of a revenge-fantasy uprising of coal-mine canaries. A dark humor is again present in these tiny bolshie birds who strip themselves naked and propose to revolt against a world that used their suffering as an exploitable tool to assist fossil fuel extraction. It challenges us to reflect upon all the different "canaries in the coal mine"—those we have relegated to being our early warning signal, the climate casualties who pay for our safety and convenience with their lives—and how we might instead leverage the privilege of our own bodies to protect theirs.

"And they are almost forgotten
In the silence of their absence
Forgetting also
That their silence
Is the warning"

—Canary

Our minds are formed and reformed through the medium of culture—that is to say story, which means text but which also means image and movement and shared experience. My performances committed the subversive act of telling the stories that society is trying to hide, of showing things we try to avoid—our own fragility, our culpability as oppressors—for us to sit in the discomfort required to instigate change.

These artworks are not just stories but actions: the act of placing one's body in a state of precarity to illustrate a hidden reality, the act of transforming a moment of real private suffering into a public political message, the act of standing in or speaking for beings who cannot, the act of breathing air with an audience and making them aware of what is in that air, the act of creating a visible image for the invisible effects of our actions. The process of creating these artworks was also an action of revolt against the unsustainable systems that I, as an artist, was guilty of perpetuating.

THE SHOW MUST NOT GO ON

Just as healing the climate crisis requires not individual solutions but an overhaul of our current social and economic system, creating these artworks revealed to me that accessing these stories within my body would require entirely new modes of working. Becoming disabled forced me to become aware of not just how my body was a stage on which our damage to the planet played out, but how the "extractivist" mindsets of our culture underpinned my relationship with my body and my art. I used to treat my body as if it were a limitless resource for me to use to achieve my aims; I worked grueling hours and pushed myself until I collapsed, I believed I could mold my body into a machine in which any weakness was to be conquered through trying harder. While I preached the need for sustainability, social justice, and relationships between ourselves and our planet that prioritized communal and interdependent care, my most intimate of relationships, and perhaps therefore the most honest—with myself—was championing these capitalist, hyper-extractive ideals.

In the past, if a task was too large, a hurdle insurmountable, a deadline too close, I'd dig in and push through, and accomplish the "impossible." I was willing to burn up every part of myself in the service of my art—and quite specifically in service of producing proliferate results from increasingly scarce resources: time, sleep, food, headspace, energy. But this new awareness forced me to embrace attributes I would previously have derided—slowness, incapability, surrender—and to preference a sustainable relationship with my body over productivity; to treat my body as I would want to treat the earth, and to admit that, sometimes, the show must not go on.

Exhaustion, overwork, proliferative output, and stress are lauded in theatre; how many artists are in multiple projects at once, working multiple jobs to make ends meet, demanding impossible hours and physical/mental/emotional energy from their bodies without adequate physical, mental, or emotional nourishment? But when I became disabled, that "resource" of energy was suddenly precarious and finite, and I had to admit that I was not capable of doing everything alone—whether that meant getting in and out of my wheelchair, feeding myself, or making artwork. The web of connectivity that we exist within became tangible and necessary to my survival.

"I dug deeper and deeper into that dwindling reservoir of energy
With no thought for how or if it could replenish
I wanted to take my health back by force"

—The Mermaid

We fetishize strength and independence, and we label weakness and dependency as things to be conquered—but it is precisely this conquering narrative (how industrialist, how colonialist...) that prevents us from learning how to work in cooperation. We do not need to conquer and mold nature, and we do not need to conquer or "cure" our bodies. We need to work with them.

Interdependence is our resilience. Radical connectivity is our rebellion. An inclusive, sustainable design of our spaces and society needs to reject the anthropocentric attitudes of modern human culture—our societal structures should also cater to animals, plants, and complex ecosystems in recognition of how we are all connected as one planet.

And so, in this climate crisis life, my art and the way I made it have had to change. I still struggle. It will always be a struggle so long as I am within an industry that idolizes extractive behavior, in an environment that is built for a very particular type of species with a very particular type of body. But if our stories change, what we value changes— and then our practices can change too.

HANNA CORMICK

Hanna Cormick creates across fields of performance art, theatre, dance, curation, and crip activism with a creative ethos that prioritizes anti-extractivism, climate justice, and access rights. Hanna's current practice is a reclamation of body through radical visibility. Hanna has worked as a physical artist for twenty years, performing in Australia, Europe, and Asia, and is a graduate of Charles Sturt University (Australia) and École internationale de théâtre Jacques Lecoq (France).

WE DON'T WANT YOUR STATEMENTS, AMERICAN THEATRE

OR...

THE SOLIDARITY WE ACTUALLY NEEDED

II JUNE 2020

KELVIN DINKINS, JR. AND AL HEARTLEY

This past Memorial Day, an unarmed forty-six-year-old Black man was killed by a white police officer who restrained him by holding a knee to his neck for nine minutes.

This Black man's name was George Floyd. His name, along with the names of Breonna Taylor, Tony McDade, and Ahmaud Arbery, have been ceremoniously inscribed onto signs, petitions, and social media posts, and commemorated in demonstrations, over the past few weeks. The continued racialized killings of Black Americans at the hands of white men and police officers is one of the few things a pandemic could not stop.

The day after Memorial Day was just another day in the American theatre. But for Black activists and theatre practitioners, something shifted seismically.

By Friday, theatres across the country had begun frantically wordsmithing their best attempts to speak out about Black Lives Matter.

How many of the people who authored those statements actually visited the Black Lives Matter website before posting is unknown. What is known, however, is that the stirrings of support statements coming from the American theatre community was too late and certainly not enough.

On Saturday, 30 May, producer Marie Cisco, in a coordinated effort with her collaborators, launched a now-famed Google spreadsheet that names all of the theatre institutions that had not made a public statement about Black Lives Matter.[1] Marie, in a post on Facebook, stated: "When this is all over, we must remember who loves us ONLY when it profits them." The list includes some four hundred–plus theatre organizations, tracking when and where their statements were posted, and there is also a

---

1   Marie Cisco and Victor Vazquez, "Theatres Not Speaking Out," Google Sheets, accessed 14 January 2022, https://docs.google.com/spreadsheets/d/1vbTjlhaBY-MefEdh3N9sJqtT5ie-6zfHJ-90FOUhmTNs/edit#gid=0.

column that qualifies whether the statement was "business as usual"—which is to say lacking.

By the following Monday, a tidal wave of statements of "solidarity" had poured in from regional theatres, Broadway shows, and corporations highlighting anti-racism and support for Black Lives Matter. The irony is that many of the Black, Indigenous, and people of color (BIPOC) working for these theatres were not centered, or even included, in the drafting and release process. The folks spearheading these statements must have consulted similar playbooks—as evidenced from the seemingly hollow sentiments used to acknowledge the protests, police brutality, and, maybe, racism.

While both of us—Black theatre managers working in predominantly white American theatres—appreciated many of the sentiments and affirmations shared from these theatres, we were both somewhat bereft, struggling with one question that eluded us in this newfound solidarity: Where have you been?

The conversation regarding change in the American theatre—the work often labeled "equity, diversity, and inclusion" (EDI)—has happened not only for the last few years but for several decades in various iterations not couched in comfortable acronyms. The civil rights movement and the regional theatre movement are not too-distant cousins, yet the aspirations of Dr. King's table of brotherhood have almost exclusively been relegated to the stage—the programming of Black plays for Black—but predominantly white—audiences once a season, usually in February.

Executive leaders have been preoccupied with soliciting donors and foundations to pour money into training, EDI statements, reaffirming their values, coming up with EDI plans, and putting education programs in place to help train people of color to become leaders. Yet these same theatres have failed to commit to consistent training of their white board members and executive search firms, who are the designated gatekeepers in the pursuit of leadership.

In conjunction, there have been painstaking conversations about how to reform the system. Conversations, but not action. People of color have been shepherded into organizations, often as celebrated "diversity hires" in proximity to power to help make change. These same people of color arrive only to see their efforts fail, challenged, or co-opted by the institution to check a box. The problem that stems from diversity without equity or inclusion is a false expectation of lasting change without the system actually being challenged or reliable accountability measures being implemented. The box these statements failed to check: authenticity.

To the predominantly white theatres across the country, we ask you this:

Where was your statement when board nominating committees claimed they didn't have the time to attend a workshop on EDI or anti-racism?

Where was your statement when you had the opportunity to promote or hire a Black leader and chose not to because they were not afforded the same privileges of "experience" as other white candidates?

Where was your statement when countless BIPOC departed your theatres and the field because the constant presence of microaggressions and oppressive, white supremacist culture that was too toxic for them?

Your silence was deafening. Where were your statements when Black people truly needed them?

Now that theatres have finally decided to speak out, in a moment spurred by national and global crises, the resounding backlash and criticism has prompted the refrain: "Where are the receipts?" Of the many statements we consumed from theatres across the United States, so many neglected to put forward questions they were struggling with in their efforts to be anti-racist. If it had been us, instead of sprinting to draft a response, we would have pushed the leadership to consider how to use this time to frame an important question followed by an even more important and difficult discussion. We would have invited these theatres to consider what their Black staff members need right now. How is the individual theatre responsible? What has the leadership and staff done to shape and maintain an exclusionary culture in pursuit of what is supposed to be the public good? Did any of these theatres consider the Black staff they had to lay off and what they could say to those folks in this moment that could be truly authentic?

What is unconscionable is that some theatres wish to act only when there is staggering evidence of racism and oppression rather than believe the lived experiences of their Black artists, administrators, board members, and audiences.

If only our phones had been at the ready during the staff meetings and performance reviews where countless microaggressions and problematic behavior went unchecked. If only we had pressed record when wealthy board members, patrons, and donors approached us at predominantly white galas, mistaking us for catering staff or expressing shock at our actual titles. We remained silent not from a lack of courage but in the interest of self-preservation. The preservation of the Black community is a radical act in 2020, and we labor after it every day we enter predominantly white spaces and Zoom rooms as we complete our work. The people in power—mostly white, mostly male—have ignored our lived experiences and made a habit of underestimating our potential. We often hear people commiserate about why the system is so "broken" only to realize that it is not; the system works, but not for us.

Watching Black people die at the hands of white men and police is not the only incentive for theatres to act. The lives of Black people in these organizations, as well as artists and audiences alike, matter before they are put in jeopardy. Their lives matter every day they show up to the theatre and attempt to gracefully navigate the white supremacist culture the organizations have maintained for so long.

As two Black men working tirelessly in this field to survive and advocate for folks who look like us, the statements made by theatres across the country are inadequate and fail to implicate individuals in the organization who have maintained a silent stance on Black Lives Matter. Despite the urgency these theatres felt to release a statement before their name got called out on Marie's list, we were not waiting on statements. We were—and still are—waiting on proof. We are waiting for acknowledgment to the harm done and an explanation from each theatre about how they plan to disrupt white supremacy culture in perpetuity. We are thankful, however, that theatres posted statements in this moment because it proved several things for which each theatre made excuses for in the past.

Theatres can take a stance on social issues. It does not take years and costly consultants to put together an institutional statement in favor of equity, diversity, and inclusion. Theatres have finally put in writing their attempts to make a commitment to all Black people. We now have something to point to when the institution is called on to do better.

For the theatres that were bold enough to claim their organization is committed to dismantling white supremacy culture and systems, we would like to speak directly to you: there is a glaring difference between addressing white supremacy culture and proactively dismantling it. Dismantling white supremacy culture means decentering power, yielding power, and, in most circumstances, having the fortitude to step aside. Please do not claim to undertake this radical endeavor if you are unwilling to sacrifice your positional power and other financial resources in the process. Some of you are not committed to ending white supremacy in the theatre but, rather, are finally choosing to admit publicly that it exists.

If theatres want to earn the trust and attention of us and our BIPOC colleagues, they will need to do more than make a statement. They will need to change. They will need to act. But first, they will need to listen.

These statements are only the beginning, and theatres will need to unlearn practices of white fragility and defensiveness that often follow BIPOC staff speaking their truth. These practices must be modeled at all levels of the theatre and in its relationships with its stakeholders. As two young Black theatre managers, we carry our advocacy into every meeting and facet of our administrative practices, which lasts well beyond the final curtain of the Black play that, for two hours, invites you, our non-BIPOC colleagues, to consider our humanity.

We are not interested in performative allyship. We will be here after the activism for Black Lives Matter is no longer in vogue. We invite all theatres to audit their relationships with Black people at their organization and to discern what it means to stand in solidarity with them. Do not ask us to sign off on empty promises and perform the additional emotional labor that is not addressed in our performance reviews. We have enough to worry about trying to survive another day in America.

KELVIN DINKINS, JR. AND AL HEARTLEY

 *Kelvin Dinkins, Jr. (he/him) is assistant dean and assistant professor adjunct in theatre management at David Geffen School of Drama at Yale and general manager of Yale Repertory Theatre. Kelvin developed his passion for theatre leadership while an undergraduate at Princeton University. Kelvin earned his MFA in theatre management and producing from Columbia University's School of the Arts and worked as a general manager at Intiman Theatre and Two River Theater. Kelvin is on the board of trustees for the League of Resident Theatres (LORT) and Theatre Communications Group; he is also co-chair of the LORT Equity, Diversity, and Inclusion Committee..*

 *Al Heartley (he/him) is a principal at ALJP Consulting, a search and strategic-planning firm working with arts organizations across the country. He co-founded the firm out of a call to bring equity and inclusion to hiring and planning. His partners have included the Lark Play Development Center, Marin Theatre Company, Oregon Shakespeare Festival, Philadelphia Theatre Company, Penumbra Theatre, Dallas Theater Center, Pasadena Playhouse, East West Players, and New York Theatre Workshop. Prior to his life as a consultant, Al was the managing director of the Wirtz Center for the Performing Arts at Northwestern University. He is a graduate of Yale School of Drama and has worked for various regional theatres across the country including the Eugene O'Neill Theater Center, Yale Repertory Theatre, the Guthrie Theater, Cleveland Play House, and Steppenwolf Theatre Company. He has taught or lectured at Northwestern, Florida State, Yale, Michigan, Syracuse, the Commercial Theater Institute, the National Theater Institute, and Shenandoah University. blogs at New York Theater and tweets as @ newyorktheater.*

HOW LIBERAL ARTS THEATRE PROGRAMS ARE FAILING THEIR STUDENTS OF COLOR

17 JUNE 2020

MIRANDA HAYMON

I'm a young, Black, queer director and a proud graduate of a liberal arts college where I studied theatre, among other subjects. Like many young artists, I intentionally attended a non-conservatory program because I had several interests surrounding theatre and wanted my academic studies to influence and complement my directing craft.

I loved time spent outside of my core classes and the conversations I had with students with completely alternate courses of study. I formed close relationships with fellow theatre students, artists in other mediums, and people who didn't interact with the arts or humanities. The topics that came up while developing my aesthetic were so varied and diverse, but the same could not be said about the department demographics—there were only a handful of theatre professors and majors of color.

Many liberal arts theatre programs have predominantly white faculties as well as declared majors. This homogeneity is often reflected in the syllabi and programming. Whenever the mainstage season was announced at my school, the playwrights skewed mostly white and male, the plays lauded as "the canon." Little space was made for writers of color, and the few glimmers of representation were advocated by the few professors of color. In some cases guest directors offered a splash of color, but they would leave after their semester. During my senior year, with such a whitewashed array of mentorship, I was conflicted about realistic professional goals for myself. I blindly applied for entry-level directing fellowships, received one offer, and didn't think much more of it. I shifted gears and redirected my attention to putting one foot in front of the other as an emerging director.

As I learned more about the places and spaces for developing as a director, suggestions to seek out opportunities directing in colleges and universities always came up in conversation. The benefits for me as a director were attractive: solid money, good resources for design, the chance to work on classics and/or contemporary plays, eager students, and no reviews. It would also provide the opportunity for real-time exploration of craft, voice, and collaboration. For each academic directing job booked, I rallied my community and networks to the performances, finally getting myself out of that dreadful, classic catch-22: you can't get a gig because you haven't had significant enough samples of work, but you need significant samples of work to get a gig.

Twice, at two different liberal arts colleges—both with predominantly white faculties—I was offered to direct a new play written by a person of color for the mainstage. While I was thrilled by the chance to work with their students of color, I was also familiar with the traditional demographics of liberal arts theatre programs. I asked the schools, "How did your department come to this programming decision and are you prepared to accurately cast the play?" Both of the schools said, "Yes, absolutely. We are ready." But in both cases not enough students auditioned for the roles called for.

Though I was a near stranger to these communities, I was called upon to recruit. I was connected to affinity groups, clubs, and the football and basketball teams to inquire about students who might want to do a play. Current students, some of whom were auditioning for the plays themselves, were also called upon to help recruit. This created added emotional and administrative labor on my part as a guest; I was being depended on to help navigate the politics of academic institutions and speak on the behalf of the white professors scrambling for a solution.

Ultimately, both times we could not cast the original plays. I had to brainstorm new ones. Since I'd been hired to direct the "diversity" play of each school's season, the replacement plays had to be written by a person of color. I know this because, in one of the experiences, I pitched *Rhinoceros* by Eugene Ionesco and the department chair replied, "Not quite." The replacement plays had to have enough roles for the students who had already auditioned, to honor their time spent waiting to hear back on a final casting decision. I needed plays I could pull together with little preparation and that could fit into what time was left in the production calendar. Twice, my months of pre-production preparation for the original play was useless, and I scrambled to prepare to direct a few different titles we had requested from the licensing company. In both instances, I lost rehearsal hours and even a chunk of my budget since set and costume building on the previous play had already commenced. I was asked to proceed with business as usual.

As a young, Black, queer director and newcomer, there were already so many ways I was in the hot seat. On top of that, though, in both cases I was expected to provide a semester-long solution for a generational, institutional failure, and I had 25 percent less rehearsal and preparation time than expected, added emotional exhaustion, and pressure on me to make sure the production turned out okay. More than anything, I felt the need to show up for the young theatre artists of color who were thrilled that I was there, come to save them from their all-white departments. If I had had a "me"—a mentor who looked like me, talked like me, or hurt like me—how different would my sense of a future have been? I wanted to share my journey with the students, provide guidance and commonality. And we were able to build very meaningful bonds. Today, I am still in contact with the majority of them. I write their recommendation letters, edit their artistic statements, bring them to my rehearsals, hire them. I hold space for them over the phone or text when they feel their department or professors are erasing them.

The dissonance between what liberal arts programs wish to accomplish by articulating their commitment to equity and inclusion, and what work they are actually ready to engage in, is evident in their inability to make space for people of color as their students and as invited guest artists. Liberal arts theatre programs are failing their students of color and we need to start a dialogue about it. Here are four concrete things that colleges and universities can adopt as a place to start.

I. EXPAND THE NOTION OF "THE CANON."

Our academic and aesthetic definition of the canon is incredibly dated, which is at the expense of anyone who does not identify as cis, white, male, middle class, able-bodied and/or college educated. It's time for liberal arts faculty to open the lens on what work should be in the required reading, especially since many students are attracted to liberal arts programs because of the breadth of topics. There are so many plays, performance texts, and styles of performance rooted in traditions from around the world that are unspoken of in the classroom. Freshen up your syllabi and radicalize your curriculums. In your classroom discussions, you may find a passion for these works in the students, which leads me to my next point.

2. INCLUDE CURRENT STUDENTS OF COLOR (AND ALUMNI) IN YOUR PROGRAMMING

It's not just about the plays chosen, but who is choosing them. When I was in school, I would eagerly await the announcement of the next season's mainstage productions only to be consistently disappointed by the selections and lack of representation. I am not encouraging departments to make students function as the arbitrator of their entire curriculum, which includes mainstage programming, but I do think they should contribute to the dialogue. If it's not every single theatre student of color contributing thoughts, there could be elected representatives that aggregate and communicate their classmates' concerns, priorities, and interests. This dialogue should be expanded to alumni of color, especially since many alumni go on to work in various rooms and with a wide spectrum of texts.

3. HIRE GUEST ARTISTS OF COLOR AND INVOLVE THEM PRIOR TO PRODUCTION.

For guest artists, arriving as a newcomer to an established ecosystem is challenging enough, particularly for guest artists of color. We are already in unfamiliar territory, which is increased tenfold when we attend the very homogenous department meetings. Departments need to cushion this alienation by involving us in paid opportunities before our official first day starts, even a get-to-know-you conversation with students or teaching a master class before auditions. Faculty can organize for current students to visit a rehearsal for another project the guest artist is working on before they arrive on campus. By doing so, students can observe the guest artist in a different habitat, which will create more avenues for somewhat familiar encounters during the upcoming directing gig. This way, when the guest artist arrives on campus, there will already be familiar faces and conversations to be continued, making it easier for the guest artist to feel part of the community and dive into the work. In addition, this allows for longer-term relationships to develop between the guest artist and the student body, even those who are graduating.

4. HIRE GUEST ARTISTS OF COLOR AGAIN.

I wish that, for every "diverse" play I was invited to direct at a college or university, I would be hired to return to direct Shakespeare, Ionesco, or Molière. Guest artists of color should not be beholden to work only related to their racial and ethnic identities, or invited as a Band-Aid to longstanding problem in colleges, universities, and the industry. The solution doesn't end at hiring guest artists of color to direct the lone ethnic show. Give these guest artists the opportunity to dive into a text they wouldn't otherwise have access to direct, as many classics and revivals are relegated to more seasoned, typically white directors. Our directorial scope, interests, and talent should not be limited to works that are related to our identities. Providing guest directors of color the opportunity to direct an array of work can start to halt the issue of us being siloed as artists and provide an ideal opportunity for students of color to be cast in roles they may lack access to as well.

As young theatremakers of color continue to choose a liberal arts education, the theatre departments that house these artists will have to engage in discourse about how pedagogy, practice, and opportunity have been part of the problem. Each element of the curriculum and season programming process calls for an interrogation so that the classes of future rising theatre artists of color can be enriched and these artists can be adequately uplifted—not just while they are students, but when they return as guest artists, eager to continue building their craft.

MIRANDA HAYMON

Miranda Haymon (they/them) is a Princess Grace Award-winning writer, director, and curator originally from Boston. As a theatre director, Miranda has developed and staged work with the Tank, NYTW, Roundabout, Ars Nova, Manhattan Theatre Club, the Public, Bushwick Starr, Signature Theater, and more. Miranda has served as visiting faculty at Fordham, Dartmouth, Sarah Lawrence, Wesleyan, and Rutgers. Past fellowships/residencies include New Georges, Space on Ryder Farm, LCT Director's Lab, Wingspace, NYTW 2050, Roundabout, Manhattan Theatre Club, and Arena Stage. Currently, Miranda is a resident director at Roundabout Theatre Company. In the brand sphere, Miranda has directed projects with Gucci, Garage magazine, Dunkin', and Spectrum. As a writer, Miranda is under commission by Jeremy O. Harris and is developing several TV, comedy, and podcast projects. Miranda is a graduate of Wesleyan University where they double majored in German studies and theatre. mirandahaymon.com.

INTERROGATING THE SHAKESPEARE SYSTEM

31 AUGUST 2020

MADELINE SAYET

I want to talk about Shakespeare. Not Shakespeare the playwright or Shakespeare the poet, but, rather, Shakespeare the system—and what it means for all of us artists, educators, and administrators to be upholding that system. For clarification, the Shakespeare system is not simply Shakespeare's written work, but the complex and oppressive role his work, legacy, and positionality hold in our contemporary society.

Feeling defensive yet? After all, the education system in the United States has trained all of us to believe Shakespeare is the best. Why else would he be the only playwright required in the American Common Core, our academic standards for education? Why else would he be the most produced playwright in the United States? Why else would he be the way children are introduced to theatre? It is that very placement of Shakespeare as the pinnacle of theatrical achievement that I suggest we interrogate. It is time to examine the factors that have led us to assume there is a "best" and that it is him. Are all of his plays good? What exactly is it that makes him superior?

Promoting Shakespeare as the "best" writer of all time is a dangerous and white supremacist viewpoint. Until the Shakespeare field as a whole learns how to examine that, theatres that produce his work cannot be welcoming spaces for people whose ancestors were beaten and forced to give up their own languages and learn Shakespeare's. As a Mohegan theatremaker, it is my duty to make clear that the immense amount of space his work currently takes up is an ongoing tool of colonization, just as his work has been used historically as a weapon to remove other people's cultures and teach them that one British playwright is superior to all other writers. To be clear: I'm not talking about scarcity—there is always room for more plays and more artists. But Shakespeare has not been positioned amongst us. He has been positioned above us, and that is something entirely different.

BARDOLATRY

Is Shakespeare a god? If not, why is "bardolatry" a word? And why is the Shakespeare missionary complex still a real one? Whenever I hear people preach about the universalism of Shakespeare the way missionaries once wielded the Bible, I think to myself, *This is dangerous.* And yet it goes unquestioned, even though not everyone interprets his work the same way—and not everyone even likes it.

If any other writer were treated as a deity it would not be tolerated, but something about Shakespeare's role in the colonization of America has made him the exception. That's right, I did not say his work has made him exceptional, but rather his work's role in the colonization of America has enabled him to occupy a hierarchical space within a system of oppression.

I have seen the recent anti-racism statements pouring out of Shakespeare institutions both in the United States and internationally—institutions that benefit from and exist to serve and uphold this very system. But in order to begin to do anti-racist work or decolonizing work, the first step for every Shakespeare institution is to ask: What does the worship of Shakespeare do within society? We have to look at the immense space he takes up and the other stories that are silenced because of this.

WHOSE LAND ARE WE ON?

It was not until my final year of my BFA at NYU's Tisch School of the Arts that I found out there were Native playwrights. This experience is not uncommon for Native theatre artists like myself, because what is funded, what is produced, and what is taught in this country is predominantly Shakespeare. As a teen, I could not go online or to the bookstore and acquire a copy of a Native play, but Shakespeare was easily available everywhere. This is no accident.

This land has an abundance of rich and complex Indigenous storytelling traditions, but Native people in America were stolen from their homes, taken to boarding schools, forced to give up their languages, and made to learn Shakespeare. In Miles P. Grier's article "Staging the Cherokee *Othello*: An Imperial Economy of Indian Watching," he chronicles newspaper articles from the 1600s to the 1800s that mocked Indigenous peoples' responses to watching Shakespeare and how these responses were used as justification for taking our lands. We live in a place where policies have been written that have made Indigenous art illegal and learning Shakespeare mandatory, and to be honest a quick look at current school curriculums would show that not much has changed. This is the foundation of Shakespeare in America. It is as rotten as the foundation of America itself.

I'm not saying Shakespeare's plays don't have merits, but they are finite and do not represent all of us. No one should be forced to see themselves through his work. He is one voice from one time period, and his existence should not render anyone else's voice, language, or culture as lesser than. It is likely there are many other playwrights who, given the same positionality, would have been equally prolific. The perpetuation of "the Great Man Theory"—that there is one example of what is best and deserving—only serves the United States' system of capitalism and oppression.

DISMANTLING THE HIERARCHY

I'm not saying that if you love Shakespeare you shouldn't, or for people to stop producing his work, but I am saying the Shakespeare system—where everything is compared to one white man's legacy—is inherently destructive. By believing there is innate virtue in his work, people overlook all the harm it is capable of doing. For example, it's often determined whether or not a student is "smart enough" based on whether they are able to translate Shakespeare's poetry into contemporary English "well"—as determined by the teacher. This is an absurd act. Poetry should be about the vast possibilities of interpretation, not limiting students to one correct answer. There is no right and wrong when interpreting Shakespeare, but, in this scenario, a teacher has been handed all of the cultural authority over interpretation, potentially silencing the voices of any student who has a different worldview.

Similarly, how is it determined if an actor is good in Shakespeare class? By having them be forced to hit the "correct" posture and pronunciation and rhythm? And where do those "correct" postures and pronunciation and rhythms come from? Again, power is handed to the oppressors and the colonial system continues. If Shakespeare is to be done at all, it should be done in ways that encourage each student, performer, and artist to interpret it for themselves.

I personally am not interested in working with any Shakespeare institution that cannot reckon with this, because this reckoning is necessary for deep work and art-making that resonates with the present moment. Without it, Shakespeare is and will always be a part of the problem.

WHAT WOULD SHAKESPEARE DO?

Shakespeare did not know his work would be amplified in this destructive manner. Idolization is a hierarchy and we must be conscious of what has been erased when one person and worldview has been lifted to the top. We cannot continue to promote the idea that a white man is unquestionably superior.

The Shakespeare field is made up of an incredible group of researchers and dramaturgs, and if these individuals can dedicate hours and hours and hours to research on what a single Shakespearean sentence meant to folks four hundred years ago, they can spend as much time on what the sentence could mean to different groups of people today. Some of their time could easily be spent learning how to practice anti-racism.

I still believe there should be spaces for joyous celebration of Shakespeare. We all know that, as a poet, he wrote some mighty fine lines. But so have many others. Shakespeare lived in one world; our world today is different. If his plays are going to continue to be done, it's important that Shakespeareans spend as much time learning about the world we are in today and how we got here. Honestly, if Shakespeare were still a person—if he were still a playwright, as opposed to a system—that's probably what he would do.

The ideas in this article have been influenced by conversations between Madeline Sayet, Mei Ann Teo, Dawn Monique Williams, and Sarah Enloe leading up to their book chapter "The Shakespeare Problem" in Troubling Traditions: Canonicity, Theatre, and Performance *in the US recently published by Routledge (2021).*

MADELINE SAYET

Madeline Sayet (she/her) is a citizen of the Mohegan Tribe, clinical assistant professor at Arizona State University with the Arizona Center for Medieval and Renaissance Studies (ACMRS), and the executive director of the Yale Indigenous Performing Arts Program (YIPAP). For her work as a director, writer, and performer she has been honored as a Forbes 30 Under 30, TED Fellow, MIT Media Lab Director's Fellow, and a recipient of the White House Champion of Change Award from President Obama. A national tour of her play Where We Belong was recently produced by Woolly Mammoth Theatre Company in association with Folger Shakespeare Library.

LIBERATING TERROR: CLOWN AND ACTIVISM

13 NOVEMBER 2020

SAYDA TRUJILLO

A s a first-generation American—a daughter of Guatemalan immigrants—with access to education, I've been programmed to juggle two things: feeling grateful and working really hard. These two things are not in opposition, but, just like in juggling, are part of a rhythm. I was raised to do both all the time—to constantly adapt to white supremacy culture, bow my head to those in power, and to keep plugging away, even without any acknowledgement. It is the opposite of what it means to have privilege.

As I've carved a path in the clown world over the past fifteen years, specifically as a woman of color, both of these truths have continued to exist.

CLOWNING AND WHITE SUPREMACY

White supremacy manifests in clown pedagogy in ways that have flown under the radar for far too long. In the clown world, bodies of color are often the minority, while the leaders in the field are often cis-het white males. I trained at a predominantly white Eurocentric physical theatre program, and my first clown teacher—a cis-het white male, considered a genius, virtuosic—told me I was a talented actress but that I would *never* be a clown. Even though I truly believe everyone is a clown, his prophecy paralyzed me. His paradigm of clown training limits the possibility that clown could manifest in a myriad of ways, especially in bodies of color.

Two conflicting things happened at that moment: the mentality *I am not a clown* became part of me, and my activism in the field began to stir. Since then, the invincible spirit of the clown has continued to shape me, seeping through every tiny crack possible to make itself present to speak, to laugh, to sing, to bounce, to witness, and to encounter. Clown has become my language, one of rhythm and delight, of wide-open eyes, smiles, tickles and chuckles, of stillness and ease.

CLOWNS WITHOUT BORDERS

In the fall of 2005, Hurricane Stan wiped out entire villages and displaced hundreds of families in the highlands of Guatemala. In early 2006, Clowns Without Borders (CWB), a nonprofit that offers joy and laughter to relieve the suffering of all persons who live in areas of crisis, especially children, invited me to join a relief trip to bring levity and laughter to the survivors who were enduring dire circumstances.

Given the mentality that lurked inside me, I sheepishly responded with: "Thank you for the invitation, but I am not a clown." CWB, confused at my reply because I had, after all, trained at one of the "top" clown schools in the world, asked me again, "But would you like to go?" My clown spirit answered, "Yes, I'd love to." This response, which sprang up from the knowledge hidden somewhere deep inside me that indeed I was a clown, surprised me. And I took a risk.

Terror came with having accepted CWB's invitation— terror and so much joy. For the first time, I was going back to Guatemala and would be able to share my work as a performer with my family. With all my terror, I met two CWB volunteers in Guatemala City and together we traveled to my grandmother's house, to the village where I had spent part of my childhood, a beautiful home surrounded by mountains, valleys, rocks, and mango and pomegranate trees. We created a clown show together in two days, on my grandmother's patio! It was fun. It was strange. It became apparent that CWB volunteers had to be able to embody "yes." All of us there, strangers to each other, were saying "yes"—not talking about the method of clown, not demanding of each other to be funny, not indulging in *via negativa*.[1] We were building trust through play, we were listening to each other's rhythms, we were working with what we brought collectively—like how David Lichtenstein, a clown and street performer who tours all over the world and who led my first CWB trip, is approximately one and half feet taller than me; when we stand next to each other it's already funny! He treated me like a clown, and so I was one.

My clown education truly began there in Guatemala under the gaze of hundreds of children and adults who circled around us, alert, seeing us, lighting us, and tickling us. I learned the stage is any open space, often just ground, dirt, not always flat under our feet. In those first performances I allowed myself to really be seen and to really see who was around me. Doing so was the first interruption to the training that asserted I would never be a clown. I began to experience clowning as connection, a game, an encounter, an exchange. Over the fifteen years since, I have clowned in Guatemala, Ecuador, Colombia, El Salvador, Palestine, India, Lebanon, Egypt, and detention centers in Texas and New York.

Clown is one of the few forms in theatre that does not distance itself from the audience. As a clown, I exchange looks, smiles, hugs, and chases with an audience; in fact, the clown can only live fully in acknowledgement of everything present. It's immensely powerful performing clown in a corner of the Earth where loss has been experienced because

---

1   Deanna Fleysher, "Via Negativa Is Actual Bullshit," *Naked Comedy* (blog), 4 January 2020, https://nakedcomedy.blogspot.com/2020/01/via-negativa-is-actual-bullshit.html?fbclid=IwAR0bPr-9RdmO_f5MOIiawtjaHY_wIKUXmx1HuOgE3HtPgVkF_5idcPacM23c&m=1.

the performance acknowledges that loss while also getting the audience to roar in laughter. That laughter is not an escape, it is activism in the body, it is collective resistance, it both redirects purpose and at the same time includes everything that is true in that moment. It is in that laughter that we—the clowns and the community—become partners.

Clown activism is about this play of listening and responding, of seeing and being seen. It embraces terror, and in this embrace there exists space for everyone involved to access resilience and buoyancy.

CLOWN AND VOICE WORK

Part of my clown activism is undoing the notion that expertise looks a certain way. Because of this, clown has found its way into other parts of my career, including voice work—specifically, the study of breath to support the spoken and sung voice, usually done with actors and theatremakers but also sometimes with non-actors in public speaking classes or with community-based art projects.

I began to connect clown and voice work on a CWB trip to Palestine, a place where I have lived and where I learned from theatre activists and storytellers who resist the injustices of occupation with the deepest clown spirit I have ever witnessed. There, I saw the way bodies inhabit both laughter and tears, how resistance has to include both, and how resistance manifests in the voice—not the technical voice, as in the spoken or sung one for art's sake, but the voice that has agency, the voice that will not be silenced. It was in these CWB settings that I began to intuit the power and freedom that comes from laughing and crying—a power that is not controlled. As a result I started to invite my students to speak from this uncontrolled place and explore things like deep listening, ease, buoyancy, musicality, rhythm, delight, and play—all elements of clown—to find their most powerful voice.

In Palestine I became curious about my own diaspora and its effect on my voice, as well as why and how terror is a bridge to laughter and tears. During our performances, a clown gag revealed the terror that is always present for residents. In the gag, three of us clowns attempted numerous times to cross a military checkpoint, getting caught in a ridiculous loop. The repetition of our attempts—a daily struggle for Palestinians, which holds anger, pain, and violence for them—broke something open! We had tapped into the ridiculousness and comedy of the repetition, and laughter erupted from that. Hundreds of children and adults roared in full recognition. There we were again, holding terror and explosive joy in collective bodies.

CLOWN AND RESILIENCE

Clown can also manifest as resilience. I am an expert in my story, my experience, and my life. To counter the lack of inclusion of voices like mine in the field, innate in theatre programs across the nation, came the need for me to write stories that center my voice. In my solo work, I address audiences directly. I tickle them. My solo shows are cries and calls and maps of stories of displacement, and the spine of my shows—the bones, the skeleton—permeates with the spirit of a clown.

For example, in my solo autobiographical piece *I Was Raised Mexican*, a character compares the experience of Guatemalans in Mexico to Mexicans in the United States, saying, "Guatemalans are the Mexicans of Mexico. And who doesn't hate Mexicans?" The first time I performed this piece outside of a theatre, and in Spanish, was at a juvenile detention center in New York. The performance took place in a clinical-like room with tiled floors, without windows, and with florescent light. The young men at the center were all Latin American from countries ranging from Colombia to Mexico.

In response to that question, one of the men raised his hand and said, "I don't hate Mexicans." One by one, others raised their hands and echoed, "I don't hate Mexicans." I stood there listening and after most of the audience had raised their hands, I raised mine and also said, "I don't hate Mexicans." There were tears and laughter. That exchange changed everything: I learned that, to them, I wasn't performing—I was talking with the spirit of the clown. Together, we found our collective voice, our sameness. What would be considered an inappropriate interruption in a theatre became the core of the encounter. These are the ways I feel the spirit of the clown seeping through.

CLOWN AND HEALING

As a facilitator of healing processes and dialogue, I listen from the belly of my clown. I play, and it is liberating to enter a space where people and communities meet me in the center. I'm terrified but I stay in that terror where we can explode, shatter, burst, chase each other, clap, and listen for the rhythm that will unify us.

When I arrive in a community so far away from what I know, my clown leads the way. Three years ago, I co-led a four-week program called Arts Bridge: Owning Our Stories, Sharing Our Stories with Laura Betancur, an expressive arts facilitator and clown at heart. Together we designed a curriculum to work with Egyptian and Syrian women in Cairo, partnering with Dawar Arts, combining visual art with physical theatre practices, playing and finding ways to express our stories with our bodies. My clown rejects power hoarding, so as a facilitator I am a clown falling and bouncing. During those four weeks in Cairo, I invited the women to fall and bounce with me, to run, to chase, to sing, to cry. The art of surrendering power I take from the spirit of my clown.

My clown activism seeps through. Juggling gratitude and hard work is no longer my deficit, or an apology, or permission to operate in the white supremacist platforms that have contaminated this earth. The spirit of the clown resists.

Something has broken and I will sing, bounce, and denounce.
I will roar, holler, and jump.
I will tickle, fall, and bounce again.
I will smile with the stillness and the spirit of the clown.

SAYDA TRUJILLO

Sayda Trujillo (she/her) is a theatre artist specializing in voice and movement, as well as devising physical theatre performances. Born in Montreal and raised in Canada, Guatemala, and the United States, Sayda's personal work is inspired by identity and storytelling, as well as collective work with actors and non-actors. Sayda has taught and performed in thirty-two countries including Guatemala, Ecuador, Chile, Singapore, Spain, Germany, Colombia, the United Kingdom, Egypt, Lebanon, Palestine with the Freedom Theatre, and India. Since 2005, Sayda has volunteered for Clowns Without Borders, performing for thousands of children in Latin America and the Middle East. Her education includes a BFA from CalArts, a graduate certificate from Dell'Arte, and an MA in voice studies from the Royal Central School of Speech and Drama in London. saydateatrera.com.